Dina Bélanger, the day of her religious profession

The Autobiography

of

Dina Bélanger

(Marie Sainte-Cécile de Rome)
Religious of Jesus and Mary

3rd Edition revised and up-dated

Translated by Mary St. Stephen, R.J.M.
Revised and up-dated by Sr. Felecity Moody, R.J.M.

Religious of Jesus and Mary
Canada

Sincere thanks to Madame Marjorie Lachance and to all those who collaborated in this edition

With the permission
of the authorities
of the Diocese of Quebec

Quebec, 19 June 1995

Création et édition électronique : *Atelier Rouge*

ISBN 2-980 4106-3-2

Dépot légal — 3ᵉ trimestre 1997
Bibliothèque nationale du Québec
Bibliothèque nationale du Canada

© 1997   Les Religieuses de Jésus-Marie
           2049, chemin Saint-Louis
           Sillery (Québec) Canada
           GIT 1P2

           Les Religieuses de Jésus-Marie
           10070, avenue d'Auteuil
           Montréal (Québec) Canada
           H3L 2K1

1st Edition 1961
3rd Edition 1997

PREFACE

Christ always did what was pleasing to the Father (cf. Jn 8,29), the Father "who sees all that is done in secret" (Mt. 6,6). This is the key to sanctity and prayer. Does not sanctity mean to become "perfect just as the heavenly Father is perfect" (Mt. 5,48) and prayer, conversing with the Father who is there in that secret place that is our private room (cf. Mt. 6,6)?

These pressing invitations are addressed without exception to all those who wish to be truly children of the Father who is in heaven (cf, Mt. 5,45). So, in all ages, the Church has seen rise from among its ranks persons who have listened to the Lord's invitation to be "holy in all their activity" (IP 1,15), "to imitate God, as his children whom he loves, and follow Christ by loving as he loves you" (Eph. 5,1), so that their thoughts, words and actions are the same as those of Christ Jesus. (cf. Phil. 2,5). Dina Bélanger is among their number.

This young Canadian girl burned with the desire to be filled with the infinite love of the Heart of Jesus. This love, which seeks only to communicate itself so as to set the world on fire, permeated her speech, her judgments and all her actions with love. It possessed her everyday life, which became the one place above all others where she could meet with him who is holy and makes holy. Her intimacy with the Lord inspired Dina to be faithful to him in the most commonplace events of her life, and her fidelity led her to live in total and trusting self-abandonment to Jesus and Mary. Adapting her spirituality to the saying of St Augustine : "Love and do as you will", she took as her maxim : "Love and let Jesus and Mary have their way".

People of all ages and all walks of life will find in Dina Bélanger a model of fidelity to the call of the Lord. John Paul II put it this way on the day following her Beatification : "May this humble mystic *support those who seek God during this era,* especially in her hometown of Quebec!" (Audience, 22 March 1993) May I apply this wish of the Holy Father, in a special way, to those men and women who feel called interiorly to live a life of total self-giving as consecrated religious?

+ Maurice COUTURE
Archbishop of Quebec

Quebec, 6 February 1995

REQUEST FOR AND FORMULA OF BEATIFICATION

His Excellency, Mgr. Maurice Couture, Archbishop of Quebec, asks the Holy Father to add the name of Dina Bélanger to the list of the Blessed and gives a brief account of her life.

Most Holy Father, the Archbishop of Quebec humbly asks your Holiness to include the name of the Venerable Servant of God, Dina Bélanger, to the list of the Blessed.

Dina Bélanger was born in Quebec, Canada, on 30 April 1897. She was baptised on that same day with the names of Mary, Margaret, Dina, Adelaide. The only daughter of a well-to-do family, Dina received a Christian education, sheltered from selfishness and vanity.

Very early in life, Dina showed a marked attraction to Jesus and Mary. On 2 May 1907, she made her first Holy Communion and received the sacrament of Confirmation. On 1 May 1910, she became a member of the Association of the Children of Mary and shortly afterwards consecrated herself to Our Lady. On the First Friday of October 1911, Dina was inspired to consecrate her virginity to the Lord, because, she already had a "great desire to abandon herself to his love".

She completed her studies with the Sisters of the Congregation of Notre Dame in Quebec, where she was a model pupil.

At the age of eight, Dina began to study piano and made rapid progress. From 1916 to 1918 she attended the New York Conservatory where she completed her musical studies. She stayed, with two companions from Quebec, at the residence 'Our Lady of Peace', run by the Religious of Jesus and Mary, the Congregation that would later become her religious family.

Dina spent from 1918 to 1921 with her parents. Concerts and a social life filled this period, but she continued to live her life of intimacy with Jesus and Mary. One day Jesus said to her clearly : "I want you at Jesus and Mary".

On 11 August 1921, Dina entered the novitiate of the Religious of Jesus and Mary at Sillery. She received the religious habit and the name Marie Ste-Cécile de Rome on 15 February 1922. On 15 August 1923 she made her temporary profession and five years later pronounced her final vows.

It was not long before her Mother Superior realised the exceptional depth of the young sister's interior life and she asked her to write her Autobiography.

Fidelity in love, this is what best characterises her. Her most ardent desire was to live and die as a "martyr of love, victim of love, apostle of love". She lived her motto, "*Love and let Jesus and Mary have their way*" so faithfully that Jesus came to live in her in such a way as to call her "my little Own Self".

The active life of Dina was interrupted by illness. On 4 September 1929, consumed rather by love than by tuberculosis, she died peacefully in the 33rd year of her life.

A worthy daughter of Claudine Thévenet, whom the Church canonized on 21 March 1993, Dina Bélanger incarnated perfectly the charism of her Foundress : that of revealing the active goodness of Christ. Her spirituality is centered on the Heart of Christ in the Eucharist, and a filial dependence on Mary. Her apostolic heart burned with the desire of making Jesus and Mary loved even to the ends of the earth. She wished to continue her mission throughout eternity and to beg for love for the good of all, for the greater glory of God.

The Holy Father responds to the request and pronounces the formula of beatification :

We, accepting the desire of our brother, Maurice Couture, the Archbishop of Quebec, that of numerous brother Bishops and of many of the faithful, and having heard the opinion of the Congregation for the Causes of Saints, declare, in virtue of our apostolic authority, that the Venerable Servant of God, Dina Bélanger, should henceforth be called Blessed, and that her feast may be celebrated, in the places and according to the rules established by law, every year on 4 September, the day of her birth into heaven.

In the name of the Father, and of the Son, and of the Holy Spirit. Amen.

THE CONGREGATION
OF THE RELIGIOUS OF JESUS AND MARY

The Congregation of the Religious of Jesus and Mary, founded in Lyon, France, in 1818, is dedicated to the education of young people. In the beginning, it met the needs of many young girls who had been left orphans or abandoned after the French Revolution, receiving the most destitute among them into 'Providences'.

As the years went by, the work grew, and was adapted to the needs of different times and places. As early as 1842, the first missionaries left for India to open a boarding school there for young girls and an orphanage for poor children.

Today, the Congregation has numerous houses in Europe, Asia, Africa, North and South America and even New Zealand. The religious devote themselves to educating young people at the primary, secondary and university levels. In addition, they collaborate in pastoral work in parishes, paying particular attention to education in the faith. In mission countries, they are also involved in typically missionary projects, for example, dispensaries, the promotion of women and visits to rural areas.

The Mother House is situated on the Promontory of Fourvière, Lyon, and the Generalate is in Rome.

The Foundress

Born in Lyon, Claudine Thévenet (1774-1837) was deeply touched by the sufferings of her time. She saw both her brothers gunned down during the Terror and knew the misfortune of those who live without any knowledge of God.

Young people, prey to so many evils, appealed irresistibly to her generosity and her spirit of dedication. Her zeal drew others to offer precious help for the most urgent works of charity, and it was with these first companions, formed initially into an Association, that she laid the foundations of her Congregation.

In the face of so many needs, Claudine Thévenet defined very precisely the aim of her mission in the Church : "To make Jesus and Mary known and loved by means of a Christian education, with a predilection for the young and, among them, the poor." Her deep faith and her confidence in God allowed her to confront with courage and serenity the difficulties experienced by every undertaking in its beginning.

She has left to her religious a Christocentric and Marial spirituality influenced by the teachings of St Ignatius and focused on the Eucharist. Like their Foundress, the Religious of Jesus and Mary strive to "find God in everything, and everything in God."

Saint Claudine Thévenet,
Foundress of the Congregation of the Religious of Jesus and Mary

ORIGIN OF THE FIRST EDITION

according to the testimony given by a Superior from Sillery

In the course of a conversation, we were talking about the order given to certain holy souls to write the story of their life ; the thought of Mother Ste-Cécile de Rome crossed my mind ; at the very same moment, a religious turned to me and whispered : "Why wouldn't Mother Ste-Cécile de Rome write her life?"

From that moment, I was obsessed by the idea which I submitted to the Council. Our Provincial Superior, taken aback by a proposal so foreign to our customs, answered : "And what about her humility?" I did not insist.

Two weeks later, in order to follow the dictates of my conscience, I raised the question once again and permission was given.

So it was, that at the beginning of March 1924, during her spiritual interview, I said to our privileged soul : "You must write your life, my dear Sister." I think this caused her some surprise and a moment of anguish, but nothing of this was apparent.

She answered : "Is that your wish, Mother?" Having explained my wish once again, I heard her answer as always : "Yes, Mother, I will do as you ask."

She obeyed with such simplicity that at the time I had no idea of how heroic she was being.

Shortly before her death, recalling this particular order given under obedience, Mother Ste- Cécile de Rome said to me : "That act cost me more than any other in my life."

THE REDISCOVERY OF A MASTERPIECE : THE AUTOBIOGRAPHY OF DINA BÉLANGER

The *Autobiography* of Blessed Dina Bélanger (in religion Marie Sainte-Cécile de Rome) is one of the brightest jewels of the spiritual literature of the XXth century. The first impression received on reading it is of the fascinating beauty of the mystery of Jesus as well as of Christian holiness which is the deepest communion with this mystery. Those who read and re-read this text, written by a saint who was also an artist, keep returning to a fundamental impression : how beautiful it is![1]. It is the treasure or the precious pearl of which Jesus speaks in the Gospel.

About thirty years after the *Story of a Soul* of St Thérèse de Lisieux, we find the same luminous witness of Love, the Infinite Love of God, revealed and given in Jesus Christ. It is again the witness, typically feminine, of a young religious of whom the personal history, so brief and so limited, becomes paradoxically, both passionate and more beautiful on account of the love with which it is filled. This *Autobiography* is a story of Love, of a very great Love, of the greatest of all Loves. It is a personal story that takes on a universal value in espousing the Mystery of Jesus ; it opens on to the widest dimensions of the History of Salvation, and thus becomes a convincing testimony to Truth itself. Such is its theological and spiritual significance, as well as its contemp-

---

[1] Such was the first reaction of Cardinal Rouleau, Archbishop of Quebec, after having read Dina's manuscript (cf. GUINDON, Henri-Marie, Une âme mariale, Ottawa-Eastview 1940, p. 6).

orary value, in the perspective of the Second Vatican Council with its strong insistence on the universal calling to holiness. Like Thérèse, Dina understood that her vocation was to become "a great saint" (p. 115) ; and it is with the same "audacious confidence" that she was able to say : **"I Will be a Saint, O Jesus"** (p. 54).

The literary genre and the sources

In order to read the text well, it is necessary to take into account the literary genre, a narrative autobiography. *Narrative theology*, the value of which is happily being rediscovered today, is expressed in a unique way in this type of autobiography, used by so many saints in the course of the history of the church. Whether it is a question of the Confessions of St Augustin, or the Autobiographies of Teresa of Avila, of Thérèse de Lisieux and of Dina, these writings present themselves as "praise of God's merciful love", a "hymm of Love", a "Magnificat" which celebrates the wonderful works of God. The Autobiographies of Saints unite in a most harmonious way the objectivity of the Mystery with the subjectivity of the person who is in communion with It.

That said, it is necessary to underline the original character of this *Autobiography*. Dina is always very "personal" ; she quotes very little, but says everything with her own words. In everything she shows great liberty and daring. Thus, contrary to the usage of the times, she decides to address Jesus with loving tender expressions (p. 137). In the same way, in order to express the limitless nature of Love she does not hesitate to use the strongest and most audacious words, but always with accuracy and confidence.

Dina's style is remarkable for its clarity, a characteristic of the French language. Blessed Dina was very precise, a quality inherited, without doubt, from her father who was an accountant. She developed this sense of precision in her studies of harmony, and, at times, she seems to be almost a "mathematician" in the spiritual life, looking for brief and clear formulae, as in theorems, in order to express what she calls "my ideal" or "my motto". She freely uses abstract concepts such as "substitution". But at the same time she remains an artist, with a preference for the symbols and images that abound in the *Autobiography*. As a musician she often speaks of the harmony of the mystery and her text is a song, a canticle of love, but she is also very "visual", making frequent use of pictures. These pictures, which have an important place in the *Autobiography*, are like interior icons, painted by an artist of great imaginative gifts, but they are also similar to the "imaginary visions" described by Saint Teresa of Avila and so many other mystics, because they speak of an inward image. The Holy Spirit uses the artistic talents of Dina, her imagination and her sensitivity.

It is necessary to relativise the sometimes extraordinary aspect of Dina's experience, because the essential element of the mystical life lies not in the phenomena, but in Faith, Hope and Charity. These phenomena, which are very evident in Teresa of Avila, are almost absent in Thérèse de Lisieux. Dina is, as it were, somewhere between the two : with her that which is extraordinary is to be found more than in Thérèse de Lisieux and less than in the great Teresa of Avila. On this point it is particularly important to interpret carefully the numerous "words of Jesus" of which Dina speaks, not as being "private revelations" but rather a dialogue d'expression of the spiritual life.

Such a dialogue is one of the modalities of spiritual experience, and it is also a well-known literary genre if one thinks of the dialogue of Saint Catherine of Siena, or the *Imitation of Christ* which is one of Dina's principal sources (as it was for Thérèse de Lisieux). In the *Imitation* the whole of the spiritual life is expressed in the form of a dialogue between Jesus and his disciple.

Dina herself gives us a valuable key, for a sound interpretation, in the most simple and ordinary way, of the "pictures" that she sees and the "words" that she hears : "I must explain, once and for all, the expressions that I shall employ such as 'I saw', 'Jesus said to me', and similar forms of speech. They signify : "I saw in my imagination, Jesus spoke to me with that interior voice that every soul hears in moments of profound recollection when favoured with divine consolations" (p. 102). In a way that differs only slightly from this, Thérèse de Lisieux had the same experience : Jesus spoke to her through the Scriptures, although she did not hear any interior words, she contemplated the Face of Jesus and marveled at its beauty.

If one enquires, now, about the sources of the *Autobiography* of Dina, one remark must be made. As she herself tells us, she read very little. For her, as for Catherine of Siena, the book that she constantly reads is the body of the crucified Christ, the Heart of Jesus. Nevertheless, she read the *Gospels* and the *Imitation* (cf. p. 190), drawing also from the sources that are proper to her Con gregation (which has an Ignatian spirituality). Nevertheless, the two great spiritual writers who had the strongest influence on her from her adolescence were St Louis-Marie Grignon de Montfort and Saint Thérèse de Lisieux. This is very significant, for the writings of Louis-Marie and of Thérèse were very widely circulated at the beginning of our 20th century and exerted such a great influence on the whole People of God, that there is now question of declaring them Doctors of the Church. Dina names them several times, without quoting literally from them, but rather expressing their doctrine very well, an indication of how well she had assimilated it. While on this question, one could compare the numerous poems that Dina includes in her *Autobiography* with those of Thérèse and of Louis Marie : they are poor from a literary point of view, but very rich from that of the spirit, for it is there that Love expressed itself in the form of a song, a canticle.

The Christocentrism of Dina

The spirituality of Dina is characterised above all by an admirable mystical christocentrism. Dina herself gives the key to this with a quotation from Scripture in the Introduction to her *Autobiography*, the words of St Paul in the letter to the Galatians (Gal 2, 20) : "It is not I who live but Christ who lives in me" (p. 39). The great spiritual theme of substitution is nothing else but the realisation of this word of the Apostle. Dina expresses it wonderfully when she writes :

"My ideal : **the substitution of Jesus in my stead**. We are no longer two, Jesus and I ; we are one, Jesus alone. He makes use of my faculties, of my senses, of my limbs. It is He who thinks, acts, prays, looks, speaks, walks, writes, teaches ; in a word, who lives. And I, buried in His Heart, am so little that He alone can see me. I have surrendered all, nothing now concerns me, my only occupation is to contemplate Him and repeat incessantly, 'Jesus, I love Thee'. This is what is sung in heaven. My eternity has begun. How happy I am" (p. 156).

Thus this very intimate union with Jesus is realised through love, expressed by Dina in that incessant, "Jesus I love you", which is in truth the canticle of heaven, because love alone will never pass away. (cf. *1 Cor 13*, 8). Like Thérèse de Lisieux, Dina lived this union with Jesus by being very small, and becoming more and more so. And in order that the substitution expressed in the words of St Paul "it is no longer I that live but Christ who lives in me", should be realised, the path traced by John the Baptist must be followed, "the friend of the bridegroom" ; "He must increase and I must decrease" (*Jn 3*, 30). Such is the mystical "annihilation" of which Dina speaks with frequency, indicating herself as "that little annihilated nothing".

On this point she synthesises admirably the teaching of Thérèse de Lisieux on evangelical littleness and that of St Louis Marie (and the entire French School) on self dispossession, in order to belong wholly to Jesus. It is always the same radical love that is expressed symbolically as "holocaust of love" by Thérèse and as "slave of love" by Louis-Marie. Following Thérèse, Dina insists on littleness, abandonment, trust and love ; following Louis-Marie she insists equally on the maternal role of Mary on this path.

Mary, Mother of Jesus, has been given to us as Mother by Jesus Himself. She is wonderfully present throughout the *Autobiography* of Dina, within a perspective that remains constantly Christo centric. It is evident for example, when Blessed Dina concisely expresses the teaching of Saint Louis. "It is she who leads us to Jesus, it is she whom we must allow to live in us in order that Christ may substitute Himself in place of our nothingness. She is the surest path, the shortest and most perfect way to raise us up to the Infinite, unite us to Uncreated Love, until we lose ourselves in Him and sink down into the abysmal source of eternal beatitude" (p. 64). According to Saint Louis-Marie, in fact, Mary leads us to the most intimate union with Our Lord, she obtains for us the grace of knowing and loving him profoundly, with her own heart. All these elements are taken up by Dina. Here, for example is what she asks in her prayer : "Mary, my tender Mother, you whom I love so well, grant me to always love Jesus and to make Him loved with His own Heart and yours" (p. 143).

Such is the meaning of the definitive motto that Dina formulated and explained : "**Love and let Jesus and Mary have their way!** At last I had discovered an expression that satisfied me. Love that could lead to folly, even to martyrdom. **Have their way**, this was perfect surrender, the self-surrender that supposes annihilation, a destruction of myself : **Let Jesus have His way** meant let the God of love act freely ; let Mary have her way, this was blindly to confide to my Mother the task of realizing Jesus, cloaked and hidden from human eyes by the mantle of my external being" (p. 171).

It is also in the Hearts of Jesus and Mary that the young religious of Jesus and Mary would learn the fraternal love that is
lived in a religious community. She expressed it very well when
she wrote : "It is a common belief in the world that the most
legitimate affections soon cool and gradually decrease in the
atmosphere of the cloister. What a regrettable error! No, there,
more than anywhere, they develop and attain their full maturity.
Friendship, freed by grace from all natural self-seeking, is rapidly
transformed into the true flower of charity. I like to represent my
affections as so many links in a chain. Two principal links of
dazzling beauty are welded together : Christ and His Blessed
Mother. Can one love more and better than with the Hearts of
Jesus and Mary!" (p. 131). This beautiful symbol of the "rings"
clarifies well the most important and yet very delicate question
of spiritual friendship in the consecrated life. Dina, who had
made a vow of virginity at the age of 14 (cf. p. 68), is an example of the real meaning of consecrated chastity[2] : there is in her
no fear of love, withering of the heart or cooling of love, but
rather the growth of love. It is a matter of loving more and better with the Hearts of Jesus and Mary. Dina who had a very affectionate nature and who had certainly experienced a spiritual
struggle in her chastity, is not afraid to speak of her "affections"
and her "human friendships". In the Hearts of Jesus and Mary,
Dina found at once a means of living such friendships well ; for
Teresa of Avila a conversion, after many years, was required!

---

[2] Dom Crenier makes precise reference to this "interior trial which tormented
her almost continually from her twentieth to her twenty-sixth year, and which
recurs, even more intensely, during the last two years of her life. It is easy to recognize, from the way she speaks, that it is a matter of temptations against purity.
Most of the saints experience this trial by fire. Being morally certain that this kind
of temptation was in question, we asked some of those who knew Mary St Cecilia
of Rome well what was meant ; they replied that our supposition was accurate." (A
Life in Christ, Vol. II, pp. 330-331)

But this very love expressed as the love of neighbour is evidently not limited to the relationships and friendships of community life, it extends to all people, each one being "a brother for whom Christ died" (*1 Cor 8*,11). With Dina as with Thérèse de Lisieux, this universal charity is expressed principally in a concern for the salvation of all, without exception ; that all should be saved, that not one be lost. "I would close the gates of Hell to them for ever" declared Dina (p. 138). With surprising accuracy she expresses her sense of obligation to cooperate in the salvation of all, even while affirming that Jesus is the only Saviour : "I thus understood how I could be an apostle of love. The divine Mendicant made me fathom this truth, that all people are interdependent in their spiritual life no less than in society. I thus understood that I had a moral responsibility towards all souls in the whole world, both those now living and those who will one day be called into existence. In the following manner, the actions of Jesus have an infinite value, one single act of love offered to His Father is sufficient to save millions of worlds. Therefore if I remained totally annihilated, the Saviour, hidden from view by the mantle of my exterior being, could freely and without hindrance achieve His apostolic mission, that is to baptise and purify souls in His Precious Blood, draw them into the path of perfection and make them follow Him, to the odour of His ointments" (p. 161). Here we have yet again one of the aspects of the substitution : in me it is Christ who saves because, in reality, "It is not I who live, but it is He who lives in me".

The two parts of the Autobiography

In the *Autobiography* of Dina two main parts can be distinguished, of more or less the same length.

The first part was written in four months. With her characteristic love of accuracy, Dina ends this first section with a very precise note : "These pages of my *Canticle of Thanksgiving or Hymn of Love* were begun in March 1924 and finished on

30 June" (p. 178). In it Dina recounts the events of her life until that date : childhood, adolescence, her life as a student and as a pianist, her entry into the Congregation of the Religious of Jesus and Mary.

The second part takes up the account "from the month of July" (p. 179) of the same year 1924. But then the literary style becomes quite different ; it resembles rather a "Spiritual Diary" and would be written over a period of five years (until the month of July 1929).

In order to understand the meaning of these two parts, it is necessary to turn to two great Doctors of the spiritual life, St Teresa of Avila and St John of the Cross. Dina had not read their works, but what she writes corresponds exactly to their teachings.

The first part of the *Autobiography* is an account of a spiritual ascent to an already high level, that of the Sixth Mansion as described by St Teresa of Avila (in the *Interior Castle*, which is her masterpiece, the best synthesis). Nevertheless, this was not yet the summit of the spiritual life, which is the transforming union which is characteristic of the Seven Mansions. Teresa herself tells us that she had not attained those heights when she wrote her own *Autobiography*.

It is, however, precisely this summit of transforming union that dominates throughout the whole of the second part of the *Autobiography* of Dina. The young religious attained it very rapidly during the following months. But in order to reach it she had, necessarily, to pass through the final purification described by St John of the Cross as the *Dark Night of the Soul*.

The night of the soul (July-December 1924)

The painful experience described by Dina after the month of July 1924, which reached its climax with the "non-death" of

15 August, corresponds exactly with the description given by
St John of the Cross[3].   Dina was convinced that she was going
to die on the 15 August, convinced that this had been revealed to
her ; from which came the impression that it had been a total
illusion.   The night of the soul is the drama[4] that the person who
is already so close to God experiences on feeling himself
paradoxically far from Him ; although being so close to holiness,
the awareness of the depth of sinfulness is felt even more
intensely.   Bathed in the purest light, this person perceives roots
of evil in the depths of his heart with such clarity that he feels
rejected by God and lost for ever. This is exactly what Dina felt :

"After the month of July, I was cast into deep obscurity.
Jesus slumbered profoundly. Not only did He sleep, but at times
He seemed to repel me as though displeased with my conduct, I
saw myself descend into Hell, but was it not the place I
deserved? My actions appeared pitifully poor, devoid of merit"
(p. 179).

At the same time, the person who experiences this purification constantly overcomes this impression by clinging ever more
closely to the Lord by the theological virtues of Faith, Hope and
Charity. St John of the Cross describes, symbolically, the person
who is undergoing this trial as being completely clothed with the
triple garment of Faith, Hope and Charity. It is this that renders

---

[3] Such was the interpretation already offered by Dom Crenier : "Although it is
very difficult to make a judgement in such matters, it would seem, however, that
one can assume that the long period of darkness which begins with the 'nondeath'
of 15 August 1924, corresponds to what St John of the Cross calls the night of the
soul. In any case, it is sure that it was then that Marie Sainte-Cécile de Rome gives
up her own thoughts, the way in which she had hitherto understood supernatural
things and desired them. From this time, she entered the night of pure faith and
was never to come forth from it"(*ibidem*, vol. II, p. 330).

[4] It is thus that F. Marie-Eugène de l'Enfant-Jesus characterises it in his book *Je
veux voir Dieu* (Venasque, éd. du Carmel, dernière édition en 1988), one of the
best syntheses of carmelite spirituality.

him invincible, even when everything else has been stripped away, finding support neither in reason or feeling. Thus, far from going backwards, a great advance in the theological life takes place, as Dina herself says so well :

"...yet my faith and confidence increased as the darkness thickened. What a signal grace my Master bestowed on me! Peace flooded my soul. It was not a perceptible peace that I could feel and enjoy, but rather the trustful assurance of love, the stubborn confidence of a will that believes and hopes in the infinite goodness of God. I lost myself more completely in my only Good and strove to annihilate myself more and more. At certain hours, I clung desperately to my anchor of trust, feeling myself suspended as it were, above the abyss of discouragement ; with the most implicit confidence did I cleave to My God..." (p. 179).

And here, Dina's account is tranformed into an admirable prayer :

"I repeated again and again, 'Jesus, I feel that you are not pleased with me, but I shall not yield to this impression. I know, I believe that You love me and You know well that I love You, that I desire to love You with the strongest, purest love. You did love Mary Magdalen... Oh! I know You will take pity on me! I love You and I surrender myself to You. Here alone is peace and happiness' " (p. 180).

This prayer to Jesus is a most beautiful expression of the three theological virtues in their reciprocal relationship. In the first place it is by an act of faith that Dina overcomes the impression of having been rejected : "I know, I believe that you love me". These words echo those of St Paul : "I live in faith in the Son of God who loved me and who gave Himself up for me" (*Gal 2*, 20). This act of faith immediately arouses an act of love : "and You, you know that I love You and that I wish to love you with the greatest and purest love". Dina uses literally the words of the Apostle Peter in his last dialogue with the resurrected Christ (*Jn 21*,15-19). To the question "Do you love me?", repeated three times, Peter replies : "You know that I love you", and it is by this triple act of love that he is forgiven his triple denial. In the same poverty Dina dares also to say "I love You" completing it with a desire to love even more. Finally, hope in God's mercy, symbolized by the anchor (*Heb* 6, 19) in the preceding lines, appears here linked to Mary Magdalen whom Jesus loved with a merciful love, forgiving her many sins (cf. *Lk* 7). All is completed with the repetition of the "I love", love being the greatest of the three theological virtues.

This very beautiful text is particularly illuminating ; it shows how this "Jesus I love you", which is like the "continual breathing" of Dina, is not sentimentality, but the most beautiful, and always Christocentric, expression of the theological virtue of love. But this does not prevent Dina, during the same period, from a sensible expression of this act of love :

"On seeing my imperfections I say to Jesus, 'See what I can do left to myself. I bring this mistake, and I beg of You to repair my fault, for this I love You, I love You, I love You'. Then I often take my crucifix, kiss the sacred wounds, the wound on the shoulder and then the divine lips saying, 'Dearest Jesus, if I had not committed this blunder,You would not have had so many kisses and so many acts of love'. I think that my Divine Master takes pleasure in my little involuntary failings in order to give me an opportunity to make acts of greater confidence. What is certain is that my shortcomings develop in my soul the virtues of love and humility" (p. 185).

Here Dina is particularly close to Thérèse de Lisieux, she demonstrates the same "loving trust" or "loving audacity", the same way of making reparation for faults by acts of love. This is characteristic of a childlike spirituality : to always dare to "throw oneself into the arms of Jesus" according to the characteristic expression of Thérèse who wrote in the final lines of her *Auto biography* : "Even if I had on my conscience all the faults that it is possible to commit, I would go heartbroken with sorrow and throw myself into the arms of Jesus"[5].

---

5 *Manuscript* C, fol. 36v.

To the summit of sanctity : transforming union as the trinitarian fulfilment of christocentrism (from January 1925)

This purification of the night of the soul ends in January 1925, with the grace of transforming union : "I no longer picture myself in the depths of Hell. Being always annihilated in the Heart of my God, it seems to me that I am in the Holy Trinity, in Heaven itself" (p. 209). All that Dina describes then, in such a personal fashion, in her own words and without copying, corresponds exactly to the teaching of St Teresa in the Seven Mansions. This transforming union, which is the plenitude of love, is essentially characterised by a very profound knowledge of the trinitarian and christological mystery and by a perfect balance between action and contemplation, symbolised by Martha and Mary.

According to Teresa of Avila, the entrance into the Seventh Mansions is characterised by a new awareness of the Holy Trinity, in an "intellectual vision", that is to say, without any images[6], immediately followed by a renewed discovery of the saintly humanity of Jesus in an "imaginary vision" that is to say, incarnated, with an interior image[7].

This is exactly what Dina experienced. Her constant christocentrism became ever deeper and wider so that it came to include the dimension of the trinitarian mystery. This new discovery of the Trinity was accompanied by a re-discovery of the Heart of Jesus, the centre of His saintly humanity :

"Since Sunday, the 25 January, I have been experiencing a new state of soul. This date seems to have opened up a series of

---

6 *Interior Castle*, VII Mansion, ch. 1.

7 *Ibidem*, ch.2.

days of much grace. I feel in an abode of infinite, unutterable marvels. There in the Heart of the Three, nothing is palpable. What purity! What love! sensible pictures of the imagination representing the Eternal Father, the adorable Trinity, [...] have faded from my mind [...]. From the heart of the Trinity, through the glorious open wound of the Heart of Jesus, descend torrents of graces, like impetuous and innumerable oceans" (p. 211).

The great theme of the "substitution" became clarified in an altogether new form, at the heart of the trinitarian communion. The substitution permits Dina to enter into the exchange of love between Jesus and His Father in the Holy Spirit :

"The Trinity of love is in search of souls to whom it may give Itself with all Its divine treasures. To give, to give Itself is the great need of infinite Goodness. The souls who give themselves up wholly and perfectly to the Sovereign Will are rare. So that God may pour out His Graces with profusion into a human soul He must find Jesus living in it. The capacity of the soul is too limited to receive the ocean of divine blessings, but Jesus, the Immensity substituted for the limited, can satisfy in some measure the boundless desires of the Eternal Father. To become an abyss fit to be flooded by the Infinite, there must be first of all, in the spiritual domain, absolute emptying out of the human, then the substitution of Jesus for this human being, and perfect and continual abandonment of the soul to the will of the Divine Operator. The adorable Trinity longs to pour out its superabundance of mercy and love upon Jesus substituted in my being. My sweet Master, in my stead, says to the Father (always in silence, I cannot express it otherwise) : Father, behold me ready to do Thy Will. Father, the hour has come, accomplish Thy designs in me" (p. 212).

Paradoxically, this summit of the transforming union is nevertheless still a constant ascension. Dina never ceases to enter more deeply into the mystery of the Trinity and the Heart of Jesus. The mystery is ever new, and Dina expresses it with lovely symbols : "innumerable flowers", the "enclosed garden", the "sanctuary", the "tabernacle" of the Holy Trinity, into which Jesus allows her to enter gradually. It is this experience of God ever new, "from beginnings to beginnings" (St Gregory of Nyssa), which will be our joy in heaven. The transforming union gives us a foretaste. It is in this sense that the "vow of perfection" should be understood, this "ever more" of the Love which never ceases.

The experience of infinite love

Dina then lived the mystery of love in its fullest dimensions, in the communion of the Holy Spirit which is at one and the same time the mutual love of Jesus and His Father, the mutual love of Jesus and His bride, the Church. A nuptial mysticism is very present in Dina's thoughts. "The gift of God, for consecrated souls, is the Heart of the Spouse" (p. 269). It attains its fullness. Having attained holiness, the consecrated person lives in the heart of the Church which is Spouse to such a degree that he/she becomes identified with it, with the love that burns within it : "In the heart of the Church I will be love, thus I will be everything" wrote Thérèse of Lisieux[8]. With Dina, as with Thérèse, charity manifests itself in the dimension of totality and infinity. According to St John of the Cross, at these summits the communion between the Bridegroom and the Bride becomes a true "equality of love"[9] : the Bride is able to love her bridegroom as much as she is loved by Him, because she loves Him with His own love. Dina expresses this in an original and striking fashion when she speaks of "exhausting the Infinite" in order to "satisfy the Infinite".

---

8 *Manuscript B*, fol. 3v.

9 *Spiritual Canticle* B, v. 38.

In Heaven, I want to fully satisfy the infinite love of God ; to realize my ideal, I must realize the infinite treasures of Our Lord ; the good Master said, *Ask and you shall receive*, well, in Heaven **I shall beg for love** : this is my mission which I can enter upon immediately. Jesus in His immense charity needs to give Himself to souls ; if He could, He would exhaust His treasures of graces for each one. Yes, I desire to exhaust the Infinite Jesus to fully satisfy infinite love (p. 238).

Like Thérèse of Lisieux, Dina expresses the "infinite desire" to receive all the love contained in the Heart of Jesus, and in this sense to exhaust it, not so much for her personal satisfaction, but rather for His satisfaction, in order to satisfy infinitely by returning this infinite love to Him. This "exchange of love" which consists in offering Jesus "love for love" is the greatest spiritual fecundity for the salvation of all. Mary is always maternally present : "I shall be a little mendicant in the name of every human heart. It is Our Lady who will distribute the wealth of the Heart of Jesus and, buried in the Heart of Mary, I shall incessantly beg its outpouring. Yes, in Heaven, until the end of the world I shall constantly beg for love" (p. 239). Like Thérèse, Dina knows that she will "spend her heaven doing good on earth". Mary is associated with this double movement, that which consists in exhausting as in satisfying : "He has given me His Heart. I can dispose of It as I will! On realizing this gift, I looked at Our Lady. I offered her my divine Treasure saying : 'O my Mother, spend it as you will, but satisfy the adorable Trinity and satisfy my Jesus' " (p. 259). In the same sense she also writes : "I surrender myself, I abandon myself and I let Thee and my Mother have your way. I take nothing upon myself, for my interfering would spoil everything ; I have but one concern — to love Thee" . "O Master, Thou hast but one desire — to give Thyself. Then exhaust Thyself in all souls, I beg of Thee, for Thy glory" (p. 264).

As Charles Peguy understood so well, "Christianity has placed the infinite everywhere". Starting from the Mystery of the Incarnation, the Infinite entered the finitude of our humanity and came into our hearts with "the gift of the Holy Spirit which has been given to us" (*Rom* 5, 5). With Dina, this is expressed principally by the desire to love Jesus infinitely : "I love my Jesus and because I love Him, I wish to be able to suffer for Him, in union with Him, as much as He suffered for me. He has loved me and He loves me unto folly ; to correspond to His excessive love I want to love Him infinitely and if it pleases Him to give me the grace, I shall love Him with His Heart unto the infinitely Infinite" (p. 330). And this desire is truly realised in the trinitarian communion : "Oh adorable Trinity, by the heart of Jesus, I love Thee with the same love that Thou hast for Thyself, infinitely, eternally and divinely, for Thyself and Thyself alone, in the name of, and in union with all creatures, in the name of and in union with all by whom Thou mayest wish to be loved, I render Thee all the homage that can be given Thee, according to the immensity of the Infinite Spirit" (p. 248). This is not a question of pious exaggerations. The saints never exaggerate, but they express the |truth, the reality of this love of which the only measure is that it is unmeasurable. Thus St Thomas explains how "love can always increase, to infinity ; there is no limit to its growth because it is a certain participation in that infinite love which is the Holy Spirit"[10]. And he explains how we are already without limits in our love, for in this life we can love *immediately, totally and unmeasurably*[11] Him whom we shall know perfectly in another life, when the obscurity of faith will have given way to the clarity of vision. It is impossible not to compare these three adverbs with those of Dina : *infinitely, eternally and divinely*. It would be appropriate at this point to quote another passage in which Dina explains each of these adverbs :

---

[10] *Summa Theologica*, II-II, q. 24 art. 4 and 7.

[11] *Ibidem*, II-II, q. 27 art. 4, 5 and 6.

"My Jesus, yes, I wish Thee to satisfy Thyself fully in me, but I also wish that Thou shouldst satisfy Thyself fully in each and every soul. I want Thy perfect satisfaction because of Thee and the adorable Trinity, and because of each one of Thy creatures, and I want it infinitely, eternally and divinely. I must explain something of what I mean by these last three words. Thy perfect satisfaction, infinitely, eternally, divinely : I desire it 'infinitely', that is, multiplied to the infinitely infinite, to the utmost capacity of the wishes of Thy power, of the desires of Thy love, of the very caprices of Thy tenderness and the unfathomable immensity of Thy boundless comprehension. I want it 'eternally', that is to say, in the ages without beginning and without end, from Thy divine, uncreated existence, from always and incessantly, at each instant of the eternity which will never have an end. I want it 'divinely' that is to say, by Thyself. A God alone can satiate the Infinite. O Jesus,' yes, by Thee, I want to satiate the eternal and sovereign Trinity ; the most Holy Father, His Adorable Word and the Spirit of Charity. O my God, by Jesus, I want to fully satisfy Thee, for Thyself, because Thou art my God, because Thou art Infinite, because of each of Thine attributes and perfections. When I express to God my desire of loving Him, I must needs add these three adverbs. By them Our Lord understands what I desire for the glory of His Father and the adorable Trinity, which is all that a human creature can desire through the Spirit and the Heart of God ; that for the consolation of His Heart, I desire the salvation and the sanctification of all souls just as He desires it Himself" (p. 338-339).

Communion with the heart of Jesus in the mystery of his agony

Dina became indeed the bride of Christ, as his "alter ego", to such a degree that she understood Him to name her **"my little ownself"** (p. 282). He then manifests to her the full love of His Heart, that love of which He gave the supreme expression in His

Passion, in His Agony. This intimate communion with the agonising heart of Jesus is one of the most beautiful of the final chapters of the *Autobiography*, in harmony with the teachings of the
greatest saints and spiritual authors.

Dina understands Jesus to say to her : "My Agonising Heart
saw in Gethsemane, besides consecrated souls, the multitude of
other souls" (p. 305). In the same way Pascal placed these
words in the mouth of Jesus "I thought of you in my agony"[12] ;
and Thérèse de Lisieux, in communion with the same mystery
said : "Jesus, you saw me"[13]. The best theological justification
for this was given by St.Thomas Aquinas : thanks to the beatific
vision that Jesus constantly enjoyed in the depths of His soul,
Jesus could really see each one of us, just as He saw God His
Father. But already St Paul had the conviction of having been
personally loved by Jesus in His Passion when He declared : "The
Son of God loved me, and gave Himself up for me" (*Gal 2*, 20).

In the agonising Heart of Jesus Dina discovers the whole of
humanity, but especially those whom Jesus loved with a special
love, by associating them more particularly with His mystery :
these are priests and consecrated persons. Every thing that Dina
writes concerning them is most powerful, very beautiful and also
of great relevance to the present day when the Church is reflecting further on identity and formation in the priestly and consecrated life. Dina has a remarkable sense of the solidarity of the
whole of humanity in Christ but more especially in the priestly
ministry and consecrated life. In the light of Vatican II, one
could interpret what she writes considering the baptismal and
the priestly ministry in relation with the unique priesthood of
Christ, as it is expressed in the great priestly offering of His
agony. In the time of Dina it was customary to speak of the

---

[12] Pensées, No. 739 (Ed. Lafuma) : Le Mystère de Jésus-Christ.

[13] Poem 24 : *Jésus, mon Bien-Aimé, rappelle-toi*, verse 21.

priest as another Christ : "sacerdos alter Christus". For Dina, this truth is a call : the priest should become what he is, as Jesus gave her to understand : "My priests should be other Christs" (p. 294). But Dina is herself a consecrated woman, the bride whom Jesus calls "my little ownself". Her entire message to priests as also to consecrated persons, read in the agonising Heart of Jesus, is a powerful call to holiness : how much Jesus loves them and calls them to love Him in refusing Him nothing. She demonstrates the wonderful beauty and fecundity of a consecrated person who refuses Jesus nothing. On seeing this she writes : "Oh my Jesus, how beautiful Thou art!" (p. 300), for she had become pure transparency of Jesus, a pure instrument of His work of salvation : "In the consecrated souls given up to me entirely, in whom I act freely, my rays attain all souls until the end of time" (p. 305). Thus Dina understood Jesus to say to her : "Do not refuse me anything, My little spouse" (p. 304), and yet again : "Your power, by My Divine Heart, is infinite ; your part is great in the salvation and sanctification of all souls in the present and in the future" (p. 305).

In all this there is evidently no "dolorisme" for the greatest of all joys, that of the victory and the triumph of love, pervades all suffering. This is the greatest paradox of Jesus the crucified one, who was, at one and the same time "happy and suffering", according to St Catherine of Siena. Dina lived this mystery in its depths and she gives a good example of it when she writes : "On the one hand I was at recreation through obedience. Jesus wished me to be in good spirits. On the other hand, His Heart wished me to taste the bitterness of His Agony" (p. 345). In the same sense Dina understood Jesus as saying to her "a soul cannot approach My heart, without being happy, because I am the source of all joy and happiness" (p. 353). In the same way it was when she was enduring the most grievous suffering that Thérèse de Lisieux could affirm "Jesus, my joy is to love You"[14]. This is

---

[14] Poem 44 : *Ma Joie*, last verse.

the meaning of all the final dialogues between Dina and Jesus, in 1929, in the last pages of her *Autobiography* "How sweet it is to love Thee Jesus!" "If you knew how sweet it is to My Heart to be loved!" (p. 360).

And just as Thérèse had defined her mission on earth as in heaven with these simple words "to love Jesus and to make Him loved"[15] Dina also could declare : "...my duty now, and my occupation during Eternity until the end of time, is, and will be, **to radiate Jesus upon all souls, through the Blessed Virgin**" (p. 266).

Fr. FRANÇOIS-MARIE LÉTHEL, o.c.d.

Professor of Theology at the Teresianum, Rome.

Rome, 28 June, 1994.

---

[15] *Letter*, 24 February 1897.

INTRODUCTION

PRAISED FOR EVER BE JESUS AND MARY!
CANTICLE OF THANKSGIVING
or
SONG OF LOVE

O Jesus, I promised not to think back to the past any-more so as to concentrate only on you, in the present, and now out of obedience I must re-live those times past that I thought were dead, at least here on earth. It is your will, I must submit to it lovingly. My only pleasure is TO LET YOU HAVE YOUR WAY. I have abandoned myself completely to your action, so that, without hindrance, you may be able to fulfil your designs in me, poor as I am ; to act freely, always and in everything. You have given me the grace to abandon myself to your love, you have blotted me out, and in the purest transport of grati-tude, I cry out : "I live now not with my own life, but with the life of Christ who lives in me."

O my loving Spouse, how can I express your infinite goodness to me! You love me to distraction, with a love that can be explained only by the insatiable thirst of your divine Heart to give and to forgive. My utter poverty, my weakness, the depth of my nothingness : these are the objects of your gifts. From the first glimmer of reason in me, you revealed yourself to my eyes to entrance them, to my soul to captivate it. Ever since then, without ceasing, at every second, you have been the jealous Lover who watches over his betrothed and never wants her to turn her gaze away from him, so that he alone will be the master of her affections. You have plunged me into the immensity of your grace and your mercy, like a tiny sponge in the ocean. Countless times, when I was cold, forgetful, ungrateful, you multiplied your invitations and your caresses.

O Jesus, write these pages yourself so as to sing my canticle of thanksgiving ; so as to reveal your goodness and your divine power in someone as despicable as I am ; so as to prove, once again, that paradise, the perfect bliss of a soul here on earth, is TO LOVE YOU AND TO LET YOU HAVE YOUR WAY.

Without a single exception, you have bestowed your graces upon me through Mary, your good Mother and mine, whom I love so much! And it is my constant desire to let her act freely in my life so as to foster your work in me. Good Master, holy Virgin, I dedicate this work to you ; I surrender it completely to you. May this act of obedience help me to understand more fully your tenderness and my extreme poverty ; may it fire me with love for you and realize the motto of our dear Institute : Praised for ever be Jesus and Mary!

To the reader,

More often than not, Dina wrote her Canticle of Thanksgiving with great difficulty and a feeling of exhaustion, and without ever re-reading it. This new edition adheres rigorously to the substance of her text ; however, we have taken the liberty of sometimes bringing it into line with the new rules of French grammar as regards punctuation and syntax.

The summary at the head of each chapter is not part of the autobiography. The footnotes are taken from *Une vie dans le Christ* by Dom. Léonce Crenier, O.S.B.

I
FAMILY LIFE
UP TO THE AGE OF SIX
1897-1903

Protection of the Queen of Heaven. — First hymns. — A novena.
— Two dreams. — A fit of anger. — First charitable works. —
Catechism and reading lessons. — A journey.

It seems to me that, at the dawn of my life, God enveloped
me in the protective cloak of the Blessed Virgin ; my eyes first
saw the light on the eve of the month of Mary, a Friday, and that
same evening, the grace of baptism banished the evil one from
my soul, leaving the Holy Spirit in command. I belonged to
Jesus, and to his mother Mary who was to watch over my earliest
years through the intermediary of two visible guardian angels,
my excellent parents.

Yes, my excellent parents! Only in heaven will I understand
the watchfulness, devotedness and love of my father and mother.
It is one of the greatest heavenly favours, to be born and to live
in a climate of peace, union, charity, sublime example and constant conformity to the designs of Providence. "O Jesus, you have
given me this choice gift! I want to thank you for it ceaselessly
and through all eternity. Thank you for having preserved to this
day these two persons who forget themselves for your sake ;
thank them for me, yourself. Bless them in their joys, their sacrifices, their troubles. Be everything to them. To prove my
gratitude to them, I have but one duty — and a very pressing
duty : to become holy. It is a sacred obligation. If I fail in this,
I am devoid of filial devotion, I do not deserve to be called their
child, I am not responding to their past and present concern.

Yes, I will be holy insofar as God wills ; and may I thus repay the trouble they have taken over my education and console them for the sacrifices imposed by separation."

My soul was to be the only plant that my dear parents would have to cultivate. I had a small brother whom I do not remember ; I love him dearly and often pray to him. Jesus came to gather this lily and take him to paradise when he was three months old. My parents saw this act of Providence as leaving them with a heavier responsibility, a more delicate mission. Their eyes were always wide open, so as to keep far away from their frail sapling even the least harmful insect ; their lips were always open to provide it with pure sap ; their hearts were always open so as to inflame it with the noblest love.

As soon as I could talk, Mama taught me to pray. She often sang during the day, especially hymns. No sooner could my ear detect a sound than she made me sing with her, as she cradled me on her knees, while I embraced her ; or else while I was playing quite near her. I never left her. Rather, I should say that she was unable to live unless she could see me at her side. The first words of a song that I can remember are the following :

> Good morning, little Jesus,
> My joy and my delight,
> Good morning, little Jesus,
> My love, my pure delight.

> I dreamt I was in Heaven
> Alas! 'twas but a dream,
> How much my soul is saddened
> Things are not what they seem.

I sang variations of this tune countless times in every possible key. My first delight, my first love was Jesus. I did not realize then the privilege that was to be mine in the future : my only delight, my only joy would be Jesus, for the joy and affection that were to be mine later would all relate to him. And can this beautiful dream of paradise, this image so often recalled, be one of the causes of the nostalgia for heaven that has haunted me throughout my life? A delightful nostalgia, because it is one of the fruits of love, but also a nostalgia as painful as martyrdom because it is a torment born of exile. And I can say : "My God, I find it trying and have always found it trying to be far away from you, here on earth." I say *far away from you* with reference to the perfect, consummate union of the soul with the Divinity, a union that can exist only in heaven. For if I reflect on the union that is possible here on earth, I know that God is in the tabernacle, that he is living continually within me and that I am close to him, that he has substituted himself for me ; but I will speak about that later.

The first hymns I can remember are these :

See here the gentle Lamb,

The true Bread of angels.

He comes from heaven for us,

Let us adore him. etc.

and

I place my trust,

Virgin, in your help, etc. etc...

Jesus and Mary are never separated in the catalogue of divine graces of which I have been the constant recipient.

I was not yet three years old when Mama began to take me to religious functions. Apart from the Mass, I remember in particular the meetings of the Ladies of the Holy Family : I felt lost at the end of a long bench for six people, in the choir-loft, near the organ. Sometimes I played. Once, during the sermon, I took out of my pocket a tiny doll, about two inches long, that I had brought on purpose. Mama looked at me : "Put that away," she said. That cost me a lot as I found it so beautiful, but I did as I was told. Five minutes later, I slipped my hand into my pocket and the toy reappeared. Mama put it in her bag. What a disappointment! When we got home, I got a scolding. Then came the following sermon... A short while before we left home, the doll vanished ; I had several others but I did not fancy being without that one. Mama thought she had hidden it in a safe place. I set about looking for it. Oh joy! I found it and silently slipped it once again into my pocket. How happy I was at my victory! I did not say a word about it as we walked along. In the middle of the sermon, Valéda (that was the name of my treasure) appeared. What a surprise for Mama! My joy was redoubled. But hardly had the small porcelain head appeared between my fingers than it escaped me once again... This time, the scolding had its effect and I no longer took playthings to church.

One day, when I was about four, I had an experience that made a deep impression on me. It was during a novena in honour of St Francis Xavier. The preacher spoke about hell. The following night, in a dream, I saw frightful demons, flame-red, rushing in and out of a long railway train. They never stopped moving and were extremely agitated. I cannot describe the fear I felt. This image is as clear today, twenty-three years later, as if I had dreamt it last night. I was terrified. It caused me physical suffering for several years : I couldn't be left alone, even for a few seconds, and in the evening, the darkness made me tremble ; I would give as a reason : "I'm frightened". Yes, I was very frightened ; I kept seeing the countless terrifying demons I had dreamt of. Oh! How ugly, frightful, nasty, repulsive they were! I wish I could think up the most despicable word to describe them. I consider this dream a great grace. Because of this horrible fear of the devil, I had a parallel hatred for sin, a prompting of the devil. Mama did not go to any more of the sermons given during this novena, because she saw I was too upset.

I had a special devotion to the recitation of the *Angelus*. At the first sound of the clock striking, I would stop playing, or taking a meal if I was at table. Often, at that moment, I would be playing within sight of Mama, at the end of the garden, waiting for Papa to return from work. At the first stroke of the clock, I would run upstairs and answer faithfully, *Amen*. As my parents said this prayer in Latin, this word was for a long time all I knew.

What a joy it was when Papa came home in the evening! Only occasionally could he come at midday. He would take me in his arms, kiss me and sometimes cuddle me for quite a long time before supper, even when he must have been quite tired. He idolized me. He spent hours playing with me and answering my endless questions. His great joy was to give me some pleasant surprise : a walk, a present of some kind, a rosary, a small statue, a toy, a piece of jewellery. As for the latter, the first pieces of jewellery I remember were a small heart-shaped locket and a small cross. A heart : symbol of the gift of my own heart to Jesus, of my love for him ; and a cross : sign of Jesus's love for me.

If my father and mother cherished me so tenderly, they also knew how to be firm and to correct me, and I often needed this. I did not like being found fault with, I was very strong-willed. How grateful I am to my parents for having known how to love me in the fullest sense of that word! For true love presupposes correction. What would have become of me had I been left to the mercy of my pride, my obstinacy, my whims, my unjustifiable roguishness. I would have been all the more ill-humoured and unbearable because of being brought up on my own, never thwarted by other children ; and later on, I would never have been able to get on with people or be tolerated without unwittingly causing everyone to suffer. "My God, thank you for making my parents teach me to obey them." In spite of the thorough formation that I received, I have been and still am a cause of suffering to others. Do I have to say that this is not intentional? I do not mean to cause the least upset to anyone! Oh, no! A thousand times no! My blunders and my sharp words are a proof of my nothingness.

One day, I had a fit of temper ; I was not yet four. I refused to do what Mama asked me to do. When she told me a second time, I got angry and began to stamp my feet, to cry and dance around. Then Papa got up and taking me by the hand calmly said : "Come on, then, I'll help you to cry and dance around and then it will be over all the sooner." Hearing my father imitate my shouting and spiteful tears, I stopped at once ; My pride was stung. I no longer wanted to dance around ; nevertheless, I had to go on jumping around, the two of us together ; that was my punishment and how it hurt my resentful inner feelings! I have not forgotten that lesson, gentle yet so salutary that I was cured for ever of the desire to show my annoyance by stamping my feet.

I used to accompany Mama on her charitable visits. All my life, I have seen my parents with their hands wide open to help the poor, give generous alms to all, and console those in trouble by their spiritual and encouraging words, by frequent and lengthy visits, and by their readiness to perform the most humble and often the most unpleasant services ; to console and help those in trouble, the sick and the suffering. Hidden suffering, unrecognised need incited them to even greater devotedness, if that were possible. It was always their delight to give silently and in secret. I have often heard them say, "Don't mention my name", or else, "This is for you, don't say anything about it" ; and there were many anonymous gifts! Individuals may not know the name of their benefactors, but God looks down more lovingly on the generosity that is shown in secret. I think my father and mother will be agreeably surprised on the day of judgment. They have no idea of the value of the sacrifices they have made in favour of all without distinction ; what is more, they forgot the good deeds they had done as soon as they were over ; but the hand of God weighed them all up and the finger of God, infinitely just, recorded them and inscribed them continually in letters of gold.

Caring for the sick is a real mission for Mama, while my father plays just as important a part in this since, by consenting to and supporting her charitable undertakings, he has had to make heroic sacrifices on many occasions. How many outings has he had to forego, how many projects have had to be abandoned so that this or that family, relative or stranger could be helped, whether by day or night, near or far, in an emergency or simply in case of need!

For a month, I accompanied Mama on her visits to a cousin who died after an illness lasting several weeks. I was five. Each morning, we had an early breakfast, tidied up quickly and then, without delay, I took Mama's hand and we set off! We nearly always went on foot, about fifteen minutes' walk. The morning at least was spent there ; sometimes we came home only in the evening.

My parents loved to give other children small treats, cakes, sweets or fruit etc. They taught me to share whatever I had with them and lend them my toys gladly. They were very anxious that I should not grow up to be selfish. They taught me to take great care of everything I had - and what a lot I had! - and to keep or put everything in order. I had to be very careful not to break anything. At the end of play-time, I put everything away myself. If I forgot, a word from Mama reminded me. After fifteen years or more, I gave away fragile toys that I had played with, and they were still in reasonable condition. I had plenty of accidents and I did not easily forget my clumsiness.

Mama, assisted by Papa, was my first catechist. In answer to my thousands of 'Why's, they would attribute everything good to God, and speak to me about the Blessed Virgin, the angels and saints. It was my mother, too, who taught me to read fluently before I ever went to school. I learnt easily and with much enthusiasm.

I had a devotion to holy pictures and would set up 'chapels' ; I would sing Mass or organise processions.

When I was five, I went on a journey to Montreal with my parents. It was not secular monuments that caught my attention but churches and statues. I realise now that Jesus put me on this earth so as to busy myself only with him. He has loved me with a love of predilection. It is the number and extent of my defects that have attracted his attention, called forth his compassion and prompted his munificence. It is only in the last few months that I have begun to understand a little what he is doing in my soul. Until then, I knew nothing of the wonderful favours God has granted me in order to keep me for himself. Oh! How aware I am of my extreme weakness and of being annihilated in my nothingness! At that time, I was present at a religious ceremony in the Hospital of the Precious Blood. One of my cousins was giving herself to Our Lord. I paid great attention to all that took place in the cloister. So that I would have a better view - there was a big congregation - my parents lifted me up in their arms. Someone offered to let Mama take me up into the pulpit. She accepted gratefully. My eyes were glued to the black grille, and everything seemed so beautiful!

As I had several relatives who were religious, I used to go with my mother to visit them in different convents. I was very observant and spoke little, but I remembered ; I pretended not to understand the conversation, especially when they would say : "I hope she will be a religious one day." Even if the question was put directly to me, I gave nothing away. The positive answer — for I had felt drawn to the religious life from my earliest years — was kept for Our Lord.

I can remember my first confession. Having prepared me, Mama told me to go to whichever priest in the parish I felt most at ease with, although she made it quite clear to me that in the confessional, we should see God and not the priest himself. "I am going to Fr. X," I told her, "because I know him." I still remember some of the kind words he spoke to me.

At that time, too, I received the Scapular of the Blessed Virgin. I felt safe when I was wearing the livery of my heavenly Mother.

I gave the devil a most original name which I had invented so as to show my disdain for him ; I called him 'Le Capidule'.

Jesus increased his kind attentions towards me. Here is one example. It is another dream, but I will tell it, nevertheless. When I was about the same age (five), I saw the Child Jesus one night in my sleep ; he was about four or five years old, breathtakingly beautiful and standing with open arms a little above the foot of my bed. I was gazing at him. Smiling, he said to me : "What would you like?" — "Will you let me have your portrait?", I answered innocently. I found him so beautiful and that is just what he was. My dream faded away but it gave me great joy and even now, the memory of it is filled with peace and love.

I did not forget my request and I was sure it would be granted. Christmas was approaching. After Midnight Mass, I found — as if it were a present from heaven — a pretty little coloured, cardboard crib. The Baby Jesus, lying in his cradle, was smiling, his arms wide open. Immediately, I exclaimed : "I knew he would send me his portrait!"

In revealing in this way some of God's favours, I feel quite confused! Only obedience can cause me to relate such things. To speak continually about myself and to repeat the pronoun I that I would prefer to see abolished for ever... Oh! (Do I have to say what I feel? Yes, since I must be perfectly open.) Oh! At a purely human, natural level, it is an indescribable torture, which turns into the sweetest joy only because Jesus wishes it. Each time I take up a pencil to continue this work, I overcome, by God's grace, a painful repugnance and I am sure that the devil is far from pleased with my submission. I am pressed for time...[1] Yet I am perfectly at peace, even though the time I have to write these lines is measured out and short.

---

[1] According to Jesus's owm words, Dina was certain she would die on the following 15 August. She had scarcely four months in which to write her *Canticle of Thanksgiving*.

"Oh Jesus! Grant me the grace to let you proclaim the truth, that is, to tell of your merciful action in me, and to reveal in full daylight the depths of my poverty."

II
FROM SIX TO TEN YEARS
1903-1907

Starting school. — The moulding of her character. — Earliest
recollections of a retreat. — A patroness. — Piano lessons.

When I was six, my parents considered sending me to school.
Two weeks before the beginning of September, my mother found
me counting the days on the calendar with my finger. "What are
you doing?", she asked. — "I want to find out how many days
there are until I go to the convent." — "Why? Are you so eager
to go ?" — "Oh, no! I'm afraid I might be lonesome."— "So
much the better, then. You will enjoy it."

I began and continued my formal schooling with the religious
of The Congregation of Notre Dame. This was a thoughtful gesture on the part of the Blessed Virgin who wanted the formation
I was to receive away from home to take place within a
Congregation specially devoted to her. And, in passing, I would
like to point out that I was born and, together with my parents,
have always lived in a parish dedicated to the Immaculate
Conception. I went morning and afternoon to the Convent of St
Roch. My mother's prophecy was fulfilled to the letter. I was
interested in the lessons from the very first day and turned to
study not simply with eagerness but with passion.

I was extremely shy and sensitive ; the slightest thing
made me cry. With unrelenting ambition, I aimed at first place ;
if I failed, I worked quickly to recover lost ground. Obedience
came easily to me. I carried out the least recommendation as
faithfully and promptly as I did the sternest commands. I did not
take advantage of any concessions ; for example, my hair was

naturally curly and, in this case, we were allowed to keep it tied back, but I sacrificed my curls and had my hair plaited so as to conform with the general rule.

My teacher's wish was law for me. One evening, at 4 o'clock, just as we were going home, my teacher handed out the *Eucharistic Newsletter*, a monthly publication in which was printed a hymn in honour of St Joseph, with the music ; she added : "If you knew this hymn, you could sing it tomorrow." This was as much a command for me as a formal order would have been. I arrived home and, after greeting Mama, asked her to teach me the hymn for the next day. If I remember rightly, the song began : *Fill me with holy joy...* I wanted to master it perfectly ; how I cried over it! I was so afraid of forgetting it overnight.

My young soul found prayer very attractive. At home, at this sacred time, it was easy to recollect myself ; I was used to joining my hands, closing my eyes and shutting out any noise there was around me. At the convent, I had numerous companions and some of them would fidget a little while speaking to God. At midday, we said the rosary. To avoid distraction, I closed my eyes, of course, but also formed a habit of covering my face with one hand. I felt at ease like this, I saw no one and had no wish to be seen. But my good teacher was keen on order and could not allow me to be different, I am grateful to her now. She called out to me and made a sign indicating that I should do as the others were doing. It was a sacrifice ; I obeyed.

Silence was no problem for me. I took care not to say a single word once the signal had been given. How God favoured me in giving me the strength to allow myself to be formed in my childhood and youth! I am only just beginning to discover the abundance of graces he showered on me so that his loving designs might be fulfilled in me!

When I was seven, I made the retreat organized annually for children. I knew that I had to take this series of spiritual exercises very seriously and to pay great attention to what was said. Our Lord drew me perceptibly to himself. On the third day, I loved my dear little Jesus so much and was so anxious to see him and have him for myself that I prayed as fervently as I could that he would take me to his beautiful heaven that very evening. This desire haunted me. During the night, I was surprised to wake up and find myself still on earth ; the next morning, I was extremely disappointed that my prayer had not been granted.

I was punctilious in following my lessons. Fatigue, cold weather, an outing, a journey - however tempting - could not keep me away from school or make me late.

As for my choice of friends, I was selective ; they were few in number ; I remained faithful to those with whom I got on well. Mama always allowed me to bring them home. She invited them for my sake, since by nature I liked to be alone. Only very seldom did she allow me to play out of her sight, even when she knew I was with excellent families. A Christian and generous mother, she watched over her frail sapling with tenderness and a jealous love. She taught me to be discreet ; at the same time, I was receiving a similar training at the convent. I was not to say anything at school or elsewhere about what went on in my family. At home, I was allowed to talk only about the pupils' outstanding achievements, without, however, distorting the truth. Oh, no! For my parents had at an early age instilled into me a horror of lying! When inquisitive or indiscreet questions were put to me, I would remain silent or talk about something else.

I enjoyed going to the church. It was only a few steps away from our house. I used to go to evening prayer. Often, during the week, my parents were unable to go. Mama would watch me from the window ; in the same way, she watched over my comings and goings between my home and the convent.

Praise and compliments made little impression on me. Besides, my father and mother taught me so effectively to attribute my childhood success and my talents to God's goodness that they dulled the potentially dazzling effect of any conceited ideas I might have had as soon as they appeared.

One day, my teacher asked me if I knew who my patron was. "No," I answered, "do I have one?" — "I think so," she said, "I'll see." She searched in vain. Jacob's daughter had the same name but it proved impossible to find any canonized saint. I said to myself : "Very well! **I will be a saint**, I will provide a patron for those who bear my name!" Was not that a divine inspiration, directing my efforts towards a particular end? That was my first ambition.

When I was eight, I began to take piano lessons with a private teacher who took a great interest in me. She came to our house for four years. During that time, I took a keen interest in practising, though with moderation because of my health.

At that time, children did not make their first Communion until they were ten. When I was nine, I was taller than other girls of my age. I understood the catechism sufficiently well to receive the Bread of Heaven. Mama came with me to the presbytery to ask the parish priest to grant me the favour of approaching the holy table. This saintly priest considered it prudent to refuse our request, since it would be an exception to the established custom. Oh! How happy I would have been to be granted such a great privilege! Our Lord wanted my poor heart to have an even greater desire for him. He asked for another year of preparation and delay.

When people spoke to me about small sacrifices, it did not scare me at all ; I felt such an interior joy at being able to offer some of them to Jesus. I tried to hide them from everyone, even from my parents. I began to conceal my interior feelings of piety and devotion. My soul was turning inwards so as to be completely open only to its Creator.

Religious ceremonies made a deep impression on me. I remember one evening, during Passiontide, I took out every black and purple ribbon I possessed, draping them over the furniture and tying them to my toys in a bow. Seeing this funereal decoration, Mama asked me to find a less dismal way of amusing myself. I obeyed. I had acted in this way out of pity. I said to myself : Our Lord died for us ; I want to show my sorrow through all these signs of mourning.

I did not always find prayer books very satisfactory. I would write down my feelings towards Jesus in the form of prayers.

I was very fond of the great St Teresa. My devotion to her became more marked over the years.

I took a great delight in flowers. I loved them all. When I went to the country, they were the nicest present anyone could give me. Just to see a single one made me think of God. I would pick wild flowers, especially daisies, and make them into wreaths. I wanted them to be covered with flowers and well-made. I had a particular liking for lilies, roses and Lady's slippers — these last on account of their name which reminded me of my heavenly Mother.

I felt drawn to the religious life. When a relative described in my presence a day in the life of a Carmelite, I hastened to write down the details after she had left. I read and re-read this order of the day with admiration.

I had an indescribable horror of criticism, of passing judgment on the actions of others. I was struck by the following truth which I heard expressed : *As you have judged your neighbour, so will God judge you. Judge not and you will not be judged.* It was a divine light, and with it, I received the strength to make a resolution always to judge others favourably, a strength that has enabled me to remain faithful to my resolution to this day. How admirable is the power of grace! In my thoughts, I attributed the best intentions to everyone, whether their actions were good or reprehensible. If their guilt seemed obvious, I found excuses. In speaking, I would defend those who were not present ; how I suffered when of necessity I had to remain silent! If they were attacked in my presence, my face

became serious ; I would attempt by my silence to show disap-
proval of disparaging or unkind remarks and I would wait for a
suitable moment to slip in a word and change the course of the
conversation.   Yes, I have been and I still am very strict with
myself on this point of fraternal charity.   I was more concerned
about the reputation of others than about my own.   Of course,
that involved sacrifice : a disregard for human respect, for what
other people might say, the courage to hold to a different opinion.   That is why I understand that it is God alone who acts in
me and through me.   Being of a shy and timid nature, how could
I possibly have withstood uncharitable comments in public? No,
I could not have done it, definitely not.   God alone kept up the
struggle.   The light that was given me from above, as well as the
help, are today my consolation and my hope.   I have no fear of
the judgments of the eternal Judge, for from that early age, I cannot remember having deliberately judged anyone. "Oh, Jesus! I
beg you to continue to grant me this precious gift, and when the
time comes for my soul to wing its way towards you, it will be
immersed trustfully in your mercy, in spite of its many miseries."

III
FROM TEN TO TWELVE YEARS
1907-1909

First Communion. — A trial. — First meditation. — Effects of Holy Communion. — The voice of Jesus. — Love of solitude. — New snares of the devil.

The time came for the retreat in preparation for my first Communion. I redoubled my spirit of recollection. I have heard it said : "A First Communion well made is a ticket to Heaven ; badly made, it is almost always a ticket to Hell." I wanted to take the train to Heaven. How meticulously I prepared for confession! I intended not to leave anything out, even the smallest fault. "My God, the list of my infidelities was very long! Thank you for forgetting them all." Nevertheless, I must proclaim, with the most heartfelt gratitude, the loving protection of Our Lord and of the Blessed Virgin, for I was clothed in my baptismal robe. Jesus had watched over me ; I repeat, *he had watched over me*, so well that one day when the devil had let loose his rage against me, I had no suspicion of the terrible danger I was in. "Good Master, my dear Mother, thank you, eternal thanks!"

The solemn morning dawned. It was the 2 May. The external arrangements were of no concern to me, I was thinking of him who was to become my sacred Guest. I can remember just one involuntary distraction ; I admitted this to Mama that very day. As I approached the holy table, the devil brought before my eyes a gold wrist-watch that I had been given as a present. I showed my contempt by making an act of desire and of love and the devil never returned to the attack. My happiness was immense. Jesus was mine and I was his. This first intimate union left me with, among other things, a hunger for his Body and Blood, a hunger that was to grow greater with every succeeding visit of his.

That same day, I was enrolled in the blue and black scapulars and became a soldier of Christ through the sacrament of Confirmation. Having been anointed, I felt ready for any battle. It was a time of rejoicing for my parents and several other members of our family gathered in our house. In the evening, Our Lord took advantage of a small incident to give me another special grace. I was not wearing my first Communion dress, which was very simple, but a white silk dress trimmed with lace. In a clumsy movement, I tore it. I felt not the least regret. Jesus made me think of him : what moments of tenderness and delight! I realized the fragility of fine clothes and worldly goods. A few moments later, I withdrew in order to rest. Oh! How happy I was to escape from the noise and to converse silently with my heavenly Treasure!

I became much more recollected at prayer, avoiding every unnecessary movement and not raising my eyes when I was reading my prayer book. My conscience was extremely delicate : the slightest suggestion (of evil) made me tremble, for fear of causing my Jesus any pain ; insignificant things seemed worthy of great fidelity. A trial awaited me : that of scruples. God sent me a holy and enlightened director who, from then on, guided my soul for thirteen years.[1] I cannot explain all I owe to this devoted priest. Our Lord will pay the debt that I could not possibly settle. To return to scruples, I suffered greatly for several months. I found peace in obedience.

It was Jesus in the tabernacle who first taught me to meditate. One afternoon, towards evening, I was alone in the church.

---

[1] M. L'abbé J.-F.-P. Cloutier

While I was praying, I felt a strong desire to meditate. Before my eyes, in my prayer book, were the words : *Lord, my God!* My mind was lost in pious reflections on these divine appellations. I lost count of time and the Master continued to enlighten me for half an hour.

Another time, present in his monstrance, he held my whole being captive. I was gazing at him, without moving ; I said to him, interiorly : "Jesus, I know that it is you who are present there in the Host. Oh! Show yourself to me, let me see you with my eyes ; I so long to see you!" I contemplated him for a very long time. I was inflamed with the desire to see him. The gentle Prisoner answered my prayer with a great increase of faith in his real presence in the Blessed Sacrament. It was a signal grace.

When I had received Communion in the morning, I had no fear of exterior events. On the first Friday in July, I was in the country, visiting an aunt. In the morning, I received the Bread of the strong. The church was a long way from the house. After dinner, as the car had not been able to wait for us, my little cousin and I had to walk back. As we were on our way, a dreadful storm was brewing. In fact, it was one of the most disastrous storms. My cousin, who was ten like myself, was justifiably scared. I said to her : "We have nothing to be afraid of ; we received Communion this morning, God is with us, he will look after us." Confidence in him took away my fear. He protected us visibly, for scarcely had we stepped indoors when the storm broke.

I used to seek out small, voluntary mortifications. So that they would not be seen, I would confine them mainly to the evening or to night-time. How I wished I had a harder pillow to sleep on!

I often thought about death. During that month of July, it haunted me for a whole day. There was no feeling of fear, just salutary reflection. During my life, Our Lord has multiplied such graces, preparing me for my eternal union with him.

The cloistered life seemed increasingly attractive to me. I thought of the day of my entry, of my clothing, of my profession. From that time on, it seemed that the 25 March and the 15 August, feasts of the Annunciation and the Assumption of the Blessed Virgin, would always be memorable days for me. That is what God has wanted. Up to now, these have been the two most solemn dates in my religious life, those most fragrant with divine perfumes, most bathed in heavenly exhilaration.

While Jesus was working in my soul, my dear parents never ceased to multiply their tokens of affection and special treats. By *'treats'*, I mean special pleasures, thoughtfulness, kind attentions that only the heart of a father and of a mother can devise. I was pampered by them in the real meaning of that word, but not spoilt in the bad sense.

That year, probably because I was well-behaved and silent, my companions at the convent began to call me Saint Dina. If only they had realized the suffering they caused me! I was grateful for their indulgence, but I realised how very mistaken they were! Today, better than ever, I can see that I deserved no credit for being studious : I was borne along by an increase of divine graces. Besides, I was clever at hiding my numerous faults and imperfections.

In the month of June following my first Communion, I began to make the nine First Fridays of the month. On the ninth and last, in February, the devil, being displeased, tried to upset me with a scruple. Jesus gave me the strength to spurn this temptation (it really was one) and I received Communion. After that, I was sure of obtaining the grace of final perseverance.[2]

---

[2] There is no question here of absolute certitude, but simply a persuasion based upon a pious belief in the efficacity of the nine First Fridays.

On the following 25 March, Holy Thursday, and also the feast of the Annunciation, Our Lord revealed himself to my soul by a new light during my thanksgiving after Communion. It was the first time that I had discerned his voice so clearly - *interiorly*, of course - a soft, melodious voice that filled me with happiness.

The devil tried to lay another snare for me : the vain habit of looking at myself in a mirror. A skilled deceiver, alas! he could register one victory after another. Jesus took pity on my stupidity and gave me the strength to work at overcoming myself. He armed my will so as to conquer this weakness. Thanks to his powerful help, I managed to destroy the seductive snare, down to the very last mesh. How good was my dear Master! In spite of my infidelities, he repeated his advances ; he held out his hand to me, more wide open and stronger, to lift me up and support me. "Thank you, Jesus, forgive me!"

A few months later, at the age of eleven, I obtained my *intermediate grade* diploma for piano All around me, I heard words of congratulation. The divine Craftsman kept my heart safe ; these small successes did not cause the slightest ruffle of conceit.

I spent the summer in the country with my parents. Nature, with its beauty and varied richness, threw me into a kind of ecstasy : twilight, moonlight, plants, flowers, fruit, streams, rivers, butterflies, birds, etc. I found the mild breezes, the rustling of leaves, the silence of the evening, the twinkling smile of the stars enthralling. Although I did not realise it, my musings were a form of devout meditation. They were to become deeper and deeper, soon being termed contemplation and reducing me to silence, lost in admiration, burning with gratitude and love for the Infinite, consumed with the desire to possess him, Beauty itself, in all its perfection.

I found solitude restful. When I had the privilege of being alone, I would slip away with some spiritual books about religious life ; I read little but would reflect deeply ; I would copy out a few lines that struck me.

In the Autumn, I was given the grace of attending a clothing at the Carmelite Monastery in Montreal. The day of the ceremony was for me like a day in heaven.

No one could give me anything more precious than pious objects or spiritual books. I wanted to have the life of St Thérèse so as to read it ; I did not ask for it.

When I was twelve, I left the Convent of St Roch because that of Jacques-Cartier, also under the direction of The Congregation of Notre Dame, had just been opened in my parish. At the time, Mama thought of sending me to finish my studies with the Ursulines. Their college was a long way from our house : my mother's concern made her apprehensive about the long journey and I went to the Academy mentioned above.

At this time, the devil tried to disturb me by another stratagem : the habit of losing patience about everything and even about trifles when I was on my own. Where would this behavior have led me? At least into some ugly fault. Jesus made me realize quickly the enemy's plan. My divine Master gave me his grace and, after a series of battles, of defeats, alas! and of victories, thank God, I corrected myself.

In this way, Our Lord kept a watchful eye on my soul and if I was so weak as to obstruct his holy action, he provided me with more powerful help or, with unflagging patience, waited for my good will to return more perseveringly. Oh! If only souls knew how merciful our Saviour is, how he loves to forgive us, they would always approach him with unlimited confidence! Our weaknesses do not deter his love ; they are for him the foundation of our holiness. All he asks is our good will, our repentance and trust in his mercy. I would like to tell of the indulgence he has shown towards me all my life, but for that I would need to understand it myself.

IV
FROM TWELVE TO FOURTEEN YEARS
1909-1911

Interior peace. — Success. — Consecration to the Blessed Virgin. — Divine workings. — A mediocre mark. — A growing desire for the religious life.

Having overcome these wiles of the devil, with the help of grace from above, I found a great interior peace. I could see clearly into my soul and nothing bothered me. A horror of every venial sin increased, and Jesus put into my heart and into my will the desire not to commit a single voluntary fault so as to please him. What sweetness there is in the divine action, as well as power! I would strive after perfect contrition with great care, begging very fervently for this gift. I venture to say that, from this time, I think I obtained this sincere sorrow for my faults ; for I aimed at loving God only for his sake, I was ready for any sacrifice in order to give greater proof of my fidelity, I wanted to love him with a perfect love. The great Craftsman of my soul drove me to pursue my original ideal of holiness, while adding to it a new inspiration : **the thirst to love him perfectly**.

I obtained permission to take advantage of the magnificent decree of His Holiness Pius X regarding frequent and daily Communion. It was my sweetest joy to approach the holy table each morning and to be united with Our Lord. To this end, how many times have I not overcome extreme physical weakness! But there I found new strength. The day came when I was not allowed to go out so early in the morning. Jesus knows how much I suffered because of having to fast so often ; but it was he who asked it of me. This sacrifice increased my hunger for and my devotion to the Eucharist.

At the convent, success continued to spur me on to work hard. No doubt, God granted it to me because he saw that I would not have had the determination of those strong souls who know how to persevere in their efforts continuously, even when they do not taste success. At school, at my piano lessons (I had been studying at the Academy since September), everything was a pleasure. I attributed that to him who crowned my efforts, I thanked him, asked for his help and never felt the least temptation to pride. One day, after a very long and particularly important competition in which I came first, my companions - and here I pay tribute to their kindness and generous hearts - my companions, I say, came to congratulate me. I replied : "Thank you, but the credit is not mine ; God did it and I am merely his instrument." I was very sincere in speaking like this and I did not have to fight against any pretension. I felt so powerless, left to myself! What a precious light I received, and it kept me firmly rooted in the truth!

On the following 1 May, I was thirteen and was admitted to the Sodality of the Children of Mary at the convent. It was sheer joy to renew solemnly the consecration to my Mother that I had pronounced on the day of my first Communion. Several days later, I chose as my motto : **Death rather than defilement**. I kept this motto until the dawn of my religious life.

At about this time, I gave myself completely to the Blessed Virgin, through the practice of the perfect devotion called *The Secret of Mary* in the spirit of Blessed Louis-Marie Grignion de Montfort. This complete abandonment of myself and all I possessed to the Queen of Heaven gave me much consolation. It is now that I understand just a little how my good Mother has repaid me a hundredfold for this total offering. In heaven, I will know what an advantage it has been to me to abandon myself completely to her wise guidance. I wish I could consecrate all souls to her, for it is she who leads us to Jesus ; it is she that we must allow to live in us so that Christ can take the place of our nothingness ; she is the safest, shortest, the most perfect way to lead us to the Infinite, to unite us with uncreated Love until we are lost in him, immersed in the Source of eternal bliss. "O sweet Virgin, Mother of all mankind, reveal to all souls without a single exception, your sublime secret ; give them the light to understand it and the generosity to make it their own. In the name of all mankind, I renew the perfect gift of myself and give you thanks."

Jesus taught me to accept with joy small annoyances and humiliations. On Holy Thursday, when the temperature was quite wonderful, I was wearing a new suit for the first time. That day, many people were visiting the Repositories, the snow was melting, I slipped and fell in the slush. I was an amusing sight but I wasn't in the least put out ; on the contrary, I was very happy since it was God's will. And, before I went into the house, I knelt on the steps and thanked God for this incident, then I kissed the ground. I was truly happy!

To kiss the ground and pray with my arms in the form of a cross were two of my favourite practices, but always in secret ; I wanted no one but my divine Master to witness my intimate gestures of tenderness towards him.

At school, each pupil received a weekly mark for conduct and application. From the age of six, my teachers had always given me a perfect report. Now, one day, I earned only a *Good* instead of the customary *Very good,* because I had been slow in lining up for the grammar lesson. How regretful I felt! I begged to be allowed to atone for my failing, but to no avail : the adverse remark was not deleted ; moreover, it remained engraved for ever on my memory. I am still extremely grateful to my good teacher for having acted as she did at that time. It was a way of ensuring that I would not allow myself to get into the habit of not obeying promptly. In addition, this discordant note was a healthy humiliation. For, during the rest of my schooling, it never happened again.

At the end of my second year at the Convent of Jacques-Cartier, when I was fourteen, I asked my parents to allow me to go to boarding school. My wish imposed a great suffering on them : that of separation. Always generous-hearted, they were unable to refuse me, knowing that this new life would be a great advantage to me from the point of view of formation. They decided that, the following September, I would go to the boarding school at Bellevue, also directed by the Notre Dame Sisters.

During the summer holidays, my longing for religious life grew much stronger. I had a serious discussion with my director about it on the 15 August, again on the feast of The Assumption of the Blessed Virgin. I felt extremely weary of the world and would willingly have left it. Why? With my parents, I enjoyed the most delicious cup of true happiness ; humanly speaking, a brilliant future, full of attractions, lay before me. Why? In spite of all this, the purest and most ardent affections could not quench my thirst ; away from home, everything seemed empty, insipid, and I repeated the words : *Vanity of vanities, all is vanity!* But why? Only God could satisfy me. This was only the prelude to a longing that Jesus was going to nurture in my soul, without fully satisfying it, for many long years, since he wanted me to remain in the world for ten more years.

Out of obedience, I began to write down some of my most intimate feelings. I tore up and burnt these notes before going to the novitiate. On the first page of the exercise book, I wrote : "God alone! *As a doe longs for running streams, so does my soul long for you, my God!* My God, I suffer for lack of suffering! I am dying for want of dying!" Then followed a series of acts of love and of desire to possess Jesus, my All. Never, to this day, have I been so clearly aware of how much Our Lord has loved me. I am a poor child on whom he has showered choice graces. How could I ever have turned my gaze or my heart away from him, since he had captivated them by his power and granted me the supreme grace of finding happiness only in him! My soul, grateful to creatures for their loving attentions yet untouched by their praise, experienced an earthly bitterness ; close to God, it drank deep of the wine of his tenderness, and was intoxicated with heavenly delights.

V
FROM FOURTEEN TO SIXTEEN
1911-1913

Boarding school. — A promise. — Intimate desires. — Influence of community life. — Reading. — An outing and a journey. — Farewell to her 'Alma Mater'.

The time came for me to leave for boarding school. I felt as if my heart were breaking. The sorrow that I was causing my parents by leaving them found an echo in my soul, yet if I was leaving them, it was not from any human desire but so as to correspond with grace. When I caught sight of the hallowed walls of my new home, as we walked up the avenue, I said the following prayer to myself : "O my God, grant that during my stay here I may not offend you by the least voluntary venial sin." I felt homesick. On the Sunday following my arrival, which had been on a Wednesday, I cried all day ; during Mass, I sobbed, I choked back my tears, and similarly in the parlour that afternoon. My parents were very upset and Papa offered to take me away : "No, thank you," I said, "I will get used to it." I cried fourteen consecutive nights ; after that, for several weeks, it was every two or three evenings ; in the end, my will grew stronger and I was comforted.

My companions were all very kind and considerate towards me, but how difficult community life seemed to me![1] I wanted to smile at everyone but I would have so loved to be alone. One night, after the final bell, my dormitory mistress

---

[1] One day, she remarked to her mother who had come to visit her : "Mama, it is no joke living with people !"

came into my cubicle. I was crying. "I know you are suffering ; you have little in common with your companions, you are too good ; they do not understand you." This remark, *you are too good*, struck me greatly ; too good! I! Oh, no! I needed to try hard to be better in order to be kinder.

On the first Friday in October, while the whole school was going into the chapel for a visit to the Blessed Sacrament, I made an offering to Our Lord : I consecrated my virginity entirely to him for ever, and I added : insofar as this promise might be pleasing to him. It surely did please my good Master, for I felt myself held fast by the most tender of bonds. Besides, this inspiration could have come only from him, and it quenched to some extent the ardent thirst I felt to abandon myself to his love.

I was inflamed with the desire to be a martyr. Often, I said : "Jesus, you died for me ; my love will never be satisfied unless you grant me the grace to die a martyr!" No torment, no tribulation held any fear for me ; how could they compare with the suffering and torment endured by the divine Lamb, scourged, sacrificed, crucified! My desire grew more and more vehement with the passing of years. Jesus is going to deny me physical martyrdom — in that respect, my desire is enough for him — but he will favour me with a martyrdom of love. Oh, what a supreme blessing! "Oh, my soul, what return can I make to the Lord? Oh, what mercy on the part of my God, you answer my great need because you are infinite! On my knees, oh, my Bridegroom, I thank you for this token of inexpressible love." Yes, in heaven, I will sing my canticle of thanksgiving with the palm (of martyrdom) in my hand.

I paid the greatest possible attention to sermons, catechism classes and religious instruction. Every devotional word that fell from the lips of the priest or of my teachers seemed to me as worthy of respect as a particle of the sacred Host : I listened to God himself speaking to me through the voice of authority. It goes without saying that during the days of retreat at the beginning of each year, I easily forgot what was going on around me in order to understand better what Our Lord was saying to me.

On my fifteenth birthday, during my thanksgiving, I asked Jesus, present in my heart, for a gift : I begged for the cross, a suffering, a trial of any kind ; I was aware that this was the Well-beloved's choicest gift. My prayer was not answered in the way I wanted ; no evident suffering came my way, but I suffered for want of suffering ; I felt how unworthy I was to receive such favours.

Free days were a burden to me, as were long periods of recreation. I had to make a great effort to join with enthusiasm in noisy games, so much so that they resulted in a feeling of intense physical fatigue.

Nevertheless, at certain times, when it was quiet, the demon of dissipation was lying in wait ; he tried to distract me with schemes that, had they been carried out, would have entertained my companions. Thank God, I did not weaken in the battle and remained faithful to the rule. I was an extremist by nature ; I was dedicated to goodness, so I was determined to achieve perfection. If, one day, when grace left me to my own devices, I had said : I am not going to follow the path of duty any longer, I would have gone to any length. How good the infinite Master was to constrain me to follow him!

During Lent, I noted down my daily sacrifices. My target was a high number. On the feast of St Joseph, I expressed my devotion and my gratitude to this great saint by a more generous offering of small acts of self-denial. At Easter, I added them up and offered them all to Our Lord as a bouquet of love. The flowers were simple, but for him alone.

I returned to the same boarding school for a second and final year. That was the year of my graduation. To complete a full course of study was to realize one of my dearest ambitions. In October, Mama became seriously ill. A devoted relative was caring for her ; all the same, I felt that if I had been near her, my presence alone would have lessened her sufferings. I had permission to go see her ; then I asked her leave not to go back to

the convent but to keep her company and lavish care on her.
"No," she answered, with all the generosity of a mother, "I do
not want that." The separation was twice as painful for her. It
was a sacrifice for me to leave her. I had made one first by offering to give up my studies, at least for that year. God accepted
all these sufferings and soon cured my dear Mama.

All my life, up to the present, the same thing has happened.
Just as I was about to fulfil some important project, on which
sometimes my future depended, Jesus asked me to sacrifice my
wish. What anguish I felt at times! What great grace I needed,
in order to abandon this or that hope with joy and do God's will!
And when I had made my act of submission, circumstances
would change or no longer present any obstacle and, each time,
on countless occasions, I achieved the aim I had set myself. I see
above all, in this course of events, the goodness and tender love
of the great Craftsman of my soul. He was teaching me how to
let myself be moulded by him like an inanimate instrument ; how
to abandon myself blindly to his action when, to my human eyes,
the most pious hopes seemed to be passing me by ; how to seek
only his glory and his interests ; how, in a spirit of detachment,
to lay at his feet, for his good pleasure, the noblest aspirations ;
how to offer up to him some dire fear, as if it were a bouquet of
myrrh. My soul overflows with gratitude towards divine Wisdom
and Mercy. These are great lights and powerful graces that I
have received. Having become detached from my intimate
desires and interior emotions, having grown to hate myself, it
was easy and natural for me to despise external, transient
objects.

I liked to know my faults ; I would ask my class and form
teachers to warn me about them. One of them told me one day
that I had shown a lack of humility when receiving a correction,
because my face had betrayed an expression of independence.
How right she was! And her kind words were a salutary lesson
for me. Yes, this daughter of pride and independence, gave me
reason to fight hard and often against my selfish liking for soli-

tude and peace. As soon as a defect appeared, I wanted to destroy it ; I was so determined to avoid everything that could displease Our Lord. In everything, I aimed at the height of perfection. Perfect order seemed to me necessary, as much in optional details as in strict duty. I was haunted by the idea that inner order, that of my soul, was closely related to what was exterior, and on the same level as the more or less careful arrangement of things I used.

I was passionate about all branches of knowledge without exception. This is all the more easily explained by the fact that none of them presented any difficulty for me. Success was always to hand, predictable on every occasion. Yet, when I had to appear in public, at competitions held in the presence of parents, where I would be praised, oh! how it cost me! It happened one day that, at the last minute, I was unable to take part in a famous oral competition because I had lost my voice ; and how I thanked God! Jesus favoured me with a strong dislike for public honour, so as to keep me truthful and humble and to strengthen my will ; he multiplied the occasions on which I had to overcome myself and master my natural timidity.

While I was at boarding-school, I read only one library book. All my spare time was spent studying. I always had a dictionary on hand and read very, very slowly. I realize now that I was occupied not in reading but in meditating. This book was a novel based on the Gospel and I am proud to say that it is the only novel I have read in the whole of my life. And as I read it, I wondered why it was considered a novel.

Besides this library book, thanks to my good friends, I skimmed through the charming life of Blessed Thérèse of the Child Jesus and of the Holy Face, written by herself. From these pages, perused in haste, I derived immense profit for my soul. The angelic Rose perfumed all my actions with a more ardent love ; she obtained for me greater enlightenment in the art of self-abandonment.

Jesus nurtured prudence in me, as a defence against the numerous difficulties I was soon to encounter in the world ; a firm yet delicate prudence based on custody of the eyes, mortification of the senses and of curiosity and constant, vigilant attention to my whole being.

A longing for heaven, a nostalgia for my true home never left me. I was more and more enthralled by nature. One evening, during recreation, two of my companions and I were admiring the sun setting behind the big trees ; the last brilliant rays turned their green branches crimson. Suddenly, I could no longer hear the conversation around me ; my two companions, one on my right, the other on my left, called to me in vain ; then, raising their voices, they succeeded in arousing me from my rapture. They were right to tease me. Truly, I had lost consciousness, confronted with the magic of the magnificent tableau unfolding before my eyes. Having thus contemplated the marvellous, living brushwork of the Creator, the earth seemed very dark to me, I longed for eternal beauty, I felt nearer to God and I loved him more and better.

With my fellow-students, I went on a visit one afternoon to the convent at Sillery. It was the first time I had met the Ladies of Jesus and Mary. While we were walking through the corridors, a group of postulants passed by. I watched them and was impressed by their recollection. I kept the best possible memories of this visit. Each of the religious we had seen had been so kind and caring ; the pupils, too, received us very kindly. Still, I was far from thinking that the divine Master would call me later to this hallowed enclosure, and that I myself would be a postulant of Jesus and Mary! No, I had no suspicion that the religious life would admit me to its paradise there!

In the month of May, again with my fellow-students - there were seven of us - and chaperoned by a teacher, I went on a journey to Montreal, mainly to attend a ceremony of profession and clothing at the Mother House of the Congregation of Notre Dame, and at the same time to gain some new light on our own vocation. I say *new light*, since we graduate students had just finished a retreat of which the sole aim was to discern God's will for our future. The boarding-school, Villa Maria, received us warmly. As for the ceremony at the Mother House, it left my soul cold and dry. It was as if my feelings of devout enthusiasm had been submerged. I paid little attention to that and my decision to enter the novitiate there was strengthened. Jesus was going to guide me along a path I ignored.

I came to the end of my time as a boarder ; my teachers manifested the wish to welcome me back for another year ; moreover, they would have liked to persuade me to undertake further studies at their College in Montreal. My parents had found it so painful to be separated from me that they rightly wanted to keep me near them. They were also fearful of the dangers of my being far away and relatively free in a distant town ; besides, they considered that the ordinary course of studies was sufficient to admit me to any profession later on. Providence allowed this and took control of events.

So I said goodbye to my Alma Mater. Within its walls, I had breathed happiness and peace. We were often told : "The years spent at boarding school are the most beautiful years in one's life ; as pupils, you may not believe that now, but you will understand it later on." I thought to myself : Yes, I do understand. I am happy, at peace and near my God, sheltered from the snares of the world. Truly, I enjoyed to the full that pleasant life. When I left, I took with me a maxim, deeply engraved in my heart : *The well-brought-up young girl must strive to remain hidden.* I wanted to remain faithful to all the advice I had been so generously given, with such maternal love, charity and patience. Was not this, together with my prayers for their intentions, the best way to prove my gratitude to my devoted teachers?

I commended to Our Lord and his holy Mother the new life that lay before me. These few years spent away from home had been a great help in forming my character. I derived an increase of energy and self-forgetfulness from life in common.

On many occasions, I had been forced to come out of myself ; a failing that one of my teachers was kind enough to point out to me in the first few months of my time at boarding school, was that of not communicating, never showing my impressions, my feelings, my wishes, always keeping them to myself, when there could be an advantage to others if I expressed them occasionally. In a word, I had been in a situation where I had to fight against selfishness and make an effort to do good. I had experienced the joy of an ordered existence, an advantage that I particularly appreciated when it came to religious exercises : meditation, each morning - it was short, just ten minutes, but a smile from Our Lord for the whole day ; recitation of the *Little Office of the Blessed Virgin* every Sunday. Oh! What delightful moments, not to mention Holy Mass and Communion each morning!

I returned home to my parents, more affectionate and stronger, and imbued with the sound religious culture that Jesus had fostered by his action and his grace, and through the intervention of consecrated persons who had enlightened me. "O my dear Alma Mater, may you be for ever blessed by the divine Hand, for the flowers that you caused to bloom in my soul, in the warmth of your greenhouse."

VI
FROM SIXTEEN TO NINETEEN
1913-1916

Rule of life. — Interior action of Our Lord. — Desire to enter the novitiate. — Love of renunciation. — Total offering.

My canticle of thanksgiving can harmonise with two different themes. First, the religious.

My motto, **Death rather than defilement**, represented for me a compelling duty. When I was with my parents, who were so Christian, and under their close supervision, I was sheltered from danger ; everything contributed to my piety ; the environment was second to none. Nevertheless, it was a worldly life, I was really beginning to be involved externally with society. How burdensome that was for me! I did not want to offend Jesus in anything, yet in how many difficult situations I found myself ! The good Master heard my sighs, was aware of my true feelings. Was not he the sole author of all my desires for him?

I drew up a rule of life : morning and evening prayers, Mass, Holy Communion, Rosary, at least ten minutes' meditation each day ; weekly confession, as had been my custom since the year of my First Communion. In this rule of life, I also wrote down my duties towards my neighbour and towards myself. I can summarise it all by saying : death with all its potential suffering rather than consent to the least venial sin ; in order to achieve this, to pray and never draw back before renunciation.

The examination of conscience every evening was, at that time, of great assistance in preserving my peace of mind ; through it, I could see clearly into my conscience and I kept it in order.

I would have liked to be able to make a day's retreat each month and say the *Little Office of the Blessed Virgin* at least once a week. I did not manage it. This is the reason : during the eight years that I spent in the world, that is from the time I left school until I entered the novitiate, I never wanted to appear more devout, in the eyes of my parents, than any other young woman from an excellent background, nor reveal the intimate action of grace in my soul, my strong attractions, my exclusive interest in the spiritual life. As I have already said : I was very reserved by nature, but it seemed to me that Our Lord's work in my soul should be known to no one, except my director in whom, in spite of my good will, I found it impossible at certain times to confide unreservedly. I realize now that Jesus wanted it that way. It was he who was Master and Craftsman of my interior life. He was teaching me, enlightening me, sculpting and chiselling. In order to have time for meditation and to prolong my prayers, I curtailed my rest periods. In the solitude of my room. nothing would show. I was very careful not to make a noise, so as not to arouse any suspicion. Still, I would be chided sometimes for being dilatory in the morning and evening ; this turned into teasing, and I changed my ways but without neglecting what God expected of me.

I suffered a great deal on account of the confusion caused by my silence. My good parents would have allowed me ample leisure and every facility if I had let them know of my desires and my inclinations. Without doubt, they would have rejoiced, having already allowed me complete freedom in this respect, a freedom of which I did not want to take advantage.

When people spoke in my presence about the spiritual life, about asceticism, I concealed my understanding of the serious subjects treated. By a ray of his light, Jesus would reveal the truth to me in an instant, far more effectively than lengthy conversations in human languages.

During my thanksgiving after Communion, a visit to the Blessed Sacrament or meditation, my divine Friend often enlightened me. At the same time, dryness and distractions did not reduce my fervour. For some time (perhaps when I was a little younger), I remember being in such a state of dryness, numbness, that I appreciated even the inexpressible grace of baptism more by reason and will than by any feeling of love. I had nothing to say to Our Lord ; I felt completely indifferent to religious matters. At these times, when I was shrouded in darkness, I would pour out my soul at the feet of Jesus, offering him my poverty and my suffering.

I read very little, so little that it might be just as true to say that I did not read at all. Many saints, I had discovered one day, derived all their knowledge from contemplating their crucifix. I felt no need to seek in books the spiritual nourishment for which my soul was so hungry. No, the fact was that Jesus was providing me with it himself. He became the Great Book in which there shone before my eyes, in large letters, the secret of happiness and the art of loving.

I asked permission to enter the novitiate seven months after leaving school, that is, the following February. What a powerful grace it took for me to speak and let my dear Mama know of my desire! I knew I would be breaking her heart and that of my affectionate Papa. My mother answered tearfully - and I too was sobbing - that she did not want to put any obstacle in the way of my vocation, only she was going to think about it for a few days, since I was so young — not yet sixteen. God enlightened those placed over me and, following their advice, I remained in the world. It was too soon to abandon my devoted parents, who were so very happy to have me near them. I was their unique flower and they had nurtured it with jealous care, at the cost of sacrifices known only to God, and already I wanted to be transplanted elsewhere for ever ; no, no! That was not what God wanted. Our Lord left me in their loving care for many years. As for me, he kept me for himself regardless ; and the path that I thought was mine was not the one along which he would lead me. "My God, thank you for the happiness you gave my parents, thank you for enlightening me so fully."

I entrusted my desires to Jesus. Since I had no cause to reproach myself for any lack of generosity, I found peace in obedience.

I found renunciation lovelier and even attractive. If only we realised the pure, sweet happiness of acts of self-denial offered up with joy! It is one of the choice blessings that have been showered on me. The more I gave to Jesus, the more I wanted to give him ; the more sacrifices I sought out, the less I felt their thorns. The saying of St Francis : "I am never so well as when I am not well," satisfied me, as it helped me appreciate the consoling effects of interior and exterior mortification. The little suggestions that I picked up here and there seemed just right for me ; and the grace within me was so powerful that I would have felt I was lacking in gratitude towards my gentle Master if I had refused him such small sacrifices. I did not season my food, I drank tea and coffee without sugar, I took less gravy with meat, etc ; I said that it was more to my taste that way. Nothing could have been more true, but it was because I wanted to offer Jesus a sacrifice that it was to my liking. What happiness it was to offer him little invisible flowers ! — And I cannot express how distasteful it is for me to bring them out into the open. Oh, no! I must correct myself. It is a joy to reveal them out of obedience so as to sing of the divine action alone. If God were not infinitely merciful, I would certainly not receive any reward for this humble bouquet of myrrh, since he transformed every offering into sweetness and delight. The honey of self-denial tasted more delicious to my palate than the vinegar of self-indulgence.

I kept a careful watch over my eyes in particular, depriving myself of a great number of legitimate pleasures so as not to risk having any regrets.

I accepted everything, even a pin, whether pretty or ugly ; I received everything I was offered with profound gratitude. I asked for nothing unless I was forced to do so. It is easy to ask for nothing when one is basking in abundance. Indeed, it is so easy as to be almost natural. Nevertheless, by God's goodness,

I found opportunities for sacrifice. My parents could not give me enough presents to satisfy their love for me. And yet, in spite of myself, I could not cling to anything.

What am I to say about clothes and finery? What a torment they were! Bright colours, excessive jewellery were distasteful to me, and yet I often wore all kinds. Yes, I found it torture to wear jewellery so often, yet opportunities were not lacking. Here, on my knees, I repeat my hymn of love. I had to dress in silks and finery, I had to follow the fashion and its vagaries regarding colours and texture, but I consistently evaded its foolish and blameworthy demands and my conscience is free from any shadow of remorse in this respect. Thoughts of vanity were far from my mind ; they were incompatible with the disdain I had for them. I often thought how sad it was, in the world, to be compelled to waste precious time on adorning one's miserable body which is doomed to be buried ; how sad it was to spend a great amount of money when so many poor people are hungry and cold and when religious institutes and missions are in need of financial help and too often, because of this, find their efforts paralysed.

People would say to me : "You know nothing about suffering ; you have never experienced any adversity." They were right, since their judgment was based on appearances, on the exterior and our normal natural inclinations. It was impossible to surmise, from the exterior, that my happiness was not complete. Only, what enthralled the world was torture to me : esteem, pleasure — even when legitimate — plunged me into boredom. In contrast, what the world dreaded and was wary of — suffering and renunciation — I loved passionately, because Jesus made me feel as he did.

And social gatherings...! I was grateful to be invited ; I appreciated the friendship and courtesy of those I knew. But I declined on the slightest pretext. If I accepted, I felt a certain repugnance.

And family or intimate gatherings...! (I am speaking of relatives, or friends usually looked upon as part of the family). I
spent many very pleasant hours in their company and recall
delightful and gratifying memories!

A year after leaving school, in the month of June, I was
enrolled as a Promoter of the Apostleship of Prayer. This little
monthly task increased my devotion to the Sacred Heart. I was
in the best possible position to hear about the reign of the divine
Heart ; with tireless zeal, Mama devoted herself constantly to
the beautiful work of the Apostleship of Prayer.

I joined the Tabernacle Guild. On the appointed days, I went
to help sewing and embroidering church vestments. At these
meetings, there was a ten-minute spiritual reading and I found
this helpful.

At the beginning of the World War in 1914, I offered myself
to Our Lord, body and soul, in a spirit of reparation and love, so
as to console him a little and save souls. I was distressed above
all by the moral evil that threatened the world. The insight I had
was so vivid that, seeing Jesus suffering so much, I could not be
happy unless I tried to dry his tears by the few means at my disposal. I felt in my heart that my intention was pleasing to him.
How is it that we fail to understand the meekness and kindness
of the divine Heart! He is pleased even with our desires! Yet, for
our desires to be good, they must be inspired by the Holy Spirit,
and when we are faithful to holy inspirations, he accepts them as
our own gift. Oh, mystery of infinite humility! "Oh, Jesus, I
gather up all the desires that your love can inspire and, through
your sacred Heart and that of Mary, I offer them to the heavenly
Father."

The evil spirit had not given up the battle in my regard.
Certainly not. But the protection of Jesus was so attentive and
strong that it prevented me from slipping down the hazardous
slope. *For those who love God, everything turns to good.* I
passed close to the abyss and did not see it. The danger was

great, yet at that moment I did not realize it. How good the
Master is to those who love him! Several times in my life, I have
found myself blinded, without suspecting it, when faced with
danger. The darkness was so intense that I could not see.
"O divine tenderness! O infinite love! How can I sing your
praises! My God, thank you for ever for protecting my soul, for
hearing my good desires!"

I used to think about death. I was not afraid of this crucial
moment. I would say to myself : Why should I be afraid of entering into eternal life, I am doing all I can to serve Jesus ; I would
have no wish to start my life all over again, I would not behave
in any other way. I felt I could lay open my soul to its very
depths and have no fear of human judgments. Alas! Of how
many faults, failings and imperfections was I not guilty! But Our
Lord, in his mercy, purified them all in his love, overlooked my
weakness and treated me as a privileged child.

One day, I heard about the offering by which a soul abandoned itself entirely to divine Love as a victim. Scarcely had I
learnt about this gift of oneself, known as the heroic offering,
than I offered myself ; I abandoned myself entirely to the will of
Jesus as his victim. I renewed the self-offering I had made much
earlier ; I felt this time that it implied more sacrifices, more acts
of reparation. Could I refuse to make use of the means others
employed to serve the infinite Master? No. Besides, when I discovered a generous practice, when I received a heavenly light, it
was always accompanied by such a powerful grace that I had to
follow the inspiration : I was carried along by an irresistible
force ; it would have taken a more painful effort to resist than to
let myself be carried along in its wholesome current.

That is why I am happy, yes, happy to acknowledge the
favours of the Beloved towards his little Bride. I repeat, if in
heaven Jesus rewards me for what I have done during my time
on earth, it will be once more through an excess of tenderness.
As for me, I have done nothing, nothing, nothing except commit
blunders. It is he alone who has done good deeds. "Immense

love of my God, who will ever understand you... O Jesus, your Heart thirsts, it needs to give itself ceaselessly to poor creatures. Oh! consume me totally in this love which is my only possible response to your gifts."

Of love, I want to live and die!

Grant, Jesus, to my heart's desire,

Your brightly burning flame.

In your heaven, all I claim

To delight in radiance above,

Is yourself, O God of love!

VII
FROM SIXTEEN TO NINETEEN
(continued)

A second 'father'. — Music studies. — Intimate convictions. — Public performances. — New York. — The study of harmony. — A trial.

I resume my hymn of thanksgiving with my leaving school, but from a different point of view. If the melody is more worldly, the rhythm is still based on divine bounty.

When I returned home to my dear parents, God gave me a second 'father' in the person of M. l'Abbé X, my parish priest at that time, and now Monsignor X,[1] Protonotary Apostolic and Vicar General. The gratitude I feel towards this devoted and distinguished prelate cannot be put into words. In his case, too, the eternal Christ will pay my debts. May the Heart of the Master repay him infinitely for the advice, attentiveness and prodigality that he so generously afforded me ; for his advice which, so many times, brought me enlightenment, warmed my heart, kindled in me the flame of divine love and of love for the Immaculate Virgin ; for his attentiveness, reflecting his fatherly goodness, which never tired of showing interest in me and encouraging my efforts in countless ways ; for his prodigality, witness of a hand ever willing to give and "whose greatest happiness is to make others happy", an apostolic spirit in love with art and poetry and as responsive as the most sensitive of lyres!

---

[1] Mgr. Omer Cloutier, P.A. who died in 1933

As my parents intended, and following the advice of this zealous priest, I continued in earnest my piano studies. Immediately after the summer holidays, in September, I renewed my studies with enthusiasm, I might even say with passion. In January, I obtained my Advanced diploma ; in June, that of Licentiate ; a year later, that of Professor. This musical study brought me closer to God ; I offered him each note I played as an act of perfect love. My hours of practice often turned into a meditation, especially when the pieces were slow and rather reflective in style. I was assiduous in assigning the prescribed number of hours each day to study. Not a minute less, when possible. I found this a welcome pretext for more cautious contacts with the world and fewer outings. On the other hand, there were concerts and charitable works that called for my cooperation and public appearance.

Before giving my impressions on appearing before an audience, I want to say what I thought of my personal endeavours.

Obstacles and difficulties never left me discouraged. Externally, I often met with a certain measure of success. I found it futile and tedious. The praise I received only served to convince me of my lack of ability. I wanted to acknowledge the talents God had given me, but I had before my eyes such a towering peak, such a sublime ideal that I knew well that I did not deserve such praise. I received it gratefully, as if it were due to people's lenience and good will or was intended as kindly encouragement. In myself, I felt resour... : unsure and, as a result, making numerous mistakes ; with a lack of personality, having a nervous, insensitive, cold manner and, sometimes, a poor memory. I was well aware of my short comings. Each wrong note went straight to my heart and I thought : That's the measure of my competence. My emotional concentration hid any warm feelings and resulted in my icy-cold fingers moving across the key-board without producing any vibrant musical chords. I had neither a flair for improvisation nor the gift of accompaniment. I was aware of that, and of so many other defi-

ciencies. I often asked Our Lord : "Why so much study? What
can be the purpose of it all? I feel so little talent!" I prayed to
St Cecilia. One day — less than a year after I had left school —
having cried over my musical shortcomings, I hung the medal of
this gentle patron and queen of harmony around my neck and
made a resolution to wear it always. I asked St Cecilia, whom I
loved so much and to whom I had such a tender and strong devotion, to take me under her protection in a special way. I confided my efforts to her lovingly and with great confidence. "O
noble virgin, you have watched over me in the world, your smile
has consoled me many times. Thank you! By God's kindness,
you have bent over me and given me a sisterly kiss in leaving me
your name, spotless lily and rose of love! May Christ, our
Bridegroom, be for ever praised and glorified! And do you,
O Cécile, make me worthy to bear your name."

My intimate convictions increased my eagerness. Since
those who were guiding me were leading me in the direction of
music, I offered my feelings of inadequacy to God, thanked him
for all that happened and worked earnestly at my studies. This
grace of persistence now seems extraordinary to me. With it, I
can identify two other graces just as great : one strengthened my
will and another kept me humble. Such was to be from then on
the loving action of Jesus in my soul. The choice favours that he
has granted me in the course of my artistic career are beyond
human comprehension. I mention one in particular : The ineffable advantage of being understood only by Jesus. No one could
imagine the sense of martyrdom — yes, I am not afraid to stress
this word martyrdom — that I experienced when surrounded by
flowers and applause. What I am saying here, about this period
of my life, I will repeat with even greater emphasis — and it will
be all the more astonishing — in a few years' time, when I would
have a certain reputation, or at least when my name would
appear on posters as that of a pianist. No, nobody could have any
suspicion of what I thought of myself. How true it is, in my case,
that we must never judge from appearances! What I am writing
just now is hardly realistic. Yet, it is the truth. It was the action

of the good Master towards a privileged child. I was never satisfied with myself. How I suffered, humanly speaking! What joy I
experienced, in the sweet-sounding language of the Spirit! To
play the piano for an audience was often a torment for me. I am
grateful to my parents for having taught me, from my earliest
years as a student, not, as a rule, to refuse my hosts' request, and
for insisting that I accept graciously and courteously. This was a
profitable training for my will, entailing a healthy detachment
from my selfish inclinations. So I did not refuse any invitation
unless I had a genuine reason. At this point, I am aware of a keen
regret. I could have afforded my father and mother more joy in
taking their taste into account. It seems to me that, too often, I
followed my own personal inclinations in choosing what to play
for them. Yes, I failed on countless occasions. Yet I did not want
to refuse anything to those who gave me everything I had and
spent themselves for me. Far from me is any thought of ingratitude ; but this is one more proof of my self-love, the list of my
blunders is growing longer. If in truth I could have been less self-
centred, may God compensate them for my selfishness with his
favours, so that those whom I love so much may say : O happy
failings which won for us so many consolations!

I had to go on the stage and hold the attention of an
audience. Jesus, by his grace, gave me such control over myself
in the eyes of my parents — whom I did not want to burden with
justifiable anxiety — that they were able to say : "It does not
bother her at all to play in public." Had they been able to see
what I was feeling, they would not have thought thus. Their
belief pleased me since it calmed their fears. After these recitals,
my ears and my eyes were soon shut to the praise and roses
I received ; had I really heard the former and seen the latter?
Yet my heart was weary.

Once, I received the blessing of pure joy, the joy of a modest
lack of success. "My God, thank you." In the presence of a vast
audience, I was to bring an evening of music and literary read-
ings to a close by playing the national anthem, known to every-

one : *O Canada*. The final phrase is repeated ; by mistake I played the closing bars the first time round. Everyone noticed. I was very grateful to God for this little humiliation. It made a better offering for him than the magnificent bouquets that had been showered on me.

Various works of charity had their place in my timetable. In that respect, I was only supporting my mother who devoted herself in every way.

Towards the end of 1915, the question of my continuing my piano studies at a foreign Conservatory began to be given serious consideration. New York was the city chosen, and the residence run by the Ladies of Jesus and Mary (Our Lady of Peace) was the ideal place. My good parents hesitated for a long time. Their concern gave rise to fears. They looked closely at the advantages and disadvantages. Mgr. X advised them strongly. I would have two young girls from Quebec as my companions and I would be entrusted to the care of devoted religious. In February, my father and mother gave their consent and promised me the generous gift of two years' study ; the course lasted for almost eight months each year. My being away from home, and at a distance, meant more sacrifices and caused them anxiety. Their main aim was to preserve me from danger ; they were allowing me to go and live far removed from their vigilance, in a country I did not know. I am sure I cannot imagine their anguish. I know that they left me completely in God's hands, asking him to protect me, since they believed they were doing his will. They were, indeed, corresponding with God's will.

As for me, I thanked God for this great opportunity. At first, nature, or rather the evil spirit, made its presence felt through thoughts of self-satisfaction, vanity and conceit caused by the planning and realization of such a project. Jesus kept ceaseless watch over my heart. He did not allow me to be deluded by the mirages of the enemy. In my own eyes, I was still convinced of my inadequacy ; while thanking God for having endowed me with a certain talent, I did not believe myself to be any the less imperfect just because I was going to study in a great American institution.

Before my parents consented to this project, I prayed for divine light, for the greater glory of God. The plan appealed to me : I was passionately fond of art and beauty, I always aimed at perfection. I foresaw my father's and mother's tears and anxieties, caused by my absence, but I cherished the hope of making them forget the hours of darkness through the consolations and joys of the future. I was eager to broaden my knowledge so as to be, in the years to come, a less clumsy instrument in the service of the Master. However, I begged Jesus not to allow me to go away if, by chance, I was going to offend him by the least fault. I abandoned myself entirely to his will, repeating my promises of love and my resolution to please him always. When my departure was settled, I thanked him and offered him my life away from home so as to win souls for him. The reflection that I could work for his glory in a distant land filled my soul with happiness and consolation ; I wanted, for his sake, to do good.

I had begun to study harmony. From the very first lesson, I felt specially attracted to this branch of music. Subsequently, my natural inclination would have led me to neglect the piano in order to link harmonies together. In February 1916, I worked at it more assiduously in preparation for the course at the Conservatory. Before each one of my study sessions of harmony, whether long or very short, from that time until this very day, before reading a single word or writing a single note, I have recited a *Veni Sancte Spiritus* and an *Ave Maria*. I do not remember omitting this pious practice even once. If my musical compositions are valueless from the artistic point of view (and that is my opinion), they are a chain of prayers. For this reason, I feel consoled ; otherwise, I would have thought my time had been wasted. Thus I am convinced that the Holy Spirit and my sweet Mother have blessed my humble efforts in some unknown way.

I was to leave (for New York) in the autumn. On the preceding 25 May, my dear Mama was hurt in an accident : she was struck by a car and it was due to God's protection that she escaped death. After all, was not the purpose of her journey, at the time the heavy vehicle struck her, the glory of the Sacred Heart? In any case, it was a very serious accident, and what was to happen? I have already said that on the eve of carrying out some important project, God would ask me to sacrifice it. It was a kindness on his part : to give me the happiness of offering him an act of self-denial and then granting my desires.

Was Mama going to recover? It was doubtful. At the time, for several months, we had been looking after a charming two and a half year-old girl whose mother was ill ; how long would she be with us? We did not know. She was delightful, but we had to look after her. In a single moment, my mission had completely changed. Though I was absorbed in my studies, I was suddenly in a trying situation and had to take charge of the house. I abandoned myself completely to Our Lord. It was a time of suffering. It is true that the constant hope that Mama would recover increased daily as she made evident and gratifying progress. All the same, I received a great grace of resignation ; the holy indifference that Jesus nurtured within me. He taught me to practice it in this painful situation. Nature felt weighed down by suffering ; but submission to the divine action held sway and I remained at peace.

Providence restored my mother to health. "Thank you, my God." Joy and thanksgiving took the place of anguish. How sweet were the moments when, after this bad fright, my parents and I found ourselves together again for the first time around the family table. The finger of the Almighty that had struck us, but healed our wounds with infinite tenderness.

During the summer, we gave back the dear little child I have already mentioned. The obstacles disappeared. I was able to leave for New York.

When there was question of something a little out of the ordinary — as in this case, my studies away from home — my parents have always exercised a prudent discretion. They set me a wonderful example. For as long as possible they said nothing, outside the house, about plans in which some people occasionally take ill-considered pride. I feel ashamed, then, not to have behaved better in the exceptional and favourable circumstances in which Heaven allowed me to grow up! Nevertheless, my desires and my thoughts were directed towards God alone. My actions were riddled with imperfections in order to convince me of the unique truth : the good within me was the work of Jesus, the perfect Craftsman, and my numerous short-comings were the shabby outcome of my own weakness.

VIII
FROM NINETEEN TO TWENTY-ONE
1916-1918

New York. — A lucky disappointment. — Influence of the environment and of fellow-students. — A proof of love for Jesus in the Host.— Character formation. — A trial. — Return home

I set out for New York at the beginning of October. My father came with me. He wanted to become personally acquainted with some of those with whom I would be dealing, the place where I would live and the distance I would regularly have to cover. I had two companions ; our purpose was the same : we were going to study music at the same Conservatory and we would board at the same residence. One of them, whom I will refer to as B., was returning for a second year of study. I knew her : we had performed together one year and, in particular, our parents used to meet at various parish activities. The other, whom I will call A., was not unknown to me : I had met her several times on the music circuit.

When I left my mother, I could not help crying. At the station, several people had been kind enough to come and see me ; I showed no more courage there. The journey was, however, pleasant and cheerful. My father and each one of us hid our inmost feelings, and to all appearances, joy reigned supreme.

Finding myself in a crowded American city, and especially when I saw 'Our Lady of Peace', my heart beat violently. The Ladies of Jesus and Mary gave us the kindest of welcomes ; this reception convinced us of the motherly care they were to bestow on the three young girls from Quebec.

Then came the question of rooms. In that big house, only one single room and one double room were available. What a disappointment! We would not be able to have separate rooms until later on. It was God's will. Mlle B. and I, on my father's advice, offered Mlle A. the single room, while we both agreed to take the double room. No doubt, my companion B. made just as much of a sacrifice at that moment as I did. She was too kind ever to admit it to me. We did not know one another intimately. I knew she was charming, and I had been told that she was also kind. But I was accustomed to being alone ; my preference, my taste for solitude thus became an occasion for mortification. I had no knowledge of the joy and the help I was going to derive from this providential incident. In November, barely a month after our arrival, we had the opportunity to fulfil our original plan. What happened? We each gave the same answer : we would stay together. It was another of those choice favours that God reserved for me.

Indeed, it was his will to give me in this companion a true friend and to allow me to savour and understand the pious saying : *Whoever has found a friend is in possession of a real treasure.* Our intimate and communal life in a foreign country, our shared joys and sorrows, our ready smiles mutually pro-voked, our tears allayed, in a word, the close relationship, lack of constraint and the trust that existed as between two sisters served to seal the bonds of a noble, loving and precious friend-ship. Jesus himself was the bond that united our two souls. It is clear to me now, from all that has happened, that he has welded our souls together in his divine Heart, since he has called both of us to be his Brides and religious of Jesus and Mary. "O eternal Christ, may you be blessed for ever, for having, in a distant land, placed a visible angel at my side, when distance prevented my parents from watching over me! Thanks be to you for ever for having brought me to this safe and happy haven where you were also inviting this delicate soul! May you be for ever glorified through my love for her and my gratitude for her devotion! Deign always to smile and look upon her with the tenderness of a Bridegroom, so as to express my gratitude!"

I return to my early days in the United States. When my father left me, I felt a deep, interior sense of shock. I began the course at the Conservatory. I had to speak English, to listen, understand and study in English! It was amusing, especially at first. Fortunately, pianos sound the same in different countries, although the names of the notes follow the whims of language!

I was happy to be living in a convent. What excellent work these religious establishments accomplish! Within those walls, I felt safe from dangers that were new to me. The greatest advantage was to have access to a chapel where the Master lived and kept constant vigil, where Mass was celebrated every morning, where the liturgical ceremonies were held. I could never enter or leave the house without passing close to Jesus without greeting him. Our Lord willed, I think, to take up that position precisely to draw souls to himself. I was favoured with light and graces in this pretty chapel, where the deeply prayerful atmosphere encouraged a spirit of recollection. Often late in the evening, by the dim glow of the sanctuary lamp, I went up close to Jesus, kneeling at the altar rail so as to hear his voice and share my secrets with him!

I admired the goodness of the religious, their kindness and the thoughtful consideration they showed me ; their example of patience and self-denial influenced me for good.

My other companion, A., was very pleasant and very kind. She could be entertaining. It is sometimes thought that it is difficult for three people to always agree with one another and people take delight in saying : "Ah! A third person spoils everything!" In our case, this was not true. We three, spent long months in the most delightful harmony. We were always together. This joyous friendship could have been all the more at risk since we were pursuing the same goal. The humility, good humour, and thoughtfulness of B. and A. were precious lessons for me. The divine Lover had set his seal, too, on A. as one of his privileged souls. Several years ago, she was admitted to the paradise of religious life. "O Jesus, shower on her your tokens of love and choice favours!"

If there was any reason to fear that, far from home, the freedom to engage in studies that inevitably launched one into an unfamiliar society, in a new world, this culture would prove a dreaded snare for any young girl, God gave us a wonderful proof of his power and his love.

I had not altered my rule of life in any way, as regards spiritual exercises. If there was some modification, it was in prolonging my meditation. I felt even more in need of prayer, as I was afraid of the many dangers surrounding me. It was Our Lord's will. For some time, my studies undermined me physically. Out of kindness, I was advised not to go to Mass every morning so that I could rest longer. I consulted the holy priest to whom I used to have recourse at that time and, although I did not let him know of the immense sacrifice he would be imposing on me were he to require me to fast from the Eucharist[1] and from Holy Mass, he refused to let me miss the Sacred Banquet even once. His decision filled me with joy. I took it as clear proof of the desire of Jesus the Victim ; I was touched by this mark of his love for me ; I realized that nothing could separate me from him. In reality, the strength that I derived from the Holy Sacrifice and from the ineffable (grace of) communion was far superior to any I might have gained from a longer period of rest. Besides, would I have been able to rest far from Jesus?

I was immersed in an artistic environment. I took advantage of this without abusing of it. I was extremely prudent when it came to attending concerts or recitals. If I had any doubts, I would seek information and advice from reliable people. As a result, I find joy in not having culpably, at any time, exposed myself to danger.

I seldom went out for pleasure ; these outings were for the purpose of acquiring knowledge. I studied assiduously. Just to waste a second seemed to me like squandering a gold mine. My will was alert all the time.

---

[1] That is depriving me of the Eucharist

I was imbued with an exceptional grace that I might describe as a conviction of my inferiority. I venture to say that one has to have lived with such sentiments in order to understand them. Many times, it came to the point when even my reasoning seemed false. I was sincere. The interior action that Jesus deigned to accomplish at that time in my soul is so delicate, so intimate that I find it impossible to explain in words ; it is so precious that when I consider it, I am lost in admiration at the way God worked. I would need a pen of fire to inscribe a more worthy expression of gratitude. In addition, this favour was reinforced by the grace which I describe as : the veiling of my deep conviction. I am moved when I reflect today on what Jesus allowed to happen. At the piano, I played in a loud, nervous manner ; my touch was unpleasant, tiring. Could that be evidence of something other than ambition? To all appearances, I seemed to consider myself a musician. The truth is that I was trying to make progress, limping as little as possible, in the career on which I had embarked. My divine Master took the shortest possible route to ensure that I soon arrived at a desire to be humiliated and despised. On his part, this was not achieved in a moment, a day or a week, but was an incessant task — an attitude which was infiltrating my mind, a truth which was taking root in my heart never to be banished. They were invaluable resources from which I learnt to cherish humility as a pearl beyond price, and one day I wanted to gain possession of it. It made me indifferent to the opinion of others. Oh! Nature had to battle, at an earthly and human level! But it is a joy to fight on when it is the Saviour who wields the weapons. I often reflect on the thought : *I am worth only what I am worth in God's sight.* Jesus did not want me to take any pleasure in my efforts, and he permitted that, by my way of acting, others could not suspect what was going on within me. What I am writing at this moment may seem very obscure ; the divine action is so profound that I am powerless to put it into words.

Other people had great credit in my eyes ; their good qualities, their success added to my happiness in proportion to the glory they brought to him who distributes his talents as he pleases. I loved to congratulate and praise them.

God granted me another form of humiliation. I am still subject to it ; I make mention of it at this period in my life because so many memories bring it to mind. It was to introduce, in the course of a conversation, a more choice word than one which had just been used quite correctly, or to slip in a cutting word ; both these tactics were unintentional — I was so anxious not to cause the least pain to anyone. My tongue would slip and... it was too late. As for myself, I suffered with good reason, but to advantage because of these short-comings. I felt bitter regret for those to whom I was speaking and who so often could not have been dearer to me.

I had great difficulty in expressing my feelings ; I would look embarrassed and give the impression of taking pleasure in hiding them. In minor matters, when there was a difference of opinion, I always agreed interiorly with other people's ideas considering them the best. Here again, I was ill at ease, and if on occasion I had wanted to argue, I could not have succeeded any better.

My powers of observation and my imagination developed rapidly through contact with people of every nationality, as well as through different experiences. I had a natural tendency to mimicry, intended for my own amusement or that of others. I had to guard not only my tongue lest I lose control of it, but also my mind and my thoughts. If I noticed anything that was open to criticism, I did not dwell on it ; whatever was out of the ordinary and bordered however slightly on an imperfection came, in my opinion, under the domain of charity, so I would look upon people and events through spectacles tinted with this virtue.

During these two years, I returned to spend the Christmas holidays with my parents. The joy of being together again equaled the pain of separation. In Springtime, they would come to spend a few days in New York with me ; the second year, my father came alone ; he enjoyed giving me a surprise and succeeded admirably. These were so many blessings from Heaven.

In March 1917, I began to suffer an interior trial which continued without respite for about six years. The fury of the enemy was to unleash its violence, multiply its assaults, its deceits and its trickery in the very depths of my soul. Jesus showered thousands of graces on me to keep me safe during these terrible struggles. The demon was determined to win ; what ruses did he not invent so as to ensure a victory! My divine Master watched over me, guided me, fought for me, consoled me. His sweet Mother was there, crushing the infernal dragon.[2]   I went through unspeakable agony ; there were times of impenetrable darkness, of great self-denial. God prevailed. By his powerful hand, he proved victorious and I have nothing to reproach myself. "O Jesus! Thank you for having kept me united to you during all this suffering! Thank you, O Blessed Virgin, for your protection!" These years alone would suffice to convince me of Our Lord's preferential love and of the unfathomable depths of my nothingness.

The Conservatory closed its doors in the early days of June. My trunk was packed without delay. Towards the end of summer, shortly before I left for a second year, my mother became ill again. She recovered quite quickly and I returned to my studies.

Our Lord took pleasure in making me accept sacrifices in advance. I felt drawn to offer him the — humanly speaking — distressing outcome of projects as yet uncompleted. Mortification became more and more attractive ; I loved to feel the effects of the cold or the wind and to deprive myself of delicacies.

On the feast of the Immaculate Conception, I visited the Ladies of the Sacred Heart at their convent in Manhattanville. They were charming. When I had toured the boarding school, I attended Benediction of the Blessed Sacrament in their chapel. I felt deeply moved, almost drawn by the Sisters' piety. I was struck by the good order and manners of the pupils.

---

2 To overthrow the demon is Our Lady's special mission. It is God, however, who gives her the power to do so, more precisely Our Lord. He is the one who conquers the demon.

The impulsive and irascible nature that had been mine when I was four was not dead ; I could feel it boil up inside me. One day, I faced a hard struggle : someone very much my superior kindly made a critical remark to me which I had deserved for a long time. I was surprised. I expressed my thanks and went up to my room. God alone knows what went on inside me. My face was white as chalk and I was shaking ; half an hour later, the tears began to flow. Why? Because my nature wanted to show anger and my will refused to utter the least complaint. Reasoning within myself, I said : this person is right, that comment is justified ; it cost me to repel contrary thoughts, to force my pride and sensitivity to accept the truth. Grace won the day ; and with it, came the peace and joy of not having caused my sweet Master any pain. That shows how weak I was, once the divine hand appeared to leave me to myself even for a short while. In this simple situation, I should truthfully have been happy to receive a word of advice. If I delighted in being humiliated, it is because Jesus wanted to carry out an immense task, by lending me his dispositions and silencing my own conceited desires.

The following June, I left the residence feeling very grateful to the Sisters of Jesus and Mary. Each and every one had been so good to me. They kindly gave me a medal of the Sacred Heart ; one of them said to me, "Wear this medal." This seemed to me like a command. It rang soothingly in my ears, and even more in my heart. I hung the pious souvenir around my neck and wore it until that blessed moment when I became a "professed religious of Jesus and Mary". That holy religious must have prayed fervently to the Heart of Jesus as she handed me the medal, because her words filled my soul with a gratifying feeling of strength. At the time, I had no thought of becoming one day a member of that particular Congregation.

I went back to enjoy family life with my parents. The freedom I had known far from their supervision had not dulled my devotion. No, I was more fervent. The sheen of gold, the glare of wealth had served only to make me more detached ; the many opportunities for enjoyment and a life of luxury had increased my desire for self-denial ; the rush of busy crowds had made me realize even more the value of time ; the error and stupidity of too many people who do not know how to appreciate it, and still less how to use it, had also made me realize the value of the one important thing : salvation.   The race for honours and renown had taught me that a person is worth only what he is worth in the eyes of the sovereign Judge.   In other words, Jesus had set himself up as the jealous guardian of my soul.   What more can I say?   And when Jesus is present, he does not remain idle.

IX
FROM TWENTY-ONE TO TWENTY-FOUR
1918-1921

The voice and behaviour of Jesus. — A mission. — The importance of corresponding with grace. — A life of union with God. — Small sacrifices. — Some prayers. — Other favours.

As I approach this period of my life, I see myself in an ocean of choice graces. First of all, I am going to sing the work of God in the inmost depths of my being, which for the most part, I have never before revealed. All was between Jesus and myself and I preserved and pondered on our colloquies as being the secrets of the Master.

I repeat that, during these three years, the terrible trial of which I spoke earlier is going to persist. Moreover, I will be continually in a state of interior aridity. After the bright light, darkness immediately returns. Devotions, assistance at Mass, thanksgiving after Communion, meditations, will very often be occasions of distraction and struggle ; I continued to accomplish them faithfully, and I even felt the need to increase them. I devoted twenty minutes, then half an hour, to meditation each day — I had no permission to go beyond that — and at least ten minutes to spiritual reading — often taking a chapter of the *Imitation*. Quite often, I said the Rosary every day, or recited the *Little Office of the Blessed Virgin*, saying at least several Hours of it. Ejaculatory prayers, such as *My Jesus, mercy*, sometimes amounted to hundreds. Of necessity, I cut down on sleep. Weariness, the lateness of the hour or the time of night were no excuse for giving up my prayers. The Way of the Cross was also included ; it was easy, during the visit to the Blessed Sacrament.

At times, I could hear the voice of Jesus in the depths of my heart. His light brought unfamiliar representations before the eyes of my imagination. I prayed a great deal about this voice and these representations. I was assured that they were my divine Master teaching me ; anything that speaks of obedience, humiliation, self-sacrifice can come only from him. I begged the grace not to allow myself to be ensnared by the evil spirit, who is capable of skillful and cunning fabrications, not to become a victim of figments of the imagination. I again told Our Lord of my ardent and sincere desire to love him with a pure love, and of my confidence in his goodness which could not allow me to give way to illusion against my will.

I noticed that Jesus spoke to my heart only when all was absolutely calm. If I was not completely at peace, he would establish it in me by his grace, incite me to feelings of humility and sorrow for my sins ; then, I could understand his mystic language. One day when I pleaded with him not to let me be deceived by any trick of the devil, he told me how to recognize his words, how to tell the difference between his divine voice and that of the demon who wants to impersonate and deceive. The Saviour is to be heard only in recollection, peace and silence. His voice is so subdued that one's interior must be totally silenced ; it is a sweet melody. The language of Satan is noisy : it is agitated, impulsive, disturbing and abrupt. Hence, it is impossible to make a mistake. I have put this distinction to the test several times. After a colloquy with Our Lord, Satan would try to ensnare me by continuing the interior dialogue along the same lines ; but, from the very first words, he made his hypocrisy clear by his way of acting.

Jesus gave me as my guide and light : the Host and the Star. The Host was himself ; the Star, his holy Mother. He showed me a path strewn with thorns along which he had walked first, desiring to see me follow. At first, the thorns were not very numerous ; they increased the more I advanced. If I was to remain faithful, I could not let the suffering they caused me bring me to a halt. The path was narrow ; the more obstructed it was with thorns, the narrower it became. They were to grow so dense, so tall and so prickly that I was surrounded on all sides. I had to keep pushing them aside ; what does it matter if one's limbs are torn provided one is on the way to heaven! And all the time I could see the Host and the Star, representing Jesus and Mary, above my path and a little ahead of me. At the end of the road which was climbing upwards all the time, as if towards a mountain peak, there was a blessed door : that of the heavenly Home! The Saviour and the sweet Virgin would open it for me in a few years' time and then, what oceans of delight...! It seemed to me that I could just make out some glints of pure light and hear echoes of angelic melodies.

All that took place in my imagination ; the picture was clear and bright. When Jesus showed it to me, I saw it more clearly than I would perceive a material image with my corporal eyes. Many times, I found myself on this path of predilection. Now, I no longer feel the thorns, love blunts and consumes them.

I want to explain once and for all the expressions that I shall use, such as : *I saw...*, *Jesus said to me...* and other similar expressions. They mean 'I saw in my imagination', 'Jesus told me by that interior voice which every soul hears in the depth of the heart in moments of divine consolation'.

Our Lord taught me that I had a mission to fulfil. He made me pray much for this mission, and showed me how necessary and important it was to prepare for it. He did not tell me what it was. I understood that it had to do with the salvation of a great number of souls.

By a very vivid insight, he taught me the incalculable value of the least grace, because it is a gift of God. Not one of God's favours can be called small, but our human language is so limited that, when we have spoken of extraordinary and signal favours as great graces, we have only lesser terms to describe the multiplicity of graces that are ours at each second of every day.

I envisaged the multitude of gifts that I received as a precious chain, made up of links ; one single infidelity would break a link and fragment the chain. And then Jesus told me that my failure to correspond with just one grace would cause me to fail in my mission. I realized how the least refusal could deprive me of an immense amount of grace ; if one fails once, the will has less resistance ; faced with the next opportunity for an act of generosity, if it hesitates again, then it grows weaker and, having slipped downwards, falls perhaps from one abyss into another. By contrast, correspondence with a divine inspiration draws down more help from heaven ; the Lord in his mercy rewards that fidelity with a more generous gift and so on. I felt an indefinable sense of responsibility. By my own fault, I could compromise my mission. More than ever, I was aware of my freedom. I did not know which grace could — if I failed to correspond with it — betray the cause of the Almighty ; it seemed to me that this grace might have to do with something quite insignificant. I saw that perhaps I would be in hell if I had the misfortune to weaken at the particular moment chosen by God. And what of all these souls who depended for light on my fidelity! I renewed before Jesus my firm resolution to fulfil his desires. I trusted in his love, in his goodness, and was overwhelmed by my extreme poverty. My sweet Master said to me :

> I want to make use of you because you are nothing, I want to demonstrate my power through your weakness.

He repeated this on other occasions in words which always come back to the same idea :

> It is precisely because you are weak and incapable of anything that I make use of you, so that my action alone will be in evidence.

He put into my heart the sincere and ardent desire for contempt and humiliation, these priceless treasures that the world
abhors because it does not appreciate their hidden value.   To
make one's nature bleed in search of humiliation, is like tearing
one's hand to pieces by trying to crack a hard nut ; but it is to
discover and relish the delicious almond that is pure joy.   Each
morning and evening, I made the following petition : "My God,
grant me the grace to be despised and humiliated as much as you
will, and let none of those who despise and humiliate me be held
guilty. If it is your will that I should experience no more joy on
this earth, I beg you not to let me taste a single one any more."
At first, I thought that this prayer meant a total renunciation of
every joy here on earth ; it was exactly the opposite. From the
very moment my soul desired nothing but sacrifice, I was overwhelmed with happiness. This is the secret of divine love. I felt
completely indifferent to everything. My food was to do the will
of God and I blessed its every manifestation : when I felt any natural satisfaction, I submitted myself to its designs ; in times of
abnegation, I had no fear since I had asked for it.

Through Jesus, I became familiar with the idea of suffering.
Once again, he made use of a picture. In his hand was a cross.
He pierced my heart with the foot of the cross once. Later, he
thrust it in more deeply. Then, he drove it right in, even the two
arms, until it was firmly fixed ; my heart had to be torn open.
This final act meant that the Saviour, and his Cross, reigned
within me. Then he placed a crown of thorns round my heart,
symbolizing his own.

It was usually in church that my sweet Master chose to
enlighten me.   Friday, and especially the First Friday of the
month when he was exposed in the monstrance, seemed to be his
favourite days. Nevertheless, he did choose other times, too.

He introduced me to a life of union with him. At first, it
seemed he was at my side, that he was walking close by me.
Then I found he was within me. I loved to speak with him interiorly when I was out alone in the street. Then he gave me his

spirit in place of my own ; his judgment so that I might appreciate things, happenings, people in the way he wished. After that,
he replaced my will with his own ; then I felt a great strength
which urged me on towards good and compelled me to refuse
him nothing.

I had a passion for holiness. At least twice a day, morning
and evening, I begged the grace to attain the highest degree of
perfection that God could wish for me. I wanted to fulfil the
ideal God had for me ; sometimes, I said to Our Lord : "If it is for
your glory that I should be the very least in heaven, I am happy
and content ; if it pleases you that I should be raised very high, I
want, with your help, to reach that degree which you expect of
me ; I have no intention of remaining a single degree lower than
that." The divine ideal seemed to require that I should become
a very great saint. I could not possibly want anything less than
that.

Jesus began to consume me in the fire of his love. During a
colloquy, he burnt my heart with a flame from his ; later, with
another, then a third time ; on one occasion with several at once.
These great favours gradually destroyed me. To make reparation
for the sacrileges committed against the divine Heart, to work
zealously for the salvation of souls became two compelling duties
for me.

One First Friday of the month, while I was making an hour's
adoration before the Blessed Sacrament exposed, in deep silence,
I seemed to see a multitude of poor souls rushing towards their
ruin, heading for eternal damnation. By God's grace, I realized
that I had to console Our Lord and pray for the conversion of
these ignorant souls.

I need hardly say that my thirst for martyrdom increased
and, at the same time, a passion for self-denial. I will mention
some small sacrifices which afforded me unspeakable joy (I mention them because obedience demands that I should sing of all
the blessings Jesus poured into my soul ; to leave out a single

note of the chords of my thanksgiving would be to fail to do justice to the infinite Craftsman and to add to my miseries yet one more instance of ingratitude) :

— Never to show a taste for this or that delicacy or sweet. When I was passing by a confectioner's, the demon, I think, took delight in making me imagine that this or that would taste very nice. I would immediately say : No, no, it is too good for me. So as to please Our Lord even more, I would turn away, offering him in addition the pleasure that it afforded my eyes. Yet, when I was at table at home, I could have everything I desired or fancied ; even more, my parents were continually asking me to tell them what I liked. When it was not obvious, I made their kindness an opportunity to mortify myself. I accepted sweets when they were given to me, but avoided taking them myself when alone.

— Feeling thirsty yet not drinking any water, sleeping with my head on a lower or harder pillow ; not crossing even my feet etc. : those were the simple means of subduing my nature that God suggested to me. Each of these trifles, that I offered to Jesus out of love, was accompanied and rewarded by such a powerful grace that I found it impossible, except with great effort, to refuse a single act of self-denial.

— I found comfort in giving, especially if it was for a good cause or for a charitable purpose. I wanted to do good. The less I had, the freer I felt. Jesus was preparing me for the blissful detachment that is found in religious life.

One day, I heard a socialite say that St Margaret Mary had made the vow of perfection. At that moment, I was inspired. I was not in the least surprised by the generosity of such an act, it seemed to me quite natural. Can love ever be bestowed so completely as to satisfy the lover? So I made up my mind to dedicate myself to doing on every occasion what was more perfect. To me, it seemed that to do anything less was a sign of half-hearted love. I could not dream of being so happy as to bind myself by vow, but I offered Our Lord my very firm decision, my ardent desire.

The good deeds of my neighbour were invested with great merit in my eyes ; their limitations were no surprise. I often reflected on the truth that God dispenses his grace and light as he pleases. Because of that, I was edified by a great number of people, seemingly underprivileged in some respects, who accomplished truly heroic deeds.

Regularly, morning and evening, I prayed for priests, as well as men and women religious. Consecrated persons have a heavy responsibility. They have the better part ; they receive choice graces from their Spouse. May those who reap correspond in every way, always and everywhere with the wishes of the divine Sower.

My prayers embraced every intention, infinitely, according to the measure of the power and love of Jesus. I prayed in union with Our Lord and the most Blessed Virgin — and with all those beings with whom I could be united —, for everyone, in the name of everyone, in a spirit of adoration of the Blessed Trinity and in praise of the angels and saints, in thanksgiving, in reparation, in petition. My desire was to make use of the merits and the infinite means that Jesus places at our disposal, he who is our God, our Redeemer and our Father. I wanted to make use of them, for all creatures, past, present and future, who might profit from them.

Jesus granted me the favour of being a member of the Third Order of St Dominic. After a year's probation, I was allowed to be professed. I asked for the name of St Catherine of Siena ; there was some hesitation about giving it to me. When I said that my birthday coincided with the feast of this gracious saint, it was immediately and kindly given me : it was a privilege. Since then, I have had a great devotion to my Dominican patron.

St Joan of Arc was often the recipient of my pious outpourings. I begged for her intercession to obtain the grace of fidelity to my mission.

One Christmas night, during my thanksgiving, I was

greatly consoled. Our Lord had prepared me for his visit the previous evening. I was in church. Interiorly, I was suffering greatly. A sentiment of peace, of recollection came over me, penetrated me, and I had a feeling that Jesus was going to communicate with my soul in some very intimate way. Indeed, when I had
received the Host, I seemed to be, like the shepherds long ago, in
the stable at Bethlehem. The Blessed Virgin handed me the
divine Child, and Jesus kissed me lovingly ; his Heart spoke to
mine, oh! so sweetly! This colloquy with the Holy Family is
characterized by unspeakable, inexpressible happiness.
Glimpses of heavenly joys can be felt, but they defy description.

The Master, I repeat, was jealous of my heart. He did not
allow me any opportunity to turn my gaze away from him, the
divine Lover, by accepting some other offer of friendship. No, he
himself purified the love for my parents and other affections that
he had fostered in my heart — they were sufficient ; as for
others that were not necessary, he removed them. It is an astonishing and choice favour.

"O Jesus, numerous and dazzling favours appear before my
poor eyes! Without doubt, a multitude of gifts of which I am
unaware will be revealed to me in heaven. May you be for ever
blessed and glorified!"

X
FROM TWENTY-ONE TO TWENTY-FOUR
(continued)

Ongoing studies.— Desire for failure. — Purpose of studies. — Darkness. — Decision to enter the Congregation of Jesus and Mary. — Submission to her parents. — Departure.

I cannot end this account of the three years that I have just been reliving without looking at them in a different light. So I will return to them.

When my father came to see me, at the end of my second year of study in New York, he gave me a piano as a gift that I was to choose myself. It was yet another proof of his generosity. The choice was made on 24 May, feast of Our Lady, Help of Christians, and the instrument arrived at our house on 2 July, feast of the Visitation. Quite definitely, Our Lady's blessing was on it. I spent the holidays in the country. My natural curiosity made me eager to see this new piano. The following day, I returned to the city. Hardly had I entered the house — I was alone — when I felt inspired to repress my natural longing. I knelt down and prayed fervently, asking Our Lord and his holy Mother to bless the present which had come, in the first place, from them ; I also asked that each chord might resonate to their praise, that each note might sing of their glory. During that time, I felt the pang of mortification go through my entire being. Then I reached the point where I no longer felt anything : it was time for me to give way to my joy because it had been blessed and sanctified.

For the first of these three years, from October to June, I continued to follow the course in Harmony provided by the New

York Conservatory, but by correspondence. It gave me joy to do the set work each week and to receive it back corrected. There were so many ideas, it seemed, in my head, and I loved to confide them to the notes and chords.

I studied piano on my own. I took Jesus as my professor. I would prepare my work for a given day ; it seemed to me that at that particular time, he was there especially to give me my lesson. He was with me at other times, too, but not in the same way. Before playing in public, I would invite him to hear the pieces I was to perform, with the Blessed Virgin and the angels and saints. Was it not for him, my dear Master, for my Mother, for my heavenly protectors, to be the first to judge my efforts? I took more care then, if that was possible, than I did in the case of live audiences. After playing each piece, I would listen interiorly and take advice from my divine Professor. When I was practicing, I imagined that I was in the presence of the angels ; I transformed the profane subject of the different pieces into a devotional picture.

This was actually the period devoted to concerts. What I have already said about this can be applied here in a much broader sense since I was obliged to appear in public. Before each concert, Jesus asked me to forego success and to desire failure. I submitted myself to his divine will ; I begged him to grant me, of his goodness, the grace of failure in the sight of all, if that would be more pleasing to him, and not merely a momentary lapse, but total failure.

One First Friday of the month, when Our Lord was communing with my soul, I asked him the following question : "What can be the purpose of my musical studies?" For I had the intimate conviction that I would never become proficient, yet I was being driven to work hard at my studies, as if by a divine compulsion. Jesus answered :

> Your musical studies will safeguard your vocation, but you will do good particularly by your writings.

I was extremely surprised to hear this last remark. Do good by my writings! Had I really understood? And Jesus went on :

Yes, in the convent you will devote yourself to literary work.

I worshiped the designs God had for me. This reply hung over me like a mystery. Now, the shadow has faded and I understand[1]

In the summer of 1920, my desire for religious life intensified still more. The time had come for me to make a decision. I was perplexed. Where should I enter? I did not know. I no longer felt called to the Congregation of Notre Dame, where I had thought of going after I left school ; no, certainly not. Whenever I visited one of the convents of that Congregation which had been so dear to me and to which I was so indebted, the walls seemed as cold as marble and I froze. The contemplative life appealed to me. In the month of August, I spent more than a week with a community of Nursing Sisters ; I was present at a clothing ceremony. During my stay, I thought I was living with angels. I found the "grilles" attractive. On the other hand, were not my studies proof that God had chosen me for teaching? I prayed a great deal. The first light I received gave me to understand that I was meant for a teaching career. Then again, the question : Where? My prayer and reflection led me to consider three Congregations : that of Jesus and Mary, the Ursulines and the Ladies of the Sacred Heart. I was fond of the Ursulines because of the cloister and grille. I went to ask for some information which was very kindly given me. Everything pleased me, yet I still hesitated. I turned to Jesus, begging him to enlighten me as to his designs, at the appropriate time. One day, he said to me :

I want you in the Congregation of Jesus and Mary.

---

[1] The testimony of her superiors prove that she believed this prophecy concerned her poems and other pious compositions written for her sisters and certainly not her Autobiography. In reality, it is the latter which does most good.

"Wherever you wish, my dear Master," I answered, "you know I have no taste for teaching, but I want to answer your call and to go anywhere, according to your good pleasure."

You will not teach for long, he replied.

On 4 September, through the voice of his minister in whom I had confided, Our Lord told me that I would be able to leave the world in six months, or, at most, a year ; this time, I had reached the end of the road. A week later, it was decided that I should apply to the Religious of Jesus and Mary. I did not leave at the end of six months ; I had to wait almost a year. At last I was close to fulfilling my lifelong desire.

I still had to discuss the time of separation with my dear parents. Though I had no doubt about their wholehearted consent, I could understand their sorrow and their tears. My departure was to break up our family life and I would be leaving them alone. No, not alone, since God was with them! They would be less alone than in the past, since Jesus himself undertook to take my place at their side! To feel that one is a cause of heartbreak to one's father and mother is to tread on one's own heart. Jesus gave me the strength to tell them of my decision. He proved admirable in the grace he gave them. In spite of their deep distress, my parents placed no obstacle in the way of the divine call. They did not try to delay my entering the convent by even one hour. Like fervent Christians, they answered me : "Since that is what God wants, we want it, too, we accept it." Their resignation was a real consolation for me.

During the last months that I was to spend with them, my father and mother multiplied the joys and pleasures they bestowed on me. Could they possibly give me more? All my life, they had acted in the same way. What an abyss of tenderness must be the infinite goodness of the Creator, if we can discover so much kindness in the heart of his creatures! They had no

intention of deterring me from my pious purpose, far from it ;
their sublime motive was to satisfy their love, to pave my way
with flowers. In June, my father suggested a trip to Niagara Falls.
During this, our last outing together, the hours passed quickly
and happily! How many delightful and amusing memories!
Heaven blessed me in every way. The beauty of the wonders that
God had sown all over our poor earth made me think of the eternal Beauty. My spirit rejoiced in this magnificent journey and
drew real spiritual profit from it.

The day of goodbyes dawned. Waiting is agonizing! I felt certain that I was leaving the family home for ever. This conviction
never left me from the moment I had made my decision. I was
certain that Jesus would bind me to himself for ever with the
bonds of love and happiness that he was offering me in his sanctuary. It was a Thursday, the 11 August. At moments of
unspeakable anguish such as this, supernatural strength invades
and transforms us. Otherwise, our frail nature could not
advance even one step up the thorny mountain that rises before
it. I left **my home** without any hope of seeing it again.

XI
THE POSTULANCY
11 August - 2 September 1921

Entry to the Convent. — First impressions. — Snares of the
Devil. — The power of grace. — A visit to the novitiate. — The
retreat. — Two graces received during the retreat.

On the day I entered, my father and mother accompanied me
to the convent. They were to hand me back to the eternal
Master who had one day entrusted me to their care. In my soul,
there was darkness and repugnance. Hardly had I crossed the
threshold of that hallowed convent, yes, just as I went in, before
the door closed, an interior impulse compelled me to say inwardly : *This is home.* These three words were a source of consolation, especially later on ; they seemed be an to expression of
God's will ; they added to my conviction that Jesus would from
then on keep me in his service, in the shelter of religious life. At
that moment, the words did not spring from my feelings. My
desire for solitude, my dreams of a cloistered life were all dor-
mant ; just when my fervent desires were about to be fulfilled,
nothing attracted me ; I was without feeling and in darkness.

That evening, when I was given the mantilla, I received it
with great devotion. I had been wanting for so long to be rid of
worldly pomp ; at last I was clothed in a simple costume. Still,
only by a constant effort of will was I able to assimilate the pious
truths that grace presented me.

The following day, there was a ceremony : several received
the habit or made their vows. I felt utterly dry. Far from experiencing the least emotion, my heart was cold as marble, as hard
as rock. Only one thing made an impression on me : when the

new Brides of Jesus gave me the kiss of peace, each one of them left me with a feeling of joy, of indescribable peace ; it seemed to me that they were pouring into my soul a few drops of their own immense, virginal happiness.   The same was true of the new novices ; however, my feelings then were less intense.

Before I entered, I had imagined that life in the convent was one continual struggle, a ceaseless assault on one's natural inclinations. I was overjoyed. The demon was waiting for me. He tried to discourage me. During my postulancy, everything seemed excessively difficult, even almost impossible. The voice of the enemy said to me : "Are you going to live here to the end of your days? Are you going to submit to these demands which are just so many burdens?" One day, in particular, the battle was terrible, in that I needed a powerful grace not to refuse Jesus anything. I considered each of the religious, one after another ; I was in admiration at the sight of their visible happiness, of their recollection, of their virtue which presupposed self-denial, and I thought : each of them is a great saint. The demon disclosed a vast, unassailable abyss between the perfection of these consecrated souls and my own devotion. Our Lord was watching over me ; I clung to his love, begging him not to let me weaken. He set his gentle and powerful inspirations against the suggestions of the devil ; then I grew more courageous, thinking : why should I not imitate these religious, are they not frail creatures like myself? Jesus will help me just as he does them. If this life demands heroism, then he will support my weakness since he has called me to it. My divine Master was waging war on my behalf, what had I to fear? Yet the dryness persisted. The devil is definitely the father of lies. His lying and deceitful fabrications were intended to keep me far removed from true joy.   Oh! Religious life is full of delights! There is a hymn that says :

Great God...!

A single moment spent in your temple

Is worth more than a century of terrestrial feasts.

And I can sing : "O Jesus! A single moment dedicated to your service, in your holy house, is sweeter that an eternity of worldly feasts." No, no, centuries without end will be too short to tell of my gratitude to Infinite Goodness for the grace and happiness of a single second of religious life.

The devil added another idle fancy : since most of the spiritual exercises were performed in common, I would not be able to speak to Our Lord intimately, in solitude. As a result, I was not to find what I was seeking : *intimate union with God*, since I did not have the time to pour out my heart freely to him, since I had to put up with vocal prayer and the ideas of others! Lies! Lies! Trickery of the evil spirit! Religious life is an uninterrupted exchange between the soul and her Bridegroom ; everywhere, one is at prayer : praying, working, sleeping, since Jesus and the soul are one. And prayers in common were to bring me so much consolation, as they united me with holy and perfect souls. What precious cause this gave me for confidence! Besides, there is an immense amount of free time to devote to personal dialogue with the Master.

It goes without saying that I was haunted by discontent and by one particular temptation. I sometimes found the night — I mean the time intended for sleep — quite dark. If Jesus was sleeping, his Heart kept watch over me ; and I renewed my protestations of fidelity. During the day, there were plenty of distractions, and I tried hard not to show what I was feeling interiorly. Alas! I often gave myself away. Once, I had some very discreet witnesses. One afternoon, as I was passing by the chicken-run, I said to the chickens : "Oh, dear little creatures, you are at home, make the most of it! Yes, make the most of it!"

I was given the grace to put into practice at once the recommendations we were given. To evade even one of them deliberately seemed to me to be an abuse of divine favours. When there was mention of interior silence, I at once made a truce with the past : it meant the severing of close and tender ties, signing the death warrant of a thousand memories ; I could not hesitate, Our Lord wanted it. Besides, before entering, had I not joyfully sacrificed everything? A blind sacrifice, but no less sincere for all that. I had given up music entirely and for ever, if such was the will of God, just as if I had never played a single note of music.

One evening, together with the numerous companions who had entered with me, I had permission to visit the novitiate. What edified me again there was the charity of the novices, their cheerfulness, their constant smiles. I wondered what it was? What is the secret that can transform a young woman of the world so happily and in such a short time? I soon understood the great secret of the soul which, totally given to Jesus, radiates the beauty and goodness of the Well-Beloved. As I watched each of the novices, the thought that I have already expressed strengthened me : it is just as possible for me as for them. As for the novitiate setting, I saw a sentence which seemed like an order addressed directly to me : *If you begin, begin perfectly.* I responded to the grace with which I had been favoured by making a firm resolution to begin perfectly, at that very moment.

Of the meditations I made as a postulant (before the retreat), the one which made the greatest impression on me, because I received divine enlightenment, was   :"On fidelity in little things". I was convinced of the truth that I would not have the strength to go against nature in matters of importance, if I had not the generosity to give way in small things.

Then we had the retreat in preparation for our entry to the novitiate. Jesus was waiting to flood me with light and, sometimes, consolations. The temptations that I had experienced earlier faded away and nothing, just nothing, appeared difficult. As before, I rejoiced in everything. I will refer to two graces that I consider the most important :

— First, a new life. I plunged my past existence into the precious Blood of the Redeemer and I left it completely behind. I forgot it as far as my will was concerned, for often after that,

I caught myself red-handed recalling memories of long ago. The break with my past was so profound that I seemed to have died and been born again.

— The second favour granted me by divine love filled my soul with unspeakable happiness. It was the last evening of the retreat. During the free time before the preparation of the next day's meditation, I went to the chapel. It was dark, silence reigned. Jesus let me hear his gentle, mystic voice ; I felt overwhelmed with sheer delight, all was peace and love. Then my good Master took hold of my poor heart, just as one picks up an object from a particular place, and replaced it with — O gift of infinite love! — his Sacred Heart and the Immaculate Heart of Mary! Again, it was an image ; but there certainly took place within me a divine transaction that no pen could describe. I was immersed in feelings of gratitude and humility. I no longer had to seek outside myself the *Host* and the *Star* : I had Jesus and Mary within me. From that moment, I have acted and loved with the Heart of Our Lord and that of his Blessed Mother. When praying privately, I no longer said :"My God, I offer you my heart" or anything similar ; no, I did not have my heart any longer, I had been relieved of it. At community exercises, each time the words, *my heart*, occurred, the thought of my two treasures came to mind ; in conversation, I managed to avoid using them. It is still the same. If I have failed at any time, I have never been aware of it. I believe that, in their love, Jesus and the Blessed Virgin have anticipated my thoughtlessness and helped me not to forget. Oh! How good it is for a poor creature to be the object of such an exchange! To enjoy such an august change of heart is heaven on earth!

At the end of the retreat, I summed up in three phrases my plan of life for the future : **to obey blindly, to suffer with joy, to love to the point of martyrdom!** I wanted to shut my eyes to everything here below so as to see only Jesus.

XII
THE NOVITIATE
September 1921 - February 1922

Life in community. — Love of the Rule. — Teaching. — God's work. — The Game of Love and the Game of the Cross. — The daily cross. — The retreat prior to clothing. — Betrothal. — A 'new name'.

The great difficulty that confronted me in the novitiate was community life. However, I loved the family that had received me with so much charity and that, above all, was going to show admirable patience with me. Sincerely, I would have been ready to give my life joyfully for any one of my sisters. The suffering that pinpricks caused me is clear proof of my excessive sensitivity, and I think that the evil one found this a source of temptations with which to torment me.

I clung to my vocation as to eternal salvation. Apart from being unfaithful to God, which is irreparable and cannot be compared to it, the most cruel suffering for me would have been to be obliged to return to the world. However, I had problems for several more weeks. Sometimes, when I was out walking on my own, I thought of going home just as I was, without hat or coat, or, at night, of escaping through a window. I despised these promptings of the evil spirit and felt that grace held me safely in its grasp! And if I have one great regret, it is that I failed on many occasions, that I allowed my natural feelings to show, that I too often allowed myself the satisfaction of crying. That my tears flowed freely was due to selfishness and self-love. My behaviour bore witness to my pride and I find it humbling.

I made more and more blunders, they came in quick succession ; every day, I seemed more imperfect. I thought to myself : I was better in the world than I am here. I strove to observe the Rule, to carry out recommendations scrupulously I venture to say ; but, all the time, I was far from being faithful, or I did just the opposite of what was asked of me. The Rule! I was bound to it by the will of God. I begged Our Lord to grant me the grace of enduring every kind of suffering rather than let me neglect voluntarily the least of its prescriptions. What I did in no way corresponded with what I wanted to do.

I strove to acquire an agreeable virtue : that of smiling at everything, at events as much as at people. I had always had a melancholy expression ; I had to overcome this ugly habit, for, as the gentle Bishop of Geneva said, "A sad saint is a sorry saint" ; this truism suited me well. Jesus gave me to understand that true interior joy is reflected in one's facial expression ; his divine lessons taught me to accept everything with a smile. Alas! Does nature get the better of my good intentions? The Master is the best judge.

I was entrusted with the task of giving piano lessons to a few students. This was my introduction to work. The supernatural goal I set myself was as far above my natural inclinations as morality is above the profane. I saw Jesus himself in my pupils ; I imagined him at the same age as each of the pupils who came for a lesson. Who was teaching? — Again Jesus, since he was living in me. How easy it was, then to gain my initial experience! I could not have been more assiduous had Our Lord been visibly at my side.

I tried to offer Jesus the entire day, that is, not refusing him anything and working only for him. I wanted my life to be an unbroken prayer, by remaining continually united to him in my prayer, my work and my rest. In the month of November, this life of union with my perfect Model became the subject of my particular examen. What joy I felt when I realised that the divine Hand was leading me in this direction! It responded to all my aspirations. In the morning, I was to think of making five acts, in union with Our Lord, in honour of his Sacred Wounds ; similarly, in the afternoon. From the moment I woke up, I hastened to make a start with the wound of the right foot, then the left foot, the right hand, the left hand and finally his Heart. Oh! I could hardly wait to reach this last! I had often reached there by the Communion time, and I stayed there.

One day, I received a most enlightening inspiration concerning the following truth : "Heaven means possessing God ; God is living in me, I possess him ; thus, I am enjoying heaven on earth." From that blessed moment, I withdrew even more into the Heart of my dear Master ; there, I experienced the delights of heavenly bliss and, in addition, the signal privilege of being able to suffer. It is a mystery of love that in heaven our happiness will be complete, and yet we will no longer have the joy of suffering for God. If the angels could wish for anything, it seems to me that, after the gift of the Eucharist, they would envy us this favour. Yes, how sweet it is to smile at Jesus in the midst of renunciation!

I was so well concealed in my sacred Fortress that at times I could have thought that the world outside the convent had ceased to exist. I lived through external events, but they did not distract me ; they were like water flowing over a stone without penetrating it.

Each morning, during my thanksgiving after Communion, I would ask Jesus for my cross for that day ; he would allow the Blessed Virgin to give it to me. It would vary in length and in weight. It always consisted, in part, of a number of humiliations that Jesus asked me to accept in advance and for which, in his kindness, he prepared me. Subsequent events never failed to correspond precisely to the number given. The next morning, before asking for my cross, I would hand back to my good Mother that of the preceding day. It seemed misshapen because of my imperfections. Mary would redress it, through her own merits and those of her Son before giving it to him. And Jesus himself presented it to his Father.

My small daily crosses, transformed into a variety of jewels through the mediation of the Blessed Virgin and added one to another, helped to build a great cross in heaven. When completed, this latter shone with precious stones embellished with the treasures of the love of Jesus and Mary ; then it would adorn the noble cross of Christ, like a small glorious jewel in the victorious sceptre of the Redeemer. I can see now that the countless multitude of jewels that Our Lord deigns to insert in his trophy, while allowing them to reflect the splendour of his glory, the fire of his love, the rich red of his Blood, is made up of the souls of the elect redeemed, saved and sanctified by his death and resurrection. They are brought together in perfect harmony and infinite variety. "O my God, in your saints, the work of your hands, I contemplate your bounteous generosity and mercy!"

At other times, always during my thanksgiving, Jesus would lead me into his **garden**.[1] Certainly, we have no idea of the magnificence and fragrance of the flowers of heaven. I was overcome with admiration, intoxicated, just looking upon the *garden* of the Well-Beloved with the eyes of my soul. And what comparison can there be between a picture and the real thing? It is as darkness compared with light. There were the most beautiful displays in every shade, especially roses and lilies. Jesus explained to me which acts of virtue caused the shoots to grow, and the flowers to open and bloom. In a place apart, the flowers were more dazzlingly splendid and more richly embellished ; He told me that these were cultivated by consecrated souls. He showed me those that he wanted me to produce. Then, one day, he took me into the **garden of privileged souls**. Oh! It was pure delight! In the centre was his divine cross, made of wood and dark-stained : the friends of Our Lord can obtain this insignia only by self-denial. The magnificent flowers, in full bloom around the cross, were the offering of perfect sacrifice, of pure love. They seemed to me to be the smile given "by those crucified out of love to crucified Love". This quotation is from St Margaret Mary.

---

[1] See St John of the Cross : Le Cantique spirituel, Strophe XVII.

At Christmas, in the white Host, I received the Baby Jesus. One morning, this sweet Child said to me :

Would you like to play a game of love?

I saw myself just as small as he was. "Oh, yes, dear Jesus!" I replied.

Well! he said, whichever of us can love the most will win.

Then I had a sudden inspiration. I had a powerful means of playing the game. "Oh yes."

I created you, continued our loving Saviour, I gave you the gift of faith from the dawn of your existence, I surrounded you with countless precious graces, I redeemed you, pardoned you, called you to religious life : all that out of love. And you?

"Jesus, I love you as much as I can and, to prove my love, I want to refuse you nothing, nothing at all."

I know, but my love is infinite, and yours?

"Mine, O divine Child, is infinite like yours, because I love you with your own Heart!"

You are right ; so it is a draw, we have both won!

Another morning, my dear little King suggested :

Let's play the game of the cross, shall we?

"Yes, Jesus." I did not feel quite as courageous about that game as about the game of love because it seemed more difficult to win.

Whoever succeeds best in carrying the cross will win.

"As you wish."

Look, in Bethlehem, I was born in poverty ; in Egypt, at Nazareth, during my public life, on Calvary, always and everywhere I endured suffering and humiliation ; and since then, in the Eucharist, complete annihilation, and of how many insults am I not the victim in the sacrament of love! And what have you suffered for me?

"Jesus, I am happy to accept all the small crosses you deign to send me, and I thank you in advance for those that in your goodness you have reserved for me."

I have borne and endured everything without complaining.

"You know that I want to carry my cross joyfully."

I chose whatever was most painful.

I began to hesitate : "My good Master, you know my sincere desire, my firm intention, never to be unfaithful to the least of your graces. I am weak, but you know my nature. And I love your cross passionately, and everything about it that is most painful."

My sufferings, went on my loving Saviour, are of infinite value. What are yours worth?

I saw that mine were poor, miserable ; I turned sadly to the Blessed Virgin, begging her to inspire me. Light dawned at once. "Jesus", I replied contentedly, "I unite mine with yours and so my poverty is clothed in your infinite merits."

All right! concluded the divine Child, we have both won again!

Jesus often took me far above the earth to talk to him in greater tranquillity. Or else, he would raise me a little above the earth and show it to me. I saw that it was dark, overcast, black. How, then, was it possible not to mourn over one's exile and long ardently for our eternal home!

One day, my good Master told me that I was not to cling to anything here below, since I had only to love him alone, and love creatures in him and for him. For that reason, to speak in human terms, he cut off my two feet, so that I would understand that nothing on earth was to get in the way of my ascent towards him. For, in order to find Jesus, it is necessary to rise higher, to take flight.

I was delighted when I heard that I was to be allowed to receive the habit. I knew I was most unworthy to become the Bride of the Son of God!

The retreat that preceded the clothing ceremony began on 6 February. Eight complete days seemed very short to me. At times, the evil spirit launched furious attacks against me ; he returned to the attack on the very morning of my clothing. Our Lord gave me unspeakable consolation. Two meditations that gave me divine light in abundance were those on 'The Agony in the Garden of Olives' and on 'The Storm', when the apostles were struggling hard and unsuccessfully against the tempestuous waves, and Jesus joined them in the fourth watch of the night, walking on the waters.

The inexpressible joy of my retreat lay in the knowledge that shortly after my clothing, my divine Betrothed would invite me to become his Spouse. No words could describe my amazement, and my happiness was ecstatic. Once I knew the date, I began to count the hours.

During this period of reflection, I settled 'my accounts with Jesus', covering six months, from the retreat I had made as a postulant. This is what I wrote in my personal notebook : Numerous failings in all our holy Rules, through weakness, inattention. Countless graces wasted, repeated thoughtlessness towards Jesus. Lack of confidence in Jesus, hesitant, tepidness ; anxiety, faltering will. I am a repentant nobody. "O divine Love! you know all my desires ; I hide myself in your heart with my sins and miseries. Grant that I may live for you alone. With the help of your grace, no matter what it costs, I will follow in the way you are pleased to mark out for me."

The practice of union with God, as I have already described it, continued to be the subject of my particular examen. I added that I wanted **to act out of love for Jesus alone** ; not seeking either myself or any created thing.

The foremost thought during my retreat, which summed up my plain duty, was : People must be able to read our holy Rules in me.

On the final day, again during the free time that preceded night prayer, I was in the chapel. Our Lord was preparing me for the following day's feast. Then, at a given moment, it seemed he was presenting me with a ring, mystic token of union, and placing it on my finger himself. My sense of insignificance and unworthiness increased, and my confidence grew. I remained engulfed in peace and happiness.

The sacred moment of betrothal arrived. It was 15 February. My joy was so pure that, to describe it, silence is more eloquent than faltering words. I asked Jesus for **my present : a chalice**, modeled on his, containing precious jewels, that is to say the instruments of his passion : cross, nails, thorns, scourge. My divine Bridegroom's response was accompanied by an inexpressibly loving and tender smile.

I received a 'new name'. I had accepted in advance the name of any patron or patroness. Oh! How happy I was to be entrusted to St Cecilia of Rome! To the Blessed Virgin first, naturally, through the name of Mary. Then St Cecilia whom I had chosen long ago as my protectress and whom I invoked lovingly! A virgin! A martyr! An apostle! Her glory fitted in well with my ambitions. "Holy Spouse of Jesus, my desire is to sing with you : *I love my Christ.* To honour you, I desire an immortal and noble crown, like yours. In heaven, I want to be adorned with the robes associated with your three claims to glory. Prepare a lyre for me, tune it to your own. Together we will sing a canticle of love, we will compose an eternal symphony of rich chords for the glory of the Eternal."

XIII
THE NOVITIATE
15 February - 15 August 1922

A portrait. — Private profession. — Motive for devotedness to the pupils. — Literary endeavours. — Abandonment. — Friendships. — Divine love. — Annual retreat.

At last! I was clothed in the religious habit ; I kissed it with devotion and love. But as has been rightly said : *The habit does not make the monk* ; I had to strive to become less unworthy of wearing the holy habit and, above all, of bearing the title Bride of the King of Kings.

During the monthly day of retreat in March, I wrote out my aspirations : **Portrait of a Fervent Novice of Jesus and Mary**. Here is a copy :

I wish this novice to be a living model of our holy Rules. I wish her to be ignored, counted as nothing, the servant of her sisters, but foremost in the service of Jesus. I wish her to be consumed with zeal for the salvation of souls, for the glory of Jesus and Mary, always recollected, always burning with love of God. I wish her days to be fully occupied, her life to be one of continual prayer, whether in light or in darkness.

All for Jesus alone. I wish her to be detached from all that is not God, to have dealings with creatures only to find God in them, and to lead them to praise him ; I wish her to submit blindly to obedience and always to suppress her selfish inclinations so as to allow Jesus alone, and his grace, to live within her. I wish her to be always humble and trusting, whether in success or in failure ; to be always charitable, kind to everyone. May God alone live in this novice, and this novice live for God alone.

"O my soul, do you find this model worthy of admiration? If Jesus wished to bring about such marvels within you, what would you do...? Jesus does not refuse his grace to those who ask him for it. Well! Do not refuse Jesus anything!" (12 March 1922)

During Lent, at the time of meditation, Our Lord favoured me several times with vivid insights into his Passion. I gained a greater understanding of his immense love and of the love I owed him.

I longed for the moment when I would surrender myself to Jesus, in reality, as his Spouse, committing myself by the holy vows. I received this special permission and the day chosen was a Saturday, 25 March, feast of the Annunciation of the Blessed Virgin. A happy coincidence! I asked for and was given the privilege of spending the preceding day in retreat, so as to ensure greater interior recollection while continuing to perform my normal duties. At last! At last, the moment came when Jesus brought to fulfilment the desire that he himself had placed and nurtured in my soul! I cannot venture to speak of my happiness. That which I felt on the occasion of my public profession, almost a year and a half later, was no greater. At this latter ceremony, the gift of myself was no more complete than at my private profession, when I gave myself totally, unreservedly and with the intention of never taking anything back. My joy was heavenly! The day was spent in almost continual silence and tranquillity, in the company of Jesus and Mary. This was yet one more favour on the part of my Bridegroom.

I continued to teach. How I loved my pupils! It has been the same ever since with each one confided to me. I loved them with an affection that desired only their good. Without exception, when I looked at them, I saw their soul, and in it, the image of God ; I looked on them as living ciboria in which the Blessed Trinity was dwelling. If I had allowed myself any preference, it would have been for the least gifted children, for those who found study, or the observance of regulations, difficult. God surely endows educators with the heart of a mother, or rather, he replaces our heart with his own.

I also had the joy of studying music privately. In addition, I had the advantage of exploring the delights of literature. Having reviewed the rules of versification, I tried to write poetry. The patience, care and consideration with which my efforts were corrected always edified me. I would rack my brains for a long time to produce four lines without mistakes. Dictionaries of words and rhymes were more often open in my hands than closed by my side. I was very far from experiencing the ease that Jesus was to give me later, in support of the declaration he had made when I was still living in the world.

I felt a holy indifference to everything. God's will for me at each moment was my only happiness. One day, among the different poetic themes to be developed, I found this : *My Favourite Time.* I was unable to deal with it. Finally, my work was entitled : *Abandonment.* I had no preference. Everything willed by the eternal Master was equally acceptable to me.

I have just spoken of abandonment, and yet I was still unaware of the true sweetness of "love's delicious fruit". I had too little confidence. I think Jesus allowed this so that my soul could be purified by suffering ; I did not understand how to cast my useless fears upon him and yet I wanted to please him in everything! I realize now that I was creating my own fears through a lack of confidence. The light that reveals the secrets of perfect abandonment is a precious grace. "O divine Craftsman of my soul, forgive the times when I failed in confidence through no fault of my own! To prove to you my present abandonment, it is my firm belief that your infinite mercy was glorified by my failures, and my weakness, strengthened.

It was difficult for me to open my heart because of my intense nature and my shyness. God gave me a 'mother' from the moment I entered. Only Jesus knows the rich treasures of love that he puts into the souls of those responsible for leading us to him, guiding our first steps, strengthening our wavering will. When I was still a 'candidate', I began to feel a rather human affection for my superior. Our Lord at once made me aware of it. I asked him for help to overcome this natural inclination without delay, and I was given the grace to understand the purity, sweetness and strength of the bond of love that should unite my youthful soul with that of my 'mother', in the early stages of my religious life. I should see in her only Jesus or the Most Blessed Virgin ; I became totally convinced of this : hence, the purity of my altogether supernatural affection. Since Jesus and Mary were acting in and through her, my love flowed from this principle and was sustained by this truth ; what gentler tie can there be! As her goodness reflected that of the Master and her advice was the expression of his holy will, the gratitude I felt made me regret my incapacity, and I revered God's action with respect : there existed a strong bond, secured by the hand of God with ties of love and the glory of God ; a bond, everlasting as is my filial obligation of gratitude.

In the world, it is sometimes thought that legitimate affections grow cold within the walls of a convent. Oh! What an unfortunate mistake this is! On the contrary, it is there that they blossom. It is there that friendship, released by grace from purely natural motivation, can be called the true flower of charity. I look on each of my affections as a link in a chain. The two principal links, dazzlingly beautiful and joined one to the other, are Christ and the Virgin. With this divine link I connect all the others, representing human friendships. Can anyone love more intensely or better than with the heart of Jesus and that of Mary...?

In my relations with my companions, with the great family that I held dear, I knew that in spite of my efforts I was often a cause of suffering. That was humiliating and an indication of what I was capable, especially as I was quite overwhelmed by the kindness and consideration shown me.

About this time, I made a pact with the adoring angels

who kept watch over all the tabernacles in the world. I asked them to take my place always and everywhere in the presence of God, held captive. And since then, every Tuesday at Holy Mass, I am more closely united with them than on other days.

At certain times, I felt a burning desire to love Jesus. When I was in the world, it found expression in a holy exhilaration. In the novitiate, my fervour intensified and I felt as if I were suffocating. Or else I felt a *passionate desire* for the cross.

In the refectory, I became indifferent to the taste of food. Often, I was unaware what dishes I was served. I had the impression of taking my meals in the company of the Holy Family and being served by the angels.

During the monthly retreat in May, on "Charity", I was struck by one point made during the conference ; in order to benefit from the example given, I wrote down the following resolution : When I meet one of my sisters, I will, in spirit, fall on my knees at her feet and kiss them humbly. It is a sweet joy for me when the Holy Spirit grants me the grace of remembering this practice.

During the annual retreat in August, **desire for total perfection** haunted me. I could be satisfied with nothing less. And I ventured to envisage making the vow later on. In this respect, my audacity is unutterable ; or rather, my confidence in an infinitely good and powerful God is boundless. I was united with Jesus, I counted on his strength. The conviction of my own weakness and imperfection was growing. In spite of that, the only means I had of bringing some relief to my soul tormented by love was to offer whatever was best.

I chose two subjects for my particular examen so as to bring variety to my efforts. To the first, of which I have already spoken, I added the saying of St John the Baptist : *Jesus must increase and I must decrease.* I substituted this for a time. Here is the second : I will perform each of my actions, however insignificant or intimate, with all the perfection of which I am capable, out of pure love for Our Lord, for *him alone*, refusing him nothing, in gratitude for his great blessings. I wanted to add : and always choosing what is more painful to my nature. I did not write this phrase down but it was engraved in my will.

At the end of the retreat, I summed up what I felt in these words : "**I want to be holy!** With your grace, Jesus, this I will be. And I want to take the shortest cut possible, to tell you of my love and to be completely hidden in you. O Jesus. you alone know how much I want to love you and to make you loved!"

I again made the resolution dating from my retreat as a postulant — changing it slightly : **To obey blindly, to suffer lovingly, to love to the point of martyrdom.**

I tried to find a motto. *Death rather than defilement* no longer satisfied me. I needed to express love. I wanted to include the names of Jesus and his most holy Mother. Although it was rather long, I adopted this one : **Jesus and Mary, the rule of my love ; and my love, the rule of my life!**

My entire being, completely taken over by the God of love, had only one aim, to consume itself for him alone!

XIV
THE NOVITIATE
15 August 1922

A sacrifice. — Fresh graces. — Writings. — Dina's ideal. — A promise at Christmas. — Intimacy with the Master. — Zeal for souls. — Complaints of the Heart of Jesus.

It did not always fall to my lot to feel fervent. However, in times of darkness, the great Craftsman of my soul would preserve and increase in my will — which was really his — my desire for perfection.

At this time, the superiors decided to send some novices from Sillery to continue their novitiate in the United States. Who would be chosen? It was several days before we knew the answer. I offered myself to Our Lord, if such was his will for me. It cost me to do so for one particular reason, and it cost my parents who would have suffered so much from my being far away. But I could not hesitate between human pretexts and the welcome opportunity to make a sacrifice for Jesus. If authority chose me, I was ready.

I applied myself to thinking of God as often as possible, I tried to be continually aware of his presence. My loving Master told me one day that he was granting me the gift of prayer ; I felt very unworthy of this favour. When I receive choice graces in this way, my sense of poverty, of nothingness, always increases.

It seemed to me sometimes that Jesus came to me laden with graces. They were like rushing torrents, numerous, immense rivers flowing from his hands and his sacred Heart. His consolation was that I should apply these treasures to souls. Oh! If only we knew how to make use of the merits of Our Lord, how rich we would become in just a short time, and what an advantage it would be to our neighbour!

In the Autumn, I spent several weeks in the infirmary. It was a time of heavenly blessings. Jesus was giving me a tiny thorn from his crown : could I have failed to thank him with a smile? And oh! How good it is to converse with him in silence and solitude, while meditating on his passion and his love. While I was convalescing, I began to write poetry. I held my crucifix in my right hand so that my good Master could guide my pencil. What a surprise! My brain was teeming with ideas ; I did not have to search for rhymes, they came spontaneously to end the lines. I was very touched by this. The ease with which I write dates from that time. Since then, but when I am alone so that it is not obvious, I never write without the One who inspires me in my hand : that is my secret, it is Jesus who is the author. And as confirmation, I can say that when in the presence of my sisters I try to put some lines together "without him", I succeed only with difficulty, or not at all. At such times, I need dictionaries which are hardly of any use.

Our Lord was beginning to fulfil his prediction :

You will do good by your writings

He takes pleasure in making me write in the seclusion of the infirmary ; it is there that he favours me to a greater extent with his inspirations. It is so manifestly his work that often I hardly know what I am writing. I am impelled by a gentle and superior force and, on reading over what I have written, I have often been surprised to find I have expressed ideas that have not passed through my mind.

Subsequently, Jesus gave me to understand that he not only wanted me to be united to him in my life, but that his action in me and through me was to be deep-rooted. At the monthly retreat in December, my ideal was formulated thus : **The most perfect union with God**. I returned to the initial subject of my particular examen : In the morning, I will make five acts of union with Our Lord, in honour of his sacred wounds, out of love, convinced that it is God himself who thinks and acts in me, poor though I am (similarly in the afternoon). All for God alone.

I made out some questions that I was to ask myself at the examen : 1. Have I been quite convinced that it is God who thinks, speaks and acts through me? 2. Have I carried out these actions as perfectly as I can? 3. Have I used my faculties to the utmost so as to achieve my ideal as quickly as possible? 4. How can I do better this afternoon (or this evening and tomorrow morning)?

I would like to point out here that I am using the expression *so as to achieve my ideal.* I did not yet understand that an ideal cannot be achieved without changing its name and being called a reality.

To satisfy my love, I prepared to make Jesus a promise at Christmas. During Advent, I stimulated my fervour, so that my offering would be pleasing to him. When night arrived, I was in great aridity of soul. During my thanksgiving after Communion, I made the following commitment : "My God, I will perform each one of my actions with all the perfection that I can bring to them. I do not want to refuse you anything. I want to use all my faculties so as to fulfil my ideal as soon as possible. I will cultivate interior silence and recollection and, to that end, will entertain no useless thought. My God, I depend entirely on your grace. Mary, my good Mother, I trust you to keep me faithful to my promise."

The darkness that enveloped my soul persisted. The Saviour made no response, in his gentle voice, to my act which in reality was pleasing to him. He at once put my will to the test by leaving me in complete darkness. It was a wisp of the cold, hard straw on which he was lying. This grace was, assuredly, more precious than consolation, since it purified my offering of even the joy I felt in making it.

During the February retreat, I added one word to the third question in my particular examen, saying : Have I used my faculties and my senses to the utmost, etc.? I dwelt on this thought : God wants me to be a perfect religious ; he is giving me his grace to be faithful and willing. I wrote : "My God, with your holy grace, I will correspond with your designs of holiness for my soul. My Jesus, I desire to live in your Heart, quite hidden, in the closest possible union with you ; I do not want to refuse you anything whatever. Mary, my good Mother, bless me, help me."

I endeavoured to avoid every unnecessary movement, so as to promote interior recollection. I had an enormous task to do. Our Lord took pity on my weakness ; my many failings in generosity were a source of humiliation.

My intimacy with Jesus grew. In speaking to him, I loved to use the pronouns : *te, tu, toi* Does a woman use *vous* when she is speaking to her husband? — Not usually. The use of *tu* contributes to greater intimacy. Until this time, I had hesitated to adopt this tone of familiarity out of respect. But then, trust gained the upper hand ; love, knowing no bounds, chose what helped it to express itself. Sometimes I used extravagant expressions in speaking to my dear Master ; yes, extravagant. And I am far more free with them now.

As proof that he wanted to live through me, Jesus gave me his eyes, his ears, his senses, that is to say, he was "the Life of my life". Eventually, he made one final change, that of my name :

It is I who act in you and through you, from now on you will be called Jesus, he said ; but when you commit some error or blunder, it will be through your own action and then you will be called Cécile.

At these words, I was totally penetrated with a sense of dignity, accompanied by a profound conviction of my own nothingness. Since then, when my conscience is clear, it is the work of the divine Craftsman ; and when I am aware of my thoughtlessness, my failures, I hear a voice saying : "Cécile is doing (or has done) that". Oh! I am immersed by my Beloved in choice graces! How ashamed I am to be still, through my own fault, so imperfect!

Our Lord asked me to console his Heart desecrated in the Holy Eucharist. One first Friday of the month, when the Blessed Sacrament was exposed. I seemed to see, during my private adoration, a multitude of souls rushing to their eternal damnation. Some were on the brink of the abyss ; they were about to fall. Jesus told me that I could save them by praying fervently for them and offering him small sacrifices out of love. I did this at once. Then I saw these same souls, won over by divine grace, abandoning the camp of the demon.

Each morning, during my thanksgiving, our loving Saviour would fix a number of souls to be won for him during the day. Now, the number is no longer predetermined, I ask him for all ; I wish I could plunge them all, without exception, into his precious Blood ; I wish I could, through the application of his merits, shut down hell for ever. His mercy is infinite. Our Redeemer longs to pardon and forget faults. Often, he is only waiting for a loving gesture or thought from us so as to grant to one sinner or another the exceptional grace that will release him from the power of Satan.

One morning, at meditation, having listened attentively to the reading, I found it literally impossible to concentrate on the subject proposed. Recognizing the intervention of Jesus, I allowed him to lead me where he willed. He wanted to be consoled. He showed me his Heart, quite disfigured, on which from every side violent blows from an infinite number of heavy hammers rained down ; then he showed it to me again, being attacked from every direction by a host of daggers that plunged in deep and tore it apart. Each blow, whether from hammer or daggers, was an outrage caused by sin. Then, I saw him pierced by incalculable needles, most of them small, even minute :

> Those, he said, are the infidelities of religious ; Oh! How much suffering they cause me, these needles, because they belong to souls that I love most of all!

The immense sorrow of my good Master filled me with compassion and inflamed me with love. What a touching scene this was! Only in eternity will we have some realization of the pain that Our Saviour suffers because of our sins, our carelessness, our lack of love. And to think that we can console him! "Why, Jesus, do you give us poor creatures the honour of wiping away some of your tears? Your holy Mother, the pure Virgin, is always there, beside you ; millions of angelic spirits belong to your court, praising you without ceasing, yet you stoop down to us, begging us to pour a few drops of balm on the wounds of your Heart! O mystery of divine Love! Infinite love of the Shepherd for his sheep!"

Our loving Saviour sometimes asked me for prayers, for sacrifices, because a great crime was, he said, about to be committed in the world, or else in anticipation of insults to which he was soon to be subjected ; these sacrifices and prayers were intended to console him on behalf of those who would offend him.

Oh! How heart-rending are Jesus' cries of pain! How he suffers, the silent Prisoner in our tabernacles, held captive[1] day and night by love! My greatest sorrow at that time was the suffering

---

[1] Jesus is not a prisoner in the tabernacles nor do the sins of men sadden him. During His Passion, he suffered all the ingratitude, the infamy that were to be heaped upon him during centuries to come in His sacrament of love. It is this suffering, and especially that caused by sins committed actually, that he shares with faithful souls.

of the Eucharistic Heart. At a human level, no well-bred soul can see those it loves fall victim to suffering or insult without being moved. How can we remain unmoved when it is Jesus who is abandoned and despised!

I have just written : *my greatest suffering*, but I ought to have said my real suffering for, under the influence of grace, love transforms into joy what the world calls pain.

XV
THE NOVITIATE
(continued)

Communions. — Retreat. — Different kinds of thanksgiving. — Martyr, victim, apostle. — A maxim. — Life in community. — Preparation for profession and death. — My bridal bouquet.

My hunger for Holy Communion was increasing all the time. Is not a day without bread like a day without sunshine, like a day when evening is slow to come? I entrusted my preparation to the Blessed Virgin. As I approached the holy table, I imagined angels hovering round the sacred ciborium, ardent seraphim in adoration or expressing their love in hymns and sweet harmonies ; I listened to their melodies and they seemed so pure that the most harmonious praises sung here on earth sounded discordant. I received Jesus from the hands of my dear Mother. Returning to my place, led by her, I imagined I was surrounded by a host of angelic spirits who formed a guard of honour for my divine King. Often during my thanksgiving, Mary would speak for me ; all I had to do was to listen to her, unite with her, contemplate my Saviour, love him. Sometimes I saw myself as a little lamb in the arms of the good Shepherd ; I would let myself be carried by him. This image gave me unspeakable consolation.

One day, again during my thanksgiving, Jesus asked me to remain continually in retreat in his Heart and, accordingly, to strive to be as recollected as possible, just as on genuine retreat days, so as to think about him more. Far from being a distraction, this interior exercise helped me to carry out my employments better. The Master did not want to see me so taken up with him that the duties of my state of life suffered ; I am reluctant even to mention this absurd hypothesis. No, no. I walked in his presence, I kept him company, and he was busy acting through me in accordance with his designs. This preoccupation did not cause me any strain ; on the contrary, it was a loving, intensive gaze, directed towards the Guest who dwells in souls as in his temple. I was so well sheltered in my hallowed solitude that I had the impression of being protected from external disturbances by four impenetrable walls. I lived there, for Jesus alone, with Mary, my Mother, free and detached from human ambition, aspiring to eternal union. Inexpressible happiness! I repeat : it is heaven on earth.

At this time, Our Lord told me to let him have his way, he was going to begin to prepare me for death in a more immediate way, What is death, really? — The beginning of life. In order to live in God, when we get to heaven, we must allow God to live in us, here on earth.

I again imagined myself as a young dove with whom Jesus played. If he slept, I would gaze on him with admiration or close my eyes as he did ; or else I flew around so as to wake him up, and then he would respond with smiles and fondle me. On every occasion, I loved to make use of this image and I would say, for example : "Jesus, you know quite well how much your little dove loves you, and you know how much she wants to love you ; or : Jesus, your little dove is in trouble ; also : you know how content she is."

Or I was a humble flower : Jesus's lily of the valley. The lily of the valley is white, frail, enveloped in a green mantle ; it is hidden from sight, betraying its presence only by its scent. I wanted to be pure, spending my life in showering attentions on the divine Gardener, hidden in his Heart ; there, I would escape from human eyes so as to let Jesus cultivate his virtues in me, just as he wished.

In addition to his unbelievable favours, my good Master told me that *he was giving me the gift of contemplation.* A little later, he added :

I love you with a love of predilection ; my little Bride, you are privileged.

I understood that my soul was a garden that Jesus watered with choice graces. I began to realise the great responsibility I had : to be the recipient of so much imposed on me the strict obligation to correspond faithfully in everything. Yet how many failures there were, the bitter fruit of my nothingness! Love was my only resource. **I began again to love** with renewed intensity.

During the monthly retreat in May, I wrote out the promise I had made at Christmas, modifying it to some extent, and I added one more point. I repeat it here in its entirety so as to bring out more clearly the progressive work of the great Craftsman :

"My God, I wish to perform each of my actions with all the perfection of which I am capable. I wish to refuse you nothing. I wish to deploy my faculties and my whole being in achieving my ideal as fully and quickly as possible. I wish to practise interior silence and recollection and, to that end, to suppress every useless thought and every useless movement." I added : "My Jesus! Oh! How I love you! I wish to live and die as a **martyr** of love, a **victim** of love, an **apostle** of love for you alone, my God! Mary, my good Mother, whom I love so much, grant that I may always love Jesus and make him loved with his own Heart and with yours."

I expressed the same ideal in a slightly different way : **The most intimate union with Our Lord**, and as a means of achieving this : **Jesus must live and I must die!** Again I wrote : "O Jesus, O my Mother, preserve me from human respect (because one of the retreat meditations had been on 'human respect'). How happy I am (to be) in your Heart, O Jesus, in the company of my Mother!"

As for the subject of the particular examen, basically it did not change ; but instead of putting it into practice in the morning and afternoon by five separate acts, I was to think of uniting myself with Our Lord through five acts of charity towards my neighbour.

I used three words with which I was familiar : martyr, victim, apostle, because they expressed my three great desires. Often during the day, I would pronounce the formula of the vows, always adding : "My God, I beg of you the grace to live and die a martyr to love, a victim of love, an apostle of love. I ardently desire to make the vow of total perfection. I renew my promises. Mary, my good Mother, I renew the complete offering of myself to you."

By the expression *I renew my promises,*, I meant those that I had made at Christmas and amplified a little later ; by the *complete offering of myself* to the Blessed Virgin, I meant complete self-abandonment in the spirit of Grignion de Montfort.

On several occasions, Jesus responded to my triple desire by his interior voice, saying that he accepted me as a victim ; at another time, as an apostle ; finally, that I would be a martyr. I thank him now for these precious favours.

One day, he came to me with a *torrent* of graces ; I use the word torrent to signify the great quantity. Then, he said to me :

I love you so much and I have granted you such great graces that I no longer know what to give you in order to satisfy my love. All these are for you.

His exceeding tenderness benefited guilty souls above all ; moreover, my Mother was there in order to distribute these infinite treasures. I remained overwhelmed by the incomprehensible love of the divine Heart for his poor creatures. "O Jesus, your love for me is sheer folly! To prove my gratitude, I love you and wish to love you to distraction. I love you so much that I no longer know how to give myself to you so as to belong to you more completely."

I again begged for heavenly light to choose my motto. I wanted it to express my aspirations. I decided on : **To love and suffer**. Shortly afterwards, through the voice of authority, Jesus asked of me a great sacrifice or, rather, he granted me a signal favour : to accept lovingly and gratefully the small crosses that God sent me, but not to desire others. I obeyed joyfully, for through this advice I was provided with the area of suffering about which I was most sensitive. Whenever 'the passion for the cross' was awakened in my soul, I would say to my sweet Master : "Jesus, you know that all my happiness consisted in the desire to suffer for you. I can no longer ask you for this privilege. Oh! I am so happy because I suffer more from having to sacrifice my desire! I offer you my obedience." The ways of God are truly admirable! In this way, he offered me the privilege of taking one more step along the path of total detachment, of the renunciation of my desires, even of those which in my blindness I thought the best.

It was a real joy for me to live community life to the full. It was Our Lord's will that very often I should be dispensed. I was afraid of dispensations, yet how many I had to ask! Each time was a fresh act of self-denial, because I found that in some respect I was not acting according to the common rule and I was afraid of giving in to my whims and fancies. I loathed being different, and yet how many times I found myself being just that! Oh! What an immense blessing it is in religious life to allow oneself to be guided by superiors! At the beginning of my novitiate, I had come across the following reflection while reading : My divine compass is Our Lord ; my boat is the holy Rule ; those who set its course are my superiors. A soul which constantly lives under obedience sails towards heaven in gentle quietude. It is so easy to obey, and it is so heroic to give orders and to direct others!

The replies to our request to be admitted to profession were soon to be known. At a time when my soul was suffering greatly, Jesus said to me :

You will be professed and then, a year later, also on 15 August, on the feast of my Mother's Assumption, I will come and take you in death.

My joy was extreme. It was the month of May. Fifteen months still lay between me and eternal union. From that time until the middle of December, I counted the months, then I began to count the days. On the feast of the Assumption! What a privilege! When meditating on this glorious mystery during the recitation of the *rosary*, or on seeing a picture of Our Lady being assumed into infinite Love, I think of that radiant moment when I will see her, my Mother, when I will be lost in Jesus. I confide to them the task of preparing me in whatever way they wish.

While waiting, I reflected on our earthly espousals. I wanted to present my divine Bridegroom with a present. I began to arrange **my bridal basket**, which I envisaged thus :

I want to offer Jesus, on the day of my profession,. a basket of pure gold, adorned with pearls and rubies ; this was to be purchased with my acts of poverty.

In the centre of this basket, I will place the glory of Jesus and Mary ablaze with diamonds secured by the perfection of my actions.

In my basket, I want to have some lilies : chastity ; red roses : acts of love of God ; white roses : acts of charity towards my neighbour ; lilies of the valley : acts of humility. For greenery, I will have asparagus fern : acts of obedience ; moss : acts of mortification.

I ask Mary, my dear Mother, to present my basket to my divine Bridegroom. To show my gratitude to the Blessed Virgin, I will perform some acts of devotion for her.

XVI
THE NOVITIATE
June - August 1923

The oratory. — Humiliations. — The importance of the novitiate.
— Two patrons. — Union with Mary. — Retreat prior to profession.
— Ideal and motto. — Profession.

Until June, the novitiate oratory was dark and chill in spite
of being flooded with light and the sun's rays, because the Victim
of love was not residing there. Jesus was waiting for the feast of
his Eucharistic Heart before coming to dwell there. What a miracle of inconceivable charity and thoughtfulness! "Thank you,
O good Master, for allowing me to savour your presence in the
novitiate, before I left it. You had reserved for me pure consolation."

I was doing more and more stupid things all the time. People
might have thought that I took pleasure in repeating them. They
proved beneficial because they humiliated me as I deserved ; for
this reason, I valued them. Very often, though, I showed an
unbelievable lack of tact in my dealings with those to whom I
owed the greatest deference and of whom I was most fond. That
is yet another proof of what I was capable of doing. I would confide my regrets to Our Lord, and ask him to make good my blunders and console those whom I had upset.

My novitiate was coming to an end. Where was I, as regards
my interior life? I asked myself this question in all seriousness.
From the beginning of my probation, I had been struck by the
axiom that a religious is, after her profession, what she has been
during the final period of her novitiate. Of course, she does not
remain static, she makes progress ; but she will be a more or less

fervent professed religious in so far as she has been a more or less
fervent novice. And religious life is a preparation for eternal life ;
it follows that eternity depends on the novitiate. Only trust in
the infinite mercy of God prevented me from trembling with fear,
for I saw myself weighed down with imperfections. Immediately,
I took refuge in love and, in spite of everything, aimed to reach
the summit of the holy mountain : Jesus could not refuse to take
me there himself, since I let myself be carried by him in his
Heart.

One morning, during my meditation in the oratory, my dear
Master gave me two patrons who were to take a fraternal and
loving interest in me : St Cecilia and Blessed Thérèse of the Child
Jesus. St Cecilia, he told me, was to give me lessons in the
authentic apostolate and supervise my active work : teaching,
assignments, the good I would do to souls ; Thérèse of the Child
Jesus was to lead me in the path of love and self-abandonment
and take care of the interior life of my soul always, of course,
under his divine guidance and that of the Blessed Virgin, and
under the protection of my Guardian Angel. With so much help
from heaven, how could I not desire to be consumed rapidly with
love for my God? It seemed then that my two dear protectors
bent down towards me and took my hand to lead me along
according to the designs of the Bridegroom. Since then, I have
been touchingly aware of the effects of their prayers and kindly
attentions. St Cecilia obtained for me the grace to understand
better those virtues that are the indispensable adornment of
an apostolic soul, among them : kindly and smiling love for
everyone, constant self-forgetfulness, ardent and considerate
zeal ; in a word, dedication to the greater glory of Jesus and
Mary, through obedience. Thérèse of the Child Jesus, through
her intercession, opened up for me the garden of trust. Then I
tasted the genuine fruit of self-abandonment. Moreover, she
helped me to advance in the way of spiritual childhood and
obtained for me great enlightenment regarding the saying of Our
Lord and his apostles : *Unless you become as little children, you
will not enter the Kingdom of Heaven.* And all her activity,
needless to say, is marked with the seal of love.

"Oh! How relaxed I feel, Cecilia and Thérèse, in your keeping! Thank Jesus for me, for confiding me to you. And, by his grace, make me holy as he desires. May I gain for him all the souls whose sanctification and salvation depend on my generous love. Pray that I may always love him to the only extent that can satisfy me : the extent to which his burning Heart loves. O Jesus, I want to love you infinitely as with your own eternal love!"

At the June retreat, I expressed as follows the subject of my particular examen : In the morning (or in the afternoon), I will perform five acts of charity towards my neighbour, in union with Our Lord, in honour of his sacred wounds, out of love, and in union with Mary, my good Mother. I need to think more often of Mary and to unite myself to her in a more sustained way than simply by the general offering of my actions. It is the quickest way to be immersed in Jesus.

I wrote out a new questionnaire : 1° Have I performed my five acts of charity this morning (or this afternoon, etc? 2° Have I endeavoured to act with the gentleness, kindness and love of Jesus? 3° Have I allowed Our Lord to act through me, so that in seeing me, my neighbour may be drawn to my good Master? 4° How can I do better this afternoon (or tomorrow morning)?

As the theme of the retreat was 'Obedience', I added : "My God, I beg you to grant me the spirit of obedience and humility : obedience of judgment, blind obedience. I do not want to refuse you anything ; grant that I may be faithful to each one of your graces. I want to serve you as perfectly as possible because I love you. Mary, my dear Mother, protect me."

Yes, I loved my God, not that I might be rewarded in heaven but solely because I loved him and to secure his glory, here on earth as well as in heaven. I never thought of the reward that is to be gained from corresponding with grace. To please Jesus and to praise him, that is my sole motivation. I am always filled with admiration when I think that, incapable as we are of doing anything by ourselves, God deigns to grant his help to us poor humans and, moreover, to glorify us in him for all eternity if we are faithful. He offers us his treasures, then he himself does the work, — we have only to **let him have his way** — and after all that, he reserves a crown for us. It is a miracle of infinite mercy that sends me into raptures of thanksgiving.

The approach of the retreat prior to profession inspired me with fervour. During the Exercises, the instructions and superb meditations left me unmoved ; the devil even made use of some of them to try and disturb me. Our Lord wanted my soul to experience dryness and aridity. Humanly speaking, I suffered greatly, but the action of Jesus was all the more mercified as I was unaware of it.

During the retreat, I wrote as follows :

My ideal : **The most intimate union with Our Lord**.

I want Jesus to live in me and to annihilate my entire being in his.

I want to understand with the mind of Jesus, judge with his judgment, act with his will, love with his Heart. I want to look and see with his eyes, hear with his ears, speak with his tongue, use his hands, walk with his feet, move and rest in him alone!

"I hide myself for ever in your Heart, O Jesus, I make my home there in this life and for eternity."

My motto : **To love and to suffer!**

"O Jesus, I wish to live and die an apostle of love, a victim of love, a martyr of love! To satisfy my desire, I must love you with your divine Heart ; I want to love Mary, my dear Mother, as you love her ; I want to love souls, above all those of sinners, with the same love you have for them, to distraction.

"O Jesus, I want to suffer so that in your Heart I may be completely effaced and allow you to live in me ; I want to suffer to console you ; I want to suffer to save souls and lessen sin on earth ; I want to suffer because I love you!

My God, I am dying for want of not dying, such is my intense desire for perfect union with you ; but I also wish to love and suffer on earth until the end of time, so as to labour longer for your greater glory."

Two days before my profession, on 13 August, I made the following promise, on my knees, in the novitiate oratory (this formula is almost entirely borrowed ; I was pleased to be able to make use of it because it expressed my own resolutions) :

"My God, with your holy grace and the help of Mary, my kind Mother, at the feet of Jesus in the tabernacle, I promise always to sacrifice to you my will, my judgment, my tastes, my entire being ; never to raise any objection to the will, or even the desires, of my superiors and those who represent them, never to allow myself to criticise however slightly or to comment on the measures taken by my superiors or those who represent them, always to ask permissions and to give an account of them. O Jesus, my divine Bridegroom, O Mary, my good Mother, bless me!"

I signed this promise as a further proof of my sincerity before God.

On the day of my profession, Jesus lavished every kindness upon me : the fact that it was 15 August, feast of the Assumption, the presence of my beloved parents, the ceremony presided over by Mgr. X...[1], the Mass celebrated by one of my cousins[2], the presence of the devoted priest who had been my director for half of my life[3] and my "little sister" at my side (the one of whom I

---

[1] Mgr. Omer Cloutier, P.A.

[2] Rev. Joseph Matte.

[3] Rev. P. Cloutier.

spoke when writing about my stay in the States). So much for exterior consolations. But what can I say of the intimate joys I felt! Silence best preserves their divine fragrance. Just one word : The Blessed Virgin offered my basket to my dear Bridegroom. Jesus, in his turn, wanted to give me a personal gift directly concerned with my soul. He let me choose it myself. As on the day of my clothing, I would have liked to ask for a chalice but, this time, I no longer had permission to ask for suffering [4]. The good Master looked kindly on my obedience and my sacrifice ; and, in his hand I saw, oh joy! a splendid chalice, overflowing with the precious jewels of his Passion, far richer and more excellent than the one I received at my clothing. He handed it to me. My joy was indescribable, and my gratitude found expression in a silent canticle of love.

At last I was a religious of Jesus and Mary, adorned with the holy cross and the blessed rosary! I belonged to the Institute which I cherished as much as I did the divine hand which had led me to it. "O Jesus! Make me worthy of the noble title in which I take pride. So as to reduce my debt of gratitude to my Congregation, mould my soul yourself according to its spirit of charity, humility and obedience which is none other than the breath of your Spirit of Love. With your gentle Mother, act in me for the greater glory of your two sacred names."

I could not leave my beloved novitiate without committing myself in writing to the faithful practice, by God's grace, of the sacred lessons I had learnt there. My profound gratitude could make no return for even the least of the countless recommendations that had guided me, but I entrust the Eucharistic Heart of Jesus and the Immaculate Virgin with the duty of paying my debts.

---

[4] Her novice Mistress had explained that abandonment to God was better than such a request.

XVII
RELIGIOUS LIFE
August 1923 - January 1924

First mission. — Isolation. — Eucharistic fast. — The Heart of Jesus. —Substitution by Our Lord. — Annihilation retreat. — Apostolate. — Heavenly harmonies. — Consolations.

At the dawn of my active life, Jesus invited me aboard his ship : I consented with joy to his wish. I went away for a short while on a mission. I stayed five weeks. How good it is to live in our Jesus and Mary houses! In every one, there is a tabernacle where Our Lord dwells for our sake, in every one there is the same charity and the same Rule. During this time, the divine Master worked hard on my soul. He was preparing me to receive a great grace of predilection. As for my employment, I was teaching music ; when the person who was to replace me arrived, I returned to Sillery.

It was the second week in October. I taught for eight days ; then I had to be isolated because of a contagious disease. First, I was isolated for a fortnight. From the very beginning of my seclusion, on the morning of 21 October, I realised that Jesus was granting me a signal favour, that he was withdrawing me from the active life and putting me into complete retreat so that he himself could work without interruption in my soul. I experienced a deep peace and a delightful sense of joy. I had no words in which to tell my good Master of my gratitude. It would be absurd to try and define my impressions in human terms. Could I rejoice in being condemned to inaction for so many weeks knowing that my beloved sisters were overburdened, having to cope with my employments in addition to their own? Could I take any natural pleasure in being denied community life altogether, in living alone, in an extremely cheerful room, it is true, but where, after all, I was under lock and key night and day?[1]And I did not have the key ; neither did I once desire to have it. That can all be explained by a loving acceptance of God's will.

So I abandoned myself completely to Our Lord's plan. He began by depriving me of holy Communion for ten days. Oh! Such an interminable fast! Each morning, he passed by my room on his way to give himself to others who were sick, and returned without coming in. I called out to him with all the strength of my desire, but always submitting myself cheerfully to his way of acting.   In his goodness, he granted me sweet consolation. During Mass, at the time when the community would usually be approaching the holy table, I would make a spiritual communion ; it seemed to me then (it was like a mental image) that an angel brought me an invisible host ; I received it as if from the hand of the priest, and my thanksgiving was one of faith and love just as if I had received a visible host.

One of these mornings, Jesus said to me :

From now on, I am giving you the awareness of my presence within you, that is, you will enjoy the felt presence of God.

Immediately, the life of the Blessed Trinity was revealed to me inwardly, with unspeakable gentleness, peace and love ; I was overcome with respect and gratitude, and confounded at my nothingness. Lost in profound adoration of my Treasure, I was inspired to "set up a court" for my God. I asked Jesus who he wanted in his court. He wanted the Most Blessed Virgin,

---

[1] A measure taken because of the risk of contagion.

St Joseph, my holy Guardian Angel, St Cecilia and Blessed Thérèse of the Child Jesus to keep him company, to concentrate on loving him and to think of him unceasingly. Thus, he would never be forgotten or alone in me when I fell victim to distractions. Each day, I would repeat : "My Jesus, who do you want at court today?" My sweet Mother and the patrons already mentioned were always there ; but, in addition, Our Lord named either angels or saints such as St Elizabeth of Hungary, St Stanislaus Kostka, St Aloysius Gonzaga, St John, St Catherine of Siena, St Joan of Arc, St John Berchmans etc., the saints who were being feasted in heaven and whose memory was honoured by the Church. Finally, and for a long time, I have invited the whole of heaven, all the angelic spirits and all the blessed to form the court of my beloved King and to remain there for ever. I felt very small beside the resplendent cherubim, my protectors and my brothers and sisters already in glory. I was consoled to think that my canticle of love, weak and poor as it was, mingled with their pure, unceasing harmonies. As Jesus had said, I remained aware of his presence : yes, it is he who is living, I know it, I sense it!

On 1 November, feast of All Saints, the divine Victim came himself into my solitude ; I was allowed to kneel at the door of my room as the priest passed by. During my thanksgiving, tears of happiness were all my prayer. After that, I received communion every day.

While I was fasting[2], my Master was busy teaching me to grow smaller so as to let him grow greater, so that soon he might bring me to perfect union with him. Up to that time, I had been concentrating on uniting myself with God in my actions. I certainly asked at the particular examen : Have I allowed Our Lord to act through me? ; but also : Have I striven to act with the gentleness, kindness and love of Jesus? In this way, I made my small contribution to the work at hand.

---

[2] The eucharistic fast.

Until 2 November, Jesus increased his inspirations so as to teach me the perfect practice of genuine self-abandonment ; I thought I had understood this sublime word ; no, I had not fathomed its delightful depths. Abandonment of the past, of the present and of the future, of joy, pain, desire, thought, word and action, abandonment of everything to his mercy and his good will : that is what Our Lord wanted from me. Complete abandonment which, as a result, brought freedom from sensitivity and all anxiety.

If I left everything in the care of Jesus, what would happen? Jesus, in return, undertook to do everything : to think, speak, act etc. not only with me, but in my place. He **substituted** himself for me and I **let him have his way**. Oh! What a choice gift it is to understand how to let the Saviour live within one's self! I wish I could obtain this grace for every soul : the earth would be a valley no longer of bitter tears, but of tears of joy.

Jesus took over everything : was my life going to be one of inactivity? — Oh! Certainly not! My share in this work was love!

On 2 November, the monthly retreat day, I united in spirit with the community, in my solitude, and this is what I wrote :

My ideal : **The substitution of Jesus for myself**

We are no longer two people, Jesus and I ; we are just one : Jesus alone. He uses my faculties, my body. It is he who thinks, wills, prays, looks, walks, writes, teaches, in a word : who lives. And I am very small in the middle of his glowing Heart, so small that only he can see me there. I have abandoned everything to him, now nothing concerns me. My sole task is to contemplate him and to say to him continually : Jesus, I love you, I love you, I love you! It is the heavenly canticle, my eternity has begun! How happy I am!

I drew up a revised questionnaire for my particular examen.

1° Have I thought five times this morning, or this afternoon, about letting Our Lord have his way? Have I thought about this in honour of his sacred wounds, out of love, and in union with Mary, my good Mother? 2° Have I remained convinced that I am dead, completely annihilated, and that it is Jesus alone who is living in me? 3° Have I been completely abandoned to the action of Our Lord? 4° How can I do better this afternoon, or tomorrow morning?

In my motto, I deleted the second word : **suffer**, retaining only the first : **Love!** It seemed to me that love combined suffering with joy ; I saw them as both coming to life in the Heart of Jesus.

On 3 November, my dear Master asked me to make a retreat of ten full days, during which he would each day effect some **transformation** so as to establish me in a state of annihilation, of death to myself. He had me begin that evening. The following day was to be the first. It in no way interfered with my timetable which was split between my spiritual exercises and spiritual writings ; I was to remain profoundly recollected and concentrate on allowing the divine Craftsman freedom of action.

On the 4th, after my Communion, Jesus revealed to me the first transformation ; on the 5th, again during my thanksgiving, the second ; and so on for six mornings ; this consisted in telling me the work he was to accomplish in me that day. It was a question of suppressing in me all that was still natural, human, worldly. My senses and faculties, in turn, came under the salutary influence of the Sculptor's chisel. Enlightened by grace, I became aware of my lack of mortification, both exterior and interior, and my self-indulgence. When there were just three days left, Jesus gave me a glimpse of the work to be done before the end of the retreat and warned me of intense darkness. Indeed, I was plunged into a dark night.

On the 13th, in the morning, the tenth day and feast of St Stanislaus Kostka, patron of novices, Our Lord returned with his consolation, laden with merciful favours. He showed me a

fairly high altar from which rose bright flames ; it was the altar
of his love. In his hand, I saw my heart, which he had taken from
me during the retreat I had made as a postulant ; he allowed me
to gaze on it, as if to give me the opportunity to abandon myself
wholly and freely to him, then he placed it on the altar ; the fire
took hold of it and I saw it consumed down to the last fibre ;
there was nothing left, absolutely nothing.

Then Jesus invited me to approach the altar myself. There
were five steps to be climbed in honour of the five sacred
wounds. I cannot explain what I experienced interiorly. I felt a
kind of revulsion, as if my nature were in rebellion ; in my soul,
I was at peace, content. I climbed the first step, then the second
and, continuing without let or hindrance, soon reached the centre of the altar. The flames drawn back on either side did not
touch me. Watching me all the time, my good Master made me
stretch out my arms in the form of a cross ; immediately, the
flames leapt out towards me ; intensely vigorous yet somewhat
slow to act, they consumed my entire being. During the divine
conflagration, my nature seemed to tremble, to groan and, finally, to die when came the moment of final destruction. When
there was nothing more to burn, the fire died down and went
out. In the middle there were ashes. Jesus came near, breathed
on them and obliterated them. At last, nothing of myself
remained.

Nevertheless, even if I was dead according to the designs of
our Saviour, was I not still living on earth? Yes, but then Jesus
took my place. **He substituted himself for me**. He had just
caused me to disappear, there was a clear field. He could act
with freedom. He showed me that my exterior was merely a
cloak which he had to make use of, a cloak which hid him from
human eyes and allowed him to continue his life here on earth.
Then he added :

> To prove to you that this image is not a figment of your imagi-
> nation and that this annihilation of your being comes in reality from
> me, Jesus, your God, I will give you a sign.

Precisely at that moment, I began to sob.

It is I, continued my good Master, who am making you shed tears ; that is the sign I am giving you.

My tears continued to flow in great abundance. When lunch time came, my red eyes, judging from the usual effect of my tears, should have betrayed some emotion ; but I felt that every trace had vanished from my face.

My joy at knowing that I no longer existed was immense and delightful.[3] I understood better the privilege that was mine in being a victim of love. I summed up my earlier promises and made them less imperfect by saying : "My Jesus, I promise, with the help of your holy grace, neither to think of the past nor to anticipate the future and, in the present, to concern myself only with you. My Jesus, I leave it entirely to you to make reparation for the past, to achieve perfection in the present and to prepare for the future. I no longer exist."

My commitment was a hymn of trust and self-abandonment. I entrusted my numerous failings to the infinite mercy of God, repeating : "I'm sorry, Jesus, but I am offering you yet another opportunity to fulfil your role as Saviour." Until those blessed days of retreat, I knew of the unbounded goodness of our Saviour, but I did not know how to put my faith into practice. When I received this grace, I understood clearly the meaning of the word of God related in the Gospel : *There will be more rejoicing in heaven over one repentant sinner than over ninety-nine virtuous souls who have no need of repentance.* I abandon all my

---

3 The substitution of Our Lord in the soul is merely the state of a soul wholly abandoned to the will of Jesus. It is the realization of the sacred words : *If anyone loves me he will keep my word, and my Father will love him, and we shall come and make our home with him.* (Jn. 14,23).

infidelities to Jesus, and ask him to redeem the graces I have wasted ; I am not worried about the present, or the future, or about my eternity, because I am letting my good Master act freely ; in return, I love him. Before long, the Blessed Virgin was to have an important role in the my practice of self-abandonment.

Following this favour, the substitution of Our Lord, his voice would very often say to me :

Let me have my way.

And I would answer : Jesus, your little non-existent nobody loves you."

In my conversations with him, during my thanksgiving, meditation or at any time, I saw no one but him since I no longer existed, having been absorbed into him.

Then, he repeated his complaint in a distressing voice :

I am thirsting for souls! I am thirsting for love! I am begging for hearts... No one is listening to me, I am rejected, insulted, buffeted...! Oh! How thirsty I am and how I am suffering...!

Some mornings he would say to me :

Today, I want to bring back many sheep who have strayed ; I am going in search of them : to obtain for them the grace of repentance, you must **let me have my way in everything.**[4]

---

[4] These words do not mean that Dina had to remain inactive, which would have amounted to quietism, but that she was to submit passively to the divine action. This is, moreover, a state in which the soul must not and can not interfere of its own accord. These words of Our Lord might be seen as an invitation to simple openness to divine promptings, an openness that everyone is capable of with the help of grace.

In this way, I realised how I was an apostle of love. The divine Mendicant convinced me of the truth that men on earth are dependent on one another, for their spiritual as well as their social life. I had a moral responsibility towards all souls throughout the world, those living at the present time and those who would be created in the future. This is the reason : the actions of Jesus are infinite in value ;[5] one single act of love offered by him to the Father could save millions of worlds. Hence, if I remained annihilated, the Saviour, hidden beneath the cloak of my exterior being, could freely carry out his pastoral mission, baptising and purifying souls in his Blood, bringing them to perfection, enabling them to run towards the fragrance of his perfume. But, alas! If I simply hesitated to remain in a state of death, if for one moment I desired to be born again out of dust, then I would interrupt the action of Jesus ; perhaps just at that moment he was ready to shed a torrent of graces on the entire universe and, if I placed an obstacle in his way, I would become responsible for the lack of good accomplished because of an absence of divine light. The Master was beginning to trace out for me the nature of the mission about which he had spoken to me some time before I entered the novitiate.

During my isolation, there occurred a whole series of religious feasts and spiritual recreations. The conduct of Jesus towards me, in respect of earthly feast days, has remained unchanged since that time, except for some rare exceptions. He is preparing me to enjoy those of heaven before long. The pure joy that I would experience when assisting at the magnificent ceremonies in the chapel, or at such profitable and pleasantly intimate reunions, are compensated for by the kind attentions of my Bridegroom, which come directly from him through the intermediary of those who surround me.

---

5 This word "infinite" which Dina often makes use of has, in her mind, a relative, rather than an absolute, meaning. Christ's merits are of themselves infinite, it is true ; but as soon as we make them our own and use them, they have only a limited value.

On 22 November, feast of St Cécile, my patron on two accounts, Jesus said to me during Mass :

> You are not able to go to Mass ; well, come and hear Mass in heaven where St Cecilia is also being fêted.

Immediately, I seemed to be in paradise. I thought I could hear harmonies whose sweetness and power are unknown on earth. Then the multitude of angels and saints intoned a hymn of praise to the eternal God : *Gloria in excelsis Deo!* This was accompanied by innumerable instruments. Without any interruption, there followed *Sanctus, Sanctus, Sanctus Dominus Deus sabaoth. Pleni sunt coeli et terra gloria tua. Hosanna in excelsis!* Oh! Only those to whom the Lord grants this grace can understand these contemplations! This *Sanctus* surpassed everything harmonious, ineffable, exhilarating that my imagination could conceive. I heard the voices of children, of confessors, of holy women, of apostles, of martyrs ; I heard voices incomparably more beautiful, sweeter and richer than any of those : it was the choir of virgins that follow the Lamb wherever he goes. These different choirs sang alternately or fused together. Then, as the instrumental accompaniment continued, they sang a canticle of thanksgiving to the Lord glorified in St Cecilia, a hymn in her honour. The whole company of angels and saints praised her ; then, the music grew very, very quiet, and Cecilia, on her own, sang a hymn of love and gratitude to the Bridegroom. What pure sounds! The choirs took up and brought this praise to a conclusion. The instruments were still playing. Jesus said to me :

> It is time to return to earth.

"Thank you, Jesus", I answered. I opened my eyes, I listened and realised that at that very moment the Mass in the chapel was ending.[6] It was over, I could no longer find pleasure in earthly har-

---

6 Strickly speaking, there is no Mass in heaven, but St Paul tells us that Christ never ceases to offer to his Father the price of our redemption. Dina did not look upon this Mass in heaven as a true Mass. What she is describing is rather the praises of God being sung in heaven. She does nos mention the Offertory, Consecration or Communion.

monies and melodies. No! No! Even at their most perfect, they are but a faint murmur, lacking warmth. Oh! How captivating are heavenly harmonies! They are Trinitarian love allowing pure waves of their charity to reverberate! They are the breath of the divine Spirit pulsating in each of his angels and his elect!

Jesus also showered visible favours on me in my seclusion. I received "written" visits. How good are those lines penned by the heart of a "mother"! Of how much benefit to the soul is the religious affection of one's sisters! The least of the attentions with which I was surrounded fanned the flame of my love for Our Lord who granted me so many favours. And the brief interviews through the window...! I felt like Jesus' privileged captive, the little dove caged in his love.

The days passed very quickly ; my dear Master had so many things to tell me and to make me write down. Often, would He repeat :

> You are my little privileged soul ; let me have my way ; let Love have its way.

Oh! Why do we not have a better understanding of how to take pleasure in God when he calls us to be alone with him! Too often, we need the company of creatures in order to be happy. When creatures lead us to God, their conversation is like a flame feeding the divine fire within us. But how unfortunate it is when some words become a useless source of distractions! God is Truth, the prime constituent of our happiness, and can our soul not be satisfied with the language of the Infinite? Yet, in our darkness and weakness, we need light and grace to savour the privilege of living with Love alone. "Jesus, you have given me this light, this grace, and you continue to give it to me ; thank you, thank you! Already, my joy is immense when I reflect that for all eternity, for millions of centuries ever renewed, I will be lost in you alone, in the Blessed Trinity!"

XVIII
RELIGIOUS LIFE
(continued)

Jesus sleeps. — Writings. — Mission. — A Desire of the Divine Heart. — End of isolation. — More sufferings. — One final desire. — Meditations. — Letting Mary have her way. — Motto.

At certain times of special consolation, Our Lord occasionally asked me to offer it in sacrifice for the salvation of a sinner or the return of several sheep who had strayed. I would joyfully do as he wished and then I would no longer hear the divine voice ; I would be in darkness and aridity.

The evil spirit did not fail to create a great commotion around my soul. I do not know when I would finish were I to begin to write about his attacks and his deceptions. I can sum up his infernal plan by saying : he was determined to tear me away from Jesus. But with St Paul, I could repeat : *Who can come between me and the love of Christ?* And I experienced the truth of St Augustine's saying : "The evil spirit is like a chained dog who can bark but cannot bite us." In passing, I would like to say that this last sentence, which was given me one day by a maternal hand, did me a great deal of good. I had nothing to fear. Jesus was living in my place, as much in war as in peace. Besides, were not my self-abandonment and my annihilation to be as complete in times of struggle as in times of calm? Sometimes, my Master would warn me of great battles :

> The devil is going to unleash his anger, he would say ; I will seem to be asleep ; you will suffer, but do not be afraid, I will watch over you ; you cannot weaken, because I myself will repel the attack and prove victorious.

Everything would turn out just as the divine Craftsman had foretold.

In the previous chapter, I said that Jesus had many things he wanted me to write down. I return to this subject. First, he asked me never to sign anything I wrote (if others, when copying, add my name, it is without my consent),

> ... because, he said, these works are mine, not yours. You no longer exist ; you can do nothing. The inspiration and the aptitude belong to me. I am using your hand, which belongs to me, to tell souls yet again that I love them with a love they do not understand, to beg for their love, to alleviate a little the thirst of my Heart.

When I finished the **Garden of Jesus**, I seemed to see the author's name written at the end of the last page : Jesus, and I regarded the work as a composition with which I had nothing to do.

I had been in isolation for about forty days. Before the end of this time, Our Lord spoke to me as follows :

> You will not leave here when your quarantine comes to an end, it is not my wish ; I will not allow you to be completely cured. I still have too much work to do in you.

In fact, the doctor came a little later and had to extend the isolation period. It lasted nine more days.

On 4 December, Jesus lifted the veil a little more on my mission. It was clearly outlined for me thus : **To be annihilated**. If I did not remain annihilated, I would be obstructing the divine action. Then, the mission of Jesus in me was **to reveal himself and to do good**.

The 6 December was the community's monthly day of retreat. I strove to remain very recollected ; I was convinced that the mission of my divine Master was soon to begin. I renewed my self-abandonment and said again to him : "My Jesus, with the help of your grace, I promise to let you have your way in everything."

One day at that time, he said to me :

> Soon I am going to send you an illness which will prove to be more serious than the one you have at present.

I accepted everything, without knowing what was in store for me ; I understood that the subsequent illness would result from the first. He added :

> You will return to the infirmary ; I want you to write there. You will be writing until the month of July ; then, it will be finished because you will be suffering too much.

Once (I am going back several days), he had given me clear details of one of his desires ; I am leaving out the colloquy in which he asked me not to sign the pages he dictated to me :

> I want, he said, to speak in one of your writings, of the exceptional love with which my Heart burns for souls ; I want to complain of being forgotten, rejected ; I want to ask for love as a poor man begs for a piece of bread. Oh! I love souls so much and yet, so often, I am not understood and not loved! No, Love is not loved![1]

---

[1] The resemblance will be noted between these words and those Our Lord addressed to St Margaret Mary : "My divine Heart loves humanity, and you in particular, so passionately that, unable to contain within itself the flames of its burning love, it needs to spread them through you..." etc. Our Lord's words to Dina resemble, too, those addressed to St Gertrude : "Through your writings, I want to testify surely and undeniably to my divine goodness, in these latter days when I am preparing to shower my graces on a great number of persons."

These words made a deep impression on me and inflamed me with love and compassion. From that time on, the designs of the Sacred Heart often came to mind ; months slipped by, they were not fulfilled ; the time was not yet ripe. And how can I describe what I feel at this moment! Through the voice of her whom he has given me as 'mother' from the very beginning of my religious life, he has just made his intentions known to me. Yes, his Eucharistic Heart wishes to speak in none other than terms of love. "O Jesus, grant that I may be and remain annihilated and perfectly submissive to your action, so as to let you say whatever you will. Then, enlighten those souls who will hear your words, consume them in the fire of your love and make them holy through love, according to the ideal you have for each one of them."

On the vigil of the Immaculate Conception, 7 December, my quarantine came to an end. I went immediately to the chapel to greet my good Master and to thank him for the ineffable graces he had bestowed on me, especially during the previous fifty days.

I went back to teaching and a few other assignments with the pupils. I was no longer concerned about anything ; Jesus was seeing to everything. I was as completely happy as it is possible to be here on earth. My only suffering, and it was certainly very acute, was to know that the wounds of the Heart of Our Lord were constantly being reopened and aggravated by the offences of so many souls, as well as by their lack of confidence and love. As for myself, I could no longer suffer, I could only love. Self-abandonment and love transformed every second of my life into pure delight.

Nevertheless, I could not help desiring one thing, the vow of the greatest perfection ; especially as Jesus had taken my place and would himself fulfil all its obligations. I very often spoke to him about this. I would say to him : "Very well, if it is you who are asking for this, fulfil your desire!" One day, he answered :

Your desire is very pleasing to me, and I give you the same merit as if you had made the vow in its most comprehensive and perfect form. Your love is all I want.

In December, I felt compelled to seek this permission. With particular fervour, I entrusted the Blessed Virgin with the task of directing everything concerning it to the honour and greater glory of her Son. At one moment, that is to say for a few hours, I thought I had been given permission, at least in the main. My joy was indescribable. Then finally it was refused outright. I felt no regret, because I clearly saw in this the intention of Jesus. Even the sacrifice that the refusal demanded of me was turned into joy, for my love would have found satisfaction in making the vow, while by accepting the refusal with complete resignation, I had the happiness of doing God's will, not my own.

A few days later, during my thanksgiving, Our Lord said to me :

> It is because I love you that I did not wish you to be given permission to make the vow of the greatest perfection. I am aware of your love and your good desires, and, as I have already told you, I grant you the same merit as if you had made it. But I want, in addition, to give you merit for being obedient : I do not want to lay you open to committing some fault or culpable imperfection ; if, out of weakness, you do fail, then you will not be bound by the vow. Do you understand my great love for you? Renew your simple promise often, it answers all my desires.

I was deeply touched by the goodness of Jesus and no less moved by another of his favours. This was that, a few days later, the words he had spoken to me in this last exchange were repeated by one of my superiors in similar terms. I was genuinely surprised to realise how identical were the phrases used. He deigned to underline, through this exterior and perceptible sign, the truth of his intimate and mystical language.

How greatly I admire his divine action in this respect! He urged me to seek permission to make the vow. I felt deeply mortified at venturing to ask so great a favour. I knew I was really unworthy even to think of this sacred commitment. I said to my good Master : "If my request is considered presumptuous and foolhardy, so much the better, since I deserve nothing but contempt ; yet my love for you feeds and thrives on humiliation ; and so I can give you greater proof of my trust and abandonment." What did Jesus want to achieve? To make me rejoice in the sweetness of obedience and to increase his generosity towards me. Who will ever understand the infinite tenderness of his Heart!

So now I no longer had any desire but for the greater glory of God. I wanted nothing for my own personal satisfaction. My only ambition was to let Jesus have his way, I could only savour his divine will at every moment. Oh! What a blissful life!

In the middle of December, I began to count not only the months, but the days that remained until the following 15 August. There were more than 220. Many times since then, Our Lord has reminded me of the delightful moment of eternal union. Especially after communion, he would say :

My little Bride, you have still this many days left on earth.

He would specify the number, for example, 215, 200, 174, etc. Sometimes it would happen that I did not know what number we had arrived at. When he allowed me to hear his voice, supposing he said, *you have 180 days left,* he would add, *count for yourself.* I would count and find it was 180 in this particular case, and at other times, the number he had given me. At Christmas, he said again, very graciously :

This is the last Christmas you will spend on earth ; next year you will be in heaven.

At meditation, I would abandon myself to the action of my divine Master, to the whisperings of his Spirit. First, I would pay great attention to the subject matter, often read in community. I would reread part of the development of the points at evening prayer ; before going to sleep, I would go over the points in my mind, and the next morning would continue to reflect on the same subject. When it came to the time of meditation, I would begin the reading ; then after calling to mind the presence of God and saying the opening prayer, I would try to envisage the scene of the first prelude as indicated in the book, but then, almost always, I found it impossible and strayed completely away from the given subject matter. Trust, abandonment, love : this was the only theme which allowed me to savour a measure of contemplation. I looked at Jesus. He loved me and I loved him. I felt I was immersed in him. I had to make my meditation in private, that is, later than the community. Often, I would forget what time it was, and Jesus would gently warn me five minutes before the end, when it was time for the review. Sometimes, I was enjoying feelings of great sweetness, up to that moment ; I would sacrifice them without differing and obey by starting the review ; I know that my act of obedience was more pleasing to God. I also experienced the aridity of the desert ; half an hour would seem a very long time when I was in desolation. Our Lord seemed asleep, and my mind, in spite of my good intentions, was distracted. I remained profoundly at peace. The time of meditation was devoted to remaining recollected and repeating interiorly only these words : "Jesus, I love you!"

During the end-of-year retreat, one day at the end of December, there was a wonderful instruction on the Blessed Virgin. I was suddenly enlightened. Until that time, I had been united to my good Mother so as **to let Jesus have his way** ; why not **let her have her way**, too? It is true, I was practising total abandonment to Mary ; still, I did not fully understand it. From then on, in every circumstance, I let Jesus and Mary have their way. To this end, I amended the first question asked at my particular examen. What happiness this grace has given me, and continues to give me! How can a human mother not choose what is best for her child, even if the latter is unworthy of her attentions? What must one think, then, of the action of our heavenly Mother, of the Mother of fair Love, in a soul which has abandoned itself to her in the fullest sense of the word?

At that moment, I discovered the motto that I had been searching for for so long, the one which corresponded to my aspirations and summed up my feelings : **Love and let Jesus and Mary have their way!** I find this formulation completely satisfying. **Love**, meaning love to the point of distraction, to the point of martyrdom. **Let them have their way**, meaning total self-abandonment which presupposes annihilation, self-destruction. **Let Jesus have his way**, which means allowing the God of love complete freedom of action ; **let Mary have her way** : entrusting to her unreservedly the task of ensuring that her Jesus would be clothed in the mantle of my exterior being. Thus, I am on the road to heaven singing, borne on wings of love, consumed in the Heart of my divine Bridegroom and lulled by the virginal and maternal melodies of the Queen of Love!

XIX
RELIGIOUS LIFE
January - 15 August 1924

New Year greetings. — Active mission. — Meditations. — A Fast. — Return to Sillery. — Infirmary. — Gratitude. — Final Canticle of Thanksgiving or First Hymn of Love.

Jesus lost no time in withdrawing me entirely from community life which I had resumed, though only partially, with such great joy. On 1 January, I returned to the infirmary for a week, but as for community life, I did not go back to it after that.[1]

On New Year's Day, in the morning at meditation, my dear Bridegroom greeted me and gave me his gift. What did he wish me? — Love! I was to let him have his way, and let his Mother and mine have her way. And his gift? — O, joy! It was suffering!

You will have much to suffer, he told me, until 15 August.

His gift? — Next, it was a magnificent crown ; he did not give it to me. I seemed to see it... angels were close to me, holding it, though not over my head, because my life had not yet come to an end, I had not earned it. The Blessed Virgin, St Joseph, my dear Angel Guardian, Ste-Cécile, Blessed Thérèse of the Child Jesus, each in turn, wished me a "Happy New Year". Then, the choir of angels and the saints gave me that joyous greeting that is traditional here on earth. Jesus's entire court (the one of

---

[1] That is, until 30 June.

which I spoke in Chapter XVII) was speaking with me. I was inundated with peace and joy. If the interior voice of God, the invisible presence of the Blessed Virgin, the angels and saints can bring to our soul through a simple meditation so much unadulterated joy here on earth, what will it be like in heaven when we contemplate the Infinite, when we are immersed in him, when we see the Immaculate Virgin and are able to admire the angelic company of the blessed! It is easy to understand the ecstasy of eternity.

In the middle of February, Our Lord prepared me to receive a gift from his hand ; then he asked me in advance to make a sacrifice of my pupils whom, in him and for him, I loved so much. I did so at once. Besides, I kept repeating : "Do as you will, Jesus, you alone are living in me."

Following his inspiration, I made sure that everything to do with my employment was in order. He had given me one more week without any change taking place. And on the Saturday, the last day of the week, I learnt that I was to go away on mission. At the first free moment, I went to the chapel to thank my good Master for the gift he was offering me and to tell him of my happiness at *letting him have his way.*

> Go to Saint-Michel, he replied, you will not be there long, you will return in April.

It should be noted that my superiors sent me to teach there until the end of the scholastic year in June.

I returned to my first mission. Once again, I experienced the joys of living in a small family. I had the same pupils who had previously given me such sweet consolation.

One hundred and seventy days before the 15 August, Jesus said to me :

> I am going to divide the days you have left between now and eternal union into groups of ten. Each period of ten days will be like a retreat which I will devote to a particular purpose.

Indeed, from the first day of these ten-day periods, until now, he has made his intention known to me.

While I was away on mission, I felt that the action of my Master was very important ; The Blessed Virgin was also busily engaged. During my meditations, it was the Child Jesus, the life of the Holy Family in Nazareth that captivated me. Sometimes, I saw the Infant Jesus in his cradle ; his Mother would be gazing upon him ; St Joseph was nearby. Beautiful little white doves were fluttering around the Child and he played with them. Thérèse of the Child Jesus, who was also symbolised by a radiant dove, led the immaculate company of those "little victims of merciful Love". It was still possible to count these privileged souls, but I realised that they were going to increase greatly and rapidly. Jesus desires to multiply his graces and inspirations so as to draw souls to himself along the path of spiritual childhood, by confidence, love and abandonment. As for me, I remained hidden in his Heart. Oh! What a good place I was in! Ste-Cécile was there too, symbolised in more or less the same way ; I say *more or less*, because she did not actually belong to the company I have just mentioned. How tenderly the Infant Jesus loved her and caressed her!

At other times, it seemed to me that the angels were coming to invite me to join them soon in paradise and sing with them. I felt possessed by a wonderful sense of peace. They had musical instruments — Oh! I cannot explain! — and, for the glory of the Most High, they rejoiced because in a few months I would be in possession of a heavenly lyre.

Or again, the Blessed Virgin would be preparing me for union with her divine Son. One morning, Jesus reminded me first of the following historic fact : St Elizabeth of Hungary, daughter of the King of Hungary, was betrothed at the age of four to the son of the Duke of Thuringia in Germany. In spite of her age, the young Princess had to be sent to the foreign country where later she would be living. Her mother, Queen Gertrude, who had the most tender motherly love for her, did everything her heart could invent in order to adorn the dear child ; she lavished on her jewels, precious stones, countless costly gifts ; in a word, she tried to do everything in her power, having at her disposal an immense fortune. Then Jesus led me to understand the action of the Blessed Virgin in my regard. My heavenly mother was preparing me not simply for betrothal but for the marriage that would take place in eternity. If Queen Gertrude's maternal love could be so great, what must be that of the Heart of Mary! Motherly love here on earth, in spite of its wealth of dedication, is like ice compared with the burning love of the Virgin Mother, the perfect creature. The Queen of Hungary showered on her daughter adornments and rare jewels that she would hand over to a human fiancé from another country. The Blessed Virgin is a queen whose power and wealth are beyond compare : She possesses the Heart of God! What would she not do to embellish my soul so as to make it pleasing not to a fiancé, but to the Bridegroom ; not to a man but to God, not to a stranger, but to her Son! And what part did little Elizabeth play in her adornment? — None at all. At four years of age, she was completely unaware of what was happening all around her, and totally in her mother's hands. In the same way, I was not to worry about anything but to let my Blessed Mother have her way ; she undertook to make reparation for and bring to perfection the past, the present and the future, making everything ready through the merits of Our Lord and her own. That is why I am certain to glorify God in heaven to the extent he desires of me. My faults and failings are great and innumerable, but my Mother is there to cover me with her cloak of perfection and give me Jesus together with his infinite treasures.

Several paragraphs earlier, I mentioned Blessed Teresa of the Child Jesus. For some time now, I have found it impossible to address her in any other way than by saying : Teresa, my little sister ; I have to use 'tu', also, in speaking to her. This intimacy gives me great joy. As for St Cecilia, I had not the courage to take this same liberty with her ; I called her, first, St Cecilia, my patron ; then I replaced the word *my patron by my big sister.*

Then I decided to address her familiarly as : Cecilia, my big sister. Very often now, I beg the protection of my two patrons or I converse with them saying over and over again : "Cécile and Teresa, pray for us, or I confide to you this intention."

To return to the days when I was on mission. Jesus made me fast from his sacred Host for six days. And I was so hungry for Communion! On the last morning, I could not restrain my tears. Nevertheless, I was content with what he did! My happiness was sustained by the purity of my sacrifice.

The divine hand was playing ball... On 2 April, I went back to Sillery. The great Craftsman wanted me once more in the silence of the infirmary. Yes, I am very privileged. In solitude, I can listen to what my God is saying, and I live on love while waiting to take off on wings of love. Or rather, I let Jesus live while I wait for him to restore me to a life of love.

I have already said, and I repeat, that I do not know how to suffer. I feel nothing but joy. That does not prevent my eyes from occasionally shedding tears ; oh! it is my miserable nature that is crying out for attention. No, no, it is dead, I want to ignore it. At these times of involuntary weakness, I say to Jesus, smiling more lovingly : "Forgive me for crying ; how good it is to shed tears for you!"

One of my joys is never to dwell on the small acts of self-denial that come my way, that is I accept them or perform them as if I did not notice them. It is my dear Master who has given me this inspiration.

I have permission to attend Mass only very rarely. As I cannot actually be present at the holy sacrifice on earth, I hear my Mass of love and often Jesus takes me up to heaven to enjoy it being offered in paradise. Many times, too, I have been there in spirit in the morning to make my meditation. I would be very small, sitting on Our Lady's lap and she would let the Baby Jesus play with me. In heaven, if it is God's will to assign me to the lowest place, I ask nothing more, because my happiness consists in corresponding with his wishes. But just now, when I fly up to him, I can see myself only in the highest place, so as to love him better and glorify him more.

On my birthday, during my thanksgiving, my dear Master and his court greeted me. It was another divine favour that filled me with consolation. I was then the same age as Ste-Cécile was when Jesus called her to eternal union with him.

My good Master also takes pleasure in sleeping. I am often in darkness, as in the depths of night, I understand nothing. As I am always given the grace to love, what more do I need?

Religious life envelops me not only in its love, its thoughtfulness, but in every form of kindness. What impresses me deeply is the maternal kindness of superiors to a child like me. The caring consideration, too, of the elderly religious and, indeed, of all my sisters. What can I say of the external circumstances of life in the infirmary? The gentleness, patience, smiles with which my numerous whims are anticipated, are a constant source of edification for me. Moreover, what a joy it is to be living in the same house as my "dear little sister"! She does not realise the good her tender and holy affection does me, and how sensitive I am to her thoughtfulness![2] Oh! Who will pay my debt of gratitude? — Jesus.

"O my divine Bridegroom, pour out the treasures of your Heart on my dear parents whom I love — oh! You know with what everlasting love ; on my religious family to which I belong for ever, with pride and gratitude ; on all those souls who have done me good. As for myself, I will not forget a single smile or flower.

---

2 Mother Mary St Omer de Luxeuil, R.J.M., the friend B... from her time at the New York Conservatory.

Now, Jesus, you are calling me to yourself ; thank you! During my life on earth, you have plunged my soul into the ocean of your graces. As an expression of my gratitude, I have only the hymn of love. O Sweet Virgin Mary, my Mother, do you yourself tune my lyre in paradise, as Jesus wills. Blessed be that moment when I will commence in heaven my canticle of thanksgiving. Blessed be the dawn of that day without end when I will set to divine harmonies the words : **Praised for ever be Jesus and Mary!** Blessed be that eternal embrace in which I will be enfolded in Love!" (30 June 1924).

Note. — These pages of my *Canticle of Thanksgiving or Hymn of Love* were begun in March 1924 ; I completed them on 30 June of the following year.

XX
RELIGIOUS LIFE
15 August - 3 October 1924

Grace of humiliation. — Dark night. — Act of obedience. — New life. — Vow of total perfection.

Alas! The 15 August passed and Jesus left me on earth![1] I say *Alas!* But I must correct myself and sing : "Thank you, my God! Thank you for the humiliation and thank you for the suffering, both of them a source of pure joy, in which, I think, nature has no part, but in which love discovers a few drops of dew to quench its burning thirst."

From July onwards, I was in intense darkness. Jesus was sleeping deeply ; not only was he asleep, but he seemed to turn me away, as if displeased with my behaviour. I saw myself going down to hell ; was not that the place I deserved? My actions seemed so poor and imperfect that each of them was worthless. My trust and self-abandonment grew in proportion to the depth of the darkness. What a signal grace my good Master was granting me! My peace increased. I was surviving not on the peace and self-abandonment that the heart feels when it is full of joy,

---

[1] Our Lord meant mystical death : that which marks the end of life *lived at a human level* and heralds the initiation of beatitude, the dawn of eternal union and the beginning of heavenly existence, in a life *lived divinely*. As one continues to read the autobiography, the sense in which during the following year Dina truly lived "in heaven" can be seen. She had in reality passed through a kind of death. To all appearances, she was the same before and after 15 August 1924 ; but, in reality, she had undergone a profound transformation. An attentive reading of her autobiography, before and after this date, makes it clear that from this time she seems to live a completely different life, a life of amazingly deep faith, in perfect union with God.

but on that firm trust based on love, that unshakeable trust that comes from the will when it believes and hopes in the infinite goodness of God. I immersed myself more deeply in my only Good, I tried to become more and more annihilated. Often, I would say : "Jesus, you seem to be turning me away. All right! Just because of that, I will hide myself deeper in your Heart. I can see myself going down to hell : Just as you wish, Jesus, only we will both go there, for we can no longer be separated since I am annihilated in you. There, in the depths of the everlasting chasms, I will love you, my divine Bridegroom : then it will no longer be hell, because in hell there can be no love!" At times, I clung to the anchor of trust and felt as if I were suspended over the abyss of discouragement ; in pure abandonment, I clung more vehemently to my God. I again repeated : "Jesus, you seem to be very displeased with me! No, no, I cannot stay under this impression. I know, I believe that you love me and you know well that I love you, that I want to love you as ardently and purely as possible. You loved Mary Magdalene... Oh! I know that you pity me. I love you and abandon myself to you : Therein lies my happiness and my peace."

For several months, I had been told to pray for my cure, if it was God's will. Never had a greater sacrifice been asked of me by obedience. I was so far from wanting to get better. I was so eager to lose myself in Jesus and to love him, to contemplate him! I begged God for the grace to pray for this intention as my superiors wished. I think I obeyed them to the letter ; but how difficult it was for me! I felt so strongly drawn towards my supreme Love, I was groaning beneath the tedium of this world and I had to plead with him to leave me in exile, far removed from him! Yet my joy lay in suffering. In all the novenas and prayers that were so charitably multiplied for my intentions, I asked Jesus for spiritual healing, for my sanctification in whatever way he wanted to achieve it. Nevertheless, I often repeated : "Yes, Jesus, I wish to remain on earth for long years to come if that is what you prefer ; I wish to remain in darkness, in impenetrable darkness until the end of the world and even for all eternity, if such is your will."

The annual retreat took place from 6 to 15 August. I could not take part in it ; I made it on my own with Our Lord. I cannot describe how gently and powerfully I felt drawn to him. A feeling of nostalgia for heaven, of thirsting to be immersed in Love was constantly increasing. Especially during the meditations, it was simply an irrepressible surge of love, a burning desire. It was as if earth no longer existed for me. And yet, I venture to say, it was not a state of consolation. My good Master did not once awake from sleep. He seemed to slumber more and more profoundly ; he seemed deaf to my entreaties. I could not hear his voice. Though the eyes of my soul were fixed on him, they encountered no smile. How many graces I received through his divine action! My faith, my trust, my love were sublimated and intensified. Jesus allowed my love to desire him, for his own delight.

Then, on 15 August, the beautiful feast of the Assumption dawned. The Virgin of love, Mary, my sweet Mother, was feasted in heaven ; and Jesus left me on earth. So I had been mistaken. Left to myself, that was all I was capable of : foolish blunders and mistakes. Praise, love, honour and glory to my divine Master, eternal Truth! To me, wretched nothingness, be humiliation and contempt! I was plunged into an abyss of darkness ; I could see nothing, I could understand nothing, especially as Our Lord continued to sleep. But I did not content myself with desiring to see, desiring to understand. I tried to make a more perfect act of self-abandonment, a purer act of love ; and **I set out again on a completely new life**, yes, I repeat, a new life.

August came to an end, September passed ; it was still night. On 2 October, the feast of the Guardian Angels, Jesus had reserved for me a joy that might be compared to that of my religious profession. In order to correspond with the will of God, I no longer desired to make the vow of total perfection. Now, on that day, spontaneously, at a time when I was least expecting it, the one permission that, almost a year earlier, I had been refused, was granted! O joy! I thought I was dreaming! And what a permission! That of making the vow as comprehensively as possible! And when? The following morning, the first Friday of the month! I was overwhelmed with gratitude towards Our Lord who by that means was offering me a sea of graces. It was evening. Only a few hours lay between me and the solemn moment when, by vow, the gift of myself to my heavenly Bridegroom would be complete. I was filled with immense peace. Totally recollected and hidden in the Heart of Jesus, I let the Blessed Virgin prepare me for this great act. I became more aware of my weakness and powerlessness ; but this sense of my wretchedness, as deep as a bottomless abyss, was precisely the reason for my audacious trust in Our Lord. I realised the seriousness of such a vow ; I was neither fearful nor wavering, because I was sure of God. Jesus had substituted himself for me, he alone was living in me, so it was also he alone who would fulfil the obligations of such a commitment. My task was to let my divine Master have his way, to thank him, to love him, to abandon myself to his action.

The closer the sacred moment drew, the more overwhelmed I felt by my nothingness, and the more calm and confident I felt in my good Master who, nevertheless, seemed still to be sleeping. Yes, he was sleeping but his Heart was watching ; what greater proof could he give me of his loving protection! Even the darkness was for me a precious grace ; I was not going to let my soul be bound by the sacred bond of the greatest perfection at a time of interior consolation or fleeting enthusiasm, no ; love alone was to give me over to infinite Love.

As soon as I was given permission, a memory, like a flash of light, came to mind illuminating for me a divine favour. It was on the first Friday in the month of the Holy Rosary that, at fourteen years of age, I had consecrated my virginity to Our Lord. Was it not wonderfully thoughtful of Jesus and Mary to want my total consecration to take place on this happy anniversary? The date was different, but the month and day were the same.

Indeed, it was a never-to-be-forgotten 3 October! I was still in the infirmary. In the morning, I received Communion and so was all alone with my divine Guest and his invisible court. I knelt down, stretched out my arms in the form of a cross, as if in sacrifice. At that moment, I was seized with an inexpressible sense of my nothingness and unworthiness ; oh, how weak and indigent I felt! At the same time, my confidence in Jesus became like a limitless ocean, engulfing my wretchedness ; my abandonment to the action of Jesus gave me firm confidence and delectable peace. In this frame of mind, I renewed my religious vows, that is to say those of obedience, poverty and chastity, adding : "My God, with your grace and the help of Mary, my good Mother, I make the vow of the greatest perfection. Jesus, I vow to let you have your way as perfectly as you desire to act in me ; I vow always to choose to do what is most perfect." I asked God's blessing and then I begged the help of the Most Blessed Virgin by reciting the *Hail Mary* three times ; and I kissed the ground as a sign of my helplessness and of my trust in God. I felt no consolation. It is true my peace was sweet but Jesus was still sleeping ; not a word from him or from the Blessed Virgin, or from anyone in heaven. The veil of darkness was not rent. I saw that as a great favour marked with the seal of pure love, and I gave thanks with joy. Human nature, not being able to enjoy what it is naturally inclined to seek here on earth, that is, consolation, found pleasure, as did my will and my entire soul, in the divine will, even though shrouded in darkness and silence.

Until the next day, it was like a spiritual wedding. How good is the Lord who allows us to taste such happiness here on earth! Yes, how sweet is the yoke of the Master, and how light his burden! Far from feeling constrained by this seemingly rigorous vow, I was more liberated than ever ; and if my liberty could increase, I would say that for two and a half months, it has been constantly growing. This is because Jesus is the Life, the Strength, the divine Activator of my being.

I made the vow of the greatest perfection in its fullest sense, according to the light that Our Lord gave me, that is to say I committed myself, under pain of sin, to do constantly and in every circumstance what was most perfect : in my thoughts, my desires, my words, my actions, from the most important order to the most insignificant, optional and intimate detail. All my earlier promises were contained in my commitment. Thus, I had promised Jesus not to think of the past any more, nor to anticipate the future and, at each moment, to think only of him, leaving it to him to make reparation for the past, to prepare for the future and to perfect the present. I had promised not to entertain any useless thought nor to allow myself willingly to make any useless physical movement ; in making the vow in its fullest sense, all this was included. First, **obedience was my rule of total perfection**. Hence, if I had to choose between a voluntary act of self-denial and some natural pleasure recommended or simply desired by my superiors, I saw the satisfaction allowed by obedience as the more perfect, since the will or desire of my superiors represents for me the will or good pleasure of God. When obedience left me free to choose, the more perfect lay in self-denial.

This vow, then, affects every second, every moment of my life. Oh! What happiness it gives me! I do not say sensible consolation, but I reaffirm that my love of Jesus finds joy in it. It seems to me that I cannot be more totally given to him, that I cannot possibly show more confidence or complete submissiveness to him. I am bound, continually tied. Sacred cords, divine bonds, I kiss and venerate you with joy and gratitude. On the other hand, this commitment is for me, at every moment, an exercise in the virtue of humility. It provides me with an unbroken succession of humiliations that grace allows me to transform into acts of love and trust, I did not make the vow of total perfection because I thought myself perfect ; oh, no! No! A thousand times no! "O Jesus, do not let me ever make such a presumptuous and ridiculous mistake!" I wanted to make this vow, and take on this commitment, solely to say to God that I loved him and counted on him alone, that I had faith in him and was abandoning myself to his action. It is none the less a fact that I am guilty of manifold imperfections, failings, blunders, though unwillingly, it is true ; but it is all proof of my wretchedness, my weakness. And when I see myself so deserving of contempt and so poor, I take flight, on eagle's wings, towards the realms of infinite Goodness. I know that my repeated lack of thoughtfulness for Jesus does not hurt him, because it is involuntary ; I would say it happens in spite of myself, but how many times in the course of a day! And if I admit that it is involuntary, it is to give praise to the loving kindness of Our Lord. Truly, while respecting my freedom, he grants me his grace that is so forceful, so powerful that it would be more difficult for me to resist it than to be faithful to it. With so much support and mercy from my divine Craftsman, how could I fail to plumb the depths of my nothingness! Recognising my imperfections, I say to Jesus : "That's just about all I am capable of doing ; I hand this foolish behaviour over to you and leave it to you to make good ; I love you for that! Oh! How I love you!" Then I often take my crucifix and kiss the sacred wounds, the wound in his right shoulder and his adorable lips, and I add : "Dear Jesus, if I had not done this stupid thing you would not have had so many kisses, so many acts of love." I think my dear Master delights in letting me fail involuntarily, so that he can act with mercy towards me and spur me on to greater acts of trust. What is certain is that my blunders foster love and humility in my soul. I am incapable of putting into words the extent to which I feel worthy of contempt.

Each morning, I renew my sacred vow in the same circumstances and the same way as on the first day. I am so happy. Human language can in no way convey my happiness...!

XXI
RELIGIOUS LIFE
3 October 1924 - 25 January 1925

I hunger. — A star. — Christmas. — God alone. — Feelings of unworthiness. — Limitations of human words. — My divine book. — Spiritual blindness. — A crown.

During the month of October, life in the infirmary continued exteriorly unchanged. Still in darkness, my soul experienced the same nostalgia for heaven, an ardent thirst for Love.

During November, I felt an unspeakable hunger for suffering and for souls. Outside the times of daily vocal prayer, my ardour was summed up in these words : "Jesus, I am hungry! I am hungry for souls, for all souls and for their perfection! Jesus, I am hungry for suffering of every kind! I am hungry for Love!" Yes, I was hungry not only for love — an expression that could suggest simply a share of the whole — but for Love, that is for the infinitely Whole. These burning desires lasted until 8 December.

On the beautiful feast of the Immaculate Conception, my heavenly Mother granted me great favours. During the preparatory novena, the particular grace I had been begging for was *love*. On the 7th, my gaze was fixed all day on the beautiful and sinless Virgin. On the 8th, in the morning, my desire to see Mary in heaven, close to Jesus, was so great that I could not help crying. However, I remained happily submissive to the will of God, yet when a child is far from its mother, can she be blamed for shedding spontaneous tears? No, no. That happened before my Communion. Then, during my thanksgiving, Our Lord was still silent, I was in darkness, yet in my soul there was peace and joy.

During the day, in my solitude, light suddenly shone forth, like a bright star shimmering in the night. I wanted all that Jesus wanted, neither more nor less. In my intense hunger for suffering, then, was there not a lack of abandonment, masked by love? That was certainly the case, and I realised it distinctly. At that very moment, I sacrificed whatever desire I had, accepting from my divine Master, with the same happiness, consolation or desolation, bitterness or sweetness and I felt that my surrender was more complete. I thanked my immaculate Mother ; it seemed that this was her answer to one of the most important intentions of my novena, namely my sanctification according to the ideal Jesus had for me.

From the beginning of Advent, there was also preparation for the lovely feast of Christmas. I wanted my poor being to provide a cradle of love where Love might find a home. Jesus and his holy Mother prepared this cradle themselves. On Christmas Eve, I experienced a sense of quiet joy ; I was overwhelmed with unaccustomed peace and I could sing interiorly : The Baby Jesus is coming to bring love to his little Bride who no longer exists (being annihilated in him). There was no midnight Mass in the chapel for me. I heard my Mass of submission to the will of God, while waiting for the Eucharistic Jesus to come to the sick. At the very moment I received the sacred Host, I again felt shrouded in even thicker darkness. It was like another black cloud adding to the obscurity that had been there before. Oh! How good this blackness was! In my soul, love could delight in it even more, given that there was no personal satisfaction.

From that day to this, that is for three weeks, there has been an unbroken succession of loving attentions on the part of the Infant Jesus. May He bless, with his choice graces, those holy souls who convey to me his divine smiles. Oh, what a loving Master! Interiorly, I feel he is still sleeping ; but I know he is watching over me, his eyes wide open : the eyes of his Heart ; I believe he can act all the more freely and surely because I am oblivious to everything.

I am happy! Yes, yes, how happy I am! Self-abandonment is the greatest happiness on earth. I want nothing more than the salvation and sanctification of souls for the greater glory of God. Love goes through martyrdom when it sees Jesus unrecognised, unknown, rejected. I wish I could travel all over the world, setting it alight with the infinite flames of the Sacred Heart. Still, I want to be an apostle in the way Our Lord wills. In my ardent zeal I see an opportunity to make an act of self-abandonment, and similarly in my thirst for love. I do not want to aim higher than Jesus wills, under pretext of glorifying him : what a mistake and what foolishness that would be! I want what Jesus wants : nothing more, but not one iota less. Thus I can say : I want nothing. Sickness, health, rest, work, solitude, the active life, suffering, loneliness, consolation, life on earth or departure for heaven, everything that comes from Jesus is a joy to me. I no longer see any distinction, unless it is in making use of each moment with purer and stronger love. Yes, I am happy, because my happiness lies not in the events that take place but in *God alone.* Each event, whatever it may be, seems like a warm ray of sunlight issuing from the very centre of the Infinite Sun that is the Heart of the Trinity. How is it possible, then, not to savour some of the joys of heaven without ever crossing the threshold of eternity? For me, it is as if earth no longer existed. Taken literally, this last sentence would be completely nonsensical ; yet, it is the least inaccurate description of my spiritual state. My eternity has begun ; I wrote that a long time ago. I live in the Heart of my God ; I am completely hidden, annihilated in him ; is that not the life of the elect in paradise? I have abandoned myself completely to the action of the Blessed Trinity within me ; for me, nothing remains but to contemplate it, to love it ; is that not what the blessed are engaged in? Undoubtedly, in heaven, the battles are over and we are confirmed in grace. I am still battling, prey to the attacks of the enemy, and I have ample proof of this ; I am free ; at any moment, I could be unfaithful to grace. Leaving Jesus to act in me, I feel I am in a state of passivity, but this passivity does not in any way interfere with my freedom. If I can say : **I let Jesus have his way and concern myself only with him**, it is because, through trust, I count on him alone so as to refuse him nothing and to correspond always to his inspiration. And my trust in God is not a human trust, wavering, insecure, such as might spring from my weakness, certainly not ; it is the trust of God himself which I borrow, which I make my own. I am sure of my divine Craftsman, I believe in his goodness, in his love.

Every day, every hour, I should say, my extreme poverty, my unworthiness seem to me more immeasurable. I see this as a precious grace which reveals something of the truth. It seems to me that if I understood my nothingness and my unworthiness in the sight of God, I would immediately die, as if crushed by the weight of my poverty ; on the other hand, it also seems to me that I would die of love for eternal holiness, the infinite Being who deigns to humble himself to my level and raise me up to himself.

I will from now on speak only of love, of trust, of self-abandonment and of annihilation in the Blessed Trinity, of the divine life of the soul. Human language no longer conveys anything to me. Its accents can no longer express what I think and feel. In order to speak fittingly of life in heaven, the language of heaven must be used... The most beautiful pages in the life of a soul given over to the action of the infinite Artist can not, I believe, be written on earth. A few intimate notes can be struck, a few melodies sung, but I believe that Jesus wants to be the only one to enjoy to the full the sweet and powerful harmonies, the unspoilt, divine ensemble. For my part, whatever I write for the glory of my good Master can not do justice to his work in my soul. It is as if I were drawing just a few drops of water from the ocean of graces he has granted me. It is as if I were gathering just a few flowers in the enclosed garden of which he himself is the adornment.

And what I am writing is not a bouquet of phrases gleaned here and there in spiritual books or in the biographies of other souls. No. Now and always it is an act of obedience, based (humanly speaking) on self-renunciation. And what about books? Leaving out the *Holy Gospel, the Imitation of Christ,* liturgical prayers and the Constitutions and Rules of our Institute, I have to confess that I have little interest in any other book ; it is a fact I can not deny. Yet, any beautiful reflection does me good and I take it as a bountiful message from God ; a devotional text fans the flame of sacred love in my soul. Although Jesus has not spoken to me for a long time, I used to hear his intimate voice and that is why the language of books no longer tempts me. The actual words of Our Lord himself addressed to privileged souls are those which best kindle the divine fire within me. Nevertheless, here too, I am aware of the slight difference between what Jesus asks of these souls and what he wants from me. What satisfies me is to read the great book that is the Heart of my dear Master. I shut my eyes to everything on earth ; in silence, I contemplate Love. Only, I venture to say, to show yet again how good Our Lord is, to show that what I have read in the Heart of Jesus epitomizes, and goes far beyond, all the teachings I have found up to now in books in general, however sublime they might be. No doubt, this is because Jesus enlightens me all the more clearly when I read, when I meditate on him. Well, that is how he wishes it to be.

That does not mean I am not in darkness. I look and I can see nothing. Yet blind people learn to read ; even if their eyes are closed to the light, they can be taught. I am a blind person whom Jesus leads, and he is the Master. In the darkness, I learn about self-annihilation and I relish the delicious chapters on abandonment ; I am intoxicated with the pleasures of silence. Silence! What a fount of joy! Is it not said that in heaven eternal silence reigns over everything! I can not imagine it being any other way. Even now, on earth, powerful emotions reduce us to silence : joy or intense pain leave us speechless. In paradise, then, amidst the ecstasy of infinite Love, I think that silence must be the pure melody of happiness. Here, the contemplation of God and his works makes the soul incapable of uttering a single word, stills one's whole being ; so it is not surprising that, in the midst of uncreated Light, silence should constitute the most perfect praise. "My God, how good it will be to be immersed in you for ever!"

Still with the intention of glorifying the Author of the whole of creation, I will reveal a mere detail. A few days ago, Mama told me for the first time that, when I was born, I had a crown on my head. A very devout person who happened to be there noticed it and pointed it out to my mother. So my mother asked : "What does it mean? Do these children die?" The woman answered : "Either they die or else they do something great in the world."

When, a few days ago, I heard these words, they found an echo in my soul in these terms : "I must be holy. Yes, to be holy in accordance with the will of God is a compelling duty for me, it is the only token of thanksgiving that Jesus is asking of me in return for his infinite graces."

Dina and her parents

Dina aged 2

Dina aged 10, the day of her first communion

Notre-Dame de Jacques-Cartier Church, Québec

Dina aged 14

Dina, student at Bellevue Convent

Bellevue Boarding School

Dina aged 20

Dina in concert dress

Programme

Variations sur le Thème de la Marche
turque des Ruines d'Athènes . . . **BEETHOVEN.**
Mlle Dina Bélanger.

On m'appelle Mimi (la "Bohème") . . . **PUCCINI.**
Madame G.-N. Blais.

INTERMÈDE

Il est doux, il est bon ("Hérodiade") . **MASSENET.**
Madame G.-N. Blais

Chaconne . . . . **BACH-BUSONI.**
Mlle Dina Bélanger.

a) **Gondoliera** . . . . **LISZT.**

Arioso . . . . **LÉO DÉLIBES.**
Madame G.-N. Blais.

b) **Scherzo en la bémol** . . . . **BEETHOVEN.**
Mlle Dina Bélanger.

14ème Rhapsodie Hongroise . . . . **LISZT.**
Mlle Dina Bélanger.

Concert programme

One of Dina's musical compositions

Jesus and Mary College of Sillery
(destroyed by fire in May 1983)

pour toujours, selon la Règle de saint Augustin et les Constitutions de la Congrégation de Jésus-Marie. Je promets, avec l'aide de Dieu, de vivre en bonne religieuse et de m'appliquer constamment aux emplois auxquels notre Révérende Mère voudra bien m'appeler selon la forme et les Règles de notre Institut. Mon Dieu, soutenez ma faiblesse afin que je sois constamment fidèle à mes saints engagements.

Marie Ste Cécile de Rome,

R. J. M.

15 août, 1928.

Dina's autograph
(expression of her vows)

Convent of Jesus and Mary at Saint-Michel de Bellechasse
(today, Dina-Bélanger Collège)

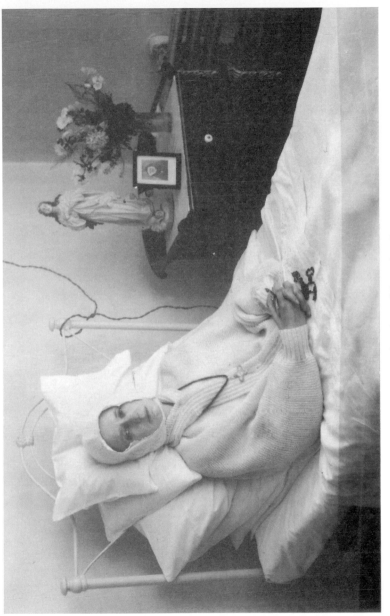

Dina, the day of her death

Tomb of blessed Dina Bélanger
Provincial house of the Religious of Jesus and Mary, Sillery

XXII
RELIGIOUS LIFE
25 January - 18 February 1925

The value of each moment. — Annihilation and life in the most adorable Trinity. — Fresh knowledge of God, of heaven. — Jesus in the Host. — God alone!. — Longing. — The only Treasure.

Joyous abandonment to the will of Jesus does not prevent me from finding every minute spent on earth very long. Poor souls in purgatory! Oh! How ignorant we are of what they are suffering, far removed as they are from the sovereign Good that they have beheld at their judgment! If we, poor, blind prisoners of our mortal body, can experience such yearning, how intense must be the pain of loss in these spirits, released from the mantle of their mortal body and, for just one moment, captivated by supreme Beauty...! "O Mary, my sweet Mother, I beg you to pour a drop of the Blood of Jesus on these souls tortured by love, then, purified, they will all enter his divine and glorious Heart."

Each moment here on earth is slow to pass because I love you, O adorable Trinity! On the other hand, every second seems to me to be laden with grace and stamped with the price of eternity. Thus every minute spent on earth is an inestimable gift. "Jesus, thank you for not destroying the veil that hides you from my eyes ; since that is your will, you grant me the joy of loving while in the midst of suffering, and suffering while I am loving."

I no longer see myself in the depths of hell. Still annihilated in the Heart of my God, it seems to me that I am in the Blessed Trinity, in heaven itself. What an apparent contradiction there is in the words I have just written : still *annihilated* and *I am,* signifying at the same time a state of death and a state of life. Yet that is what it is. I no longer exist, being consumed by the divine flame, hidden in the Heart of the Three, yet it is in paradise that I am annihilated in Love. What tranquillity! What peace! The night is fading but it is not yet daylight ; perhaps a glimmer of dawn. What calm! Yet no sensible consolation. What power! The love within my being is like an invisible force that keeps me consumed in God and exhausts me physically. I feel crushed beneath the weight of infinite love ; and yet it seems that the Trinity is allowing me to feel scarcely a single infinitesimal spark escaping from its divine Brazier. Oh! Words cannot convey what I am experiencing! If only we poor souls on earth knew how much God loves us! If only we knew how precious a soul is when it is in the state of grace! "Lord, give us the grace to know you. To know you even a little, is to love you beyond measure, you alone, for ever! I suffer and I love! How happy I am!"

The few glimmers of dawn lasted for several hours. This morning, 27 January, it is dark again, I see nothing. I am still annihilated in the Heart of the Blessed Trinity, in heaven ; it seems my dwelling is to be there for all eternity. At the same time, I am in the Heart of Mary, my dear Mother. Again, it seems that I am not just on the threshold of the Furnace of Love, but at its very centre, in the Heart of my God. There, everything is so simple and so translucent that silence is the only means I have of expressing myself.

28 January. Until these last few days, I was living in the Heart of my Jesus, in his Heart of flesh, as in a furnace of divine fire. Now, in heaven, I am in the Heart of the glorified Word. Since Sunday, 25 January, my state of soul has changed. That date seems to mark the first in a series of days of immense grace. I feel I am in a place of untold, infinite marvels. There, in the Heart of the Three, nothing is tangible. What purity! What love! Visual images, imaginary representations of the eternal Father, of the adorable Trinity, the angels, the saints or hypothetical scenes of heaven have faded away. It is unlike anything our human

intellect can suggest. I realise that my God, in whom I am anni-hilated, is granting me a signal grace in revealing to me some-thing of the truth of the beyond, but I cannot put into words what I understand. This is the truth, of that I am certain. There is nothing of a material nature such as delights our mortal eyes. Earth seems so far away, so dark, that it looks like a tiny black dot. And then, — how wonderful! — the Infinite takes care of this black abyss that is the entire universe, because he sees there souls that he has created and continues to create in his own divine image, souls that he loves, souls that he wants to enrich with his treasures. O unheard-of mystery of love! God, the Eternal, infinitely content in himself, wants to find happiness in giving himself to his creature... Lord, what goodness...! From the Heart of the Trinity, through the open and glorious wound in the Heart of Jesus, divine graces inundate the earth like count-less turbulent oceans. I say ocean so as to use a human term... There is as much difference between what I used to imagine heaven to be like and what I understand today, as between the darkest night and daylight. Yet, I cannot see the light, I am immersed in it, I am blind ; the brightness that enlightens me belongs to the Furnace in which I am plunged.

1 February. I am still annihilated in the adorable Trinity. Purity... Holiness... Love... Silence... Three Persons, yes, Three in One. By an ineffable grace, I understand something of the reality. I understand clearly, I am certain that it is the truth. But yes, *Three!* That is certain... *Only one God!* Necessarily... O infinite mystery! O divine substance...! Without the light of eternal Light, the human intellect can never envisage it... What nobility! What simplicity! God, the Father... The Word, his Son, his unique and eternal Thought... The Holy Spirit, Love...! God, Infinite Oneness...!

The senses have no part in what I understand so clearly. There are no images, no material substances. Something unknown, inconceivable, transparent... An angel, a soul : I had no idea of what a spirit was like...!

The Trinity of love is seeking souls on whom it can bestow its divine treasures.   Infinite Goodness needs to give, to give itself.   Few are those souls who abandon themselves totally to the sovereign will.   If God is to pour a profusion of his graces on a human soul, he must find Jesus living there.   A soul is too finite to contain the ocean of infinite favours ; but Jesus, the Illimitable, taking the place of what is limited, can satisfy in some way the immense desire of the heavenly Father.[1]

If a soul is to become an abyss, fit to be taken possession of by the Infinite, complete annihilation, in the spiritual sense, of what is human is essential ; then, the substitution of Jesus for this human being and perfect continuing self-abandonment to the divine Agent.   The adorable Trinity desires to pour out its treasures of mercy and love on Jesus substituted for my being. My gentle Master, taking my place, says to his Father, (still in silence, I find no other way to express it) :

> Father, here I am to do your will.   Father, the hour has come, let what you will be done in me.

2 February.

> Let what you will be done in me,

Jesus says to his Father.   I understand that it has to do with my mission.   God has chosen me out of love, he has given me a mission for his glory alone.   What are the divine plans for it? — I do not know.   I know that Jesus is speaking about it to the Blessed Trinity.   He is praying ; I hear only this request :

> Father, do not allow even one of these you have given me to be lost.

---

[1] This sentence, as well as the next few lines, provide us with the key to Dina's spirituality.

I have a clear knowledge of what my part is to be : it is annihilation, perfect, blind self- abandonment. *My part is to be nothing.* I have to allow my gentle Master complete freedom of action. I accept whatever he wills. My responsibility is immense ; it does not weigh me down because I am nothing and my faith is the faith of Jesus ; my hope, the hope of Jesus ; my love, the love of Jesus, and because I am in Mary, my immaculate Mother. On the earth, which still seems so distant, so small and so dark, there are millions of souls depending, for the graces of salvation and sanctification, on my abandonment to the divine action. The least response on my part is of great importance for the glory of God.

Jesus living in me is a fathomless abyss that the Trinity of love will fill to the brim. Eternal Love is infinitely sweet and infinitely powerful. "Jesus, Mary, pray, pray for your little annihilated nonentity. I adore, I believe, I trust, I love, consumed in them, I abandon myself to your two Hearts. Give thanks to the Blessed Trinity for the enlightenment I have been granted ; thank them for the rushing waves of love that they are soon to release, and keep me in annihilation. Dear St Joseph, my dear Guardian Angel, Cecilia, Teresa, all the heavenly court, give thanks and pray for me."

4 February. Silence... Love... God alone... Jesus : everything... Mary : my Mother... I myself : nothing.

6 February. The day before yesterday, during Benediction, I was suddenly and gently enlightened. Following on from what God has given me to understand about himself in the last few days, the presence of Jesus in the sacred Host has become eminently clear to me. Yesterday and this morning, I had the same understanding. The veil of mystery has been torn asunder. He is there, my God, infinite Unity, adorable Trinity, under the appearance of a small piece of bread. Jesus is there, in his sacred Humanity, his Heart, his precious Blood, his Soul, his eternal Divinity ; he is there, whole and entire, in each Host consecrated throughout the world and in each fragment of consecrated Host.

"Lord, I used to believe firmly by the grace of faith ; now you are granting me, in addition, the extraordinary grace of understanding. I am nothing. Deign to glorify yourself through the favours you grant my annihilated being."

7 February. I am undergoing very great interior suffering. A moment ago, as I was beginning to recite the rosary in the company of the Virgin of the Assumption, I felt crushed by the burden of life on earth. In anguish and trust, I fixed my eyes on my loving Mother. And I heard the voice of Jesus for the first time in such ages!

> You will not possess me any more completely in heaven, he said, because I have absorbed you totally.[2]

These divine, interior words consoled me. The suffering in my soul was in no way lessened, but I received a grace of strength through abandonment. I realised that I was already immersed in God ; the difference is that, at the moment, I am blind, I cannot see the splendour of the infinite ; later, when eternal beatitude begins for me, I will see the adorable Trinity. There will be no change in my surroundings. Everything will be just as it is now. O how blessed is the dwelling of the Heart of eternal Love!

10 February. God alone! Oblivion even of my nothingness. Nothing but the indivisible Trinity ; loving, contemplating it, letting it have its way in everything. No longer adverting to the insignificant being that I am ; every glance would now be simply a waste of time and a distraction. Jesus is atoning for my foolishness. He is taking charge of everything. Abandonment seems to me to be perfect when I follow this inspiration. It is an inexpressible gift of Trinitarian goodness.

---

[2] We can possess God only through the intelligence and the will. This latter faculty can arrive at full possession of God here on earth, through love ; but the intelligence can possess him only imperfectly, through faith, while in heaven it will possess him fully through a face-to-face encounter, that is, through a totally satisfying knowledge.

13 February. Aridity, dryness, aversion, temptation to discouragement and despair : that is what I am going through. By the grace of God, my will is firmly set on my decision to concern myself solely with the Blessed Trinity. If, even for one second, I turned my eyes to the insignificant creature that I am, I feel I would immediately weaken. Everything weighs me down and crushes me ; distress threatens to invade my soul. Yet I can say in all sincerity : my happiness and peace are in no way diminished when I am in this state. I am content and I find my rest in God, abandoning everything to Jesus and his immaculate Mother.

16 February : For the last two days, an unprecedented feeling of intense nostalgia. Silence is more eloquent than words to convey my state of soul...

17 February : The Trinity is revealing itself to me more fully. In addition, I have a clearer understanding of the life of the angels and saints in God. How far we are from having any idea of the delights enjoyed by the blessed in heaven! Unless we are profoundly enlightened, we remain ignorant of the true nature of eternal bliss. We will never be able to grasp the immensity of infinite goodness towards every human soul. The longest life on earth lasts in reality but one moment. How foolish we are unless we devote each instant of our life on earth to the greater glory of the sovereign Master! What a multitude of surprises will be ours at that supreme moment when the veil of truth will be torn apart! What a Tabernacle of delight is the Heart of the Trinity!

In paradise, the measure of their knowledge of God is the measure of the happiness of the elect. They are totally happy. But one single degree, I venture to say the smallest degree, of knowledge of the Eternal is worth infinitely more than all the conceivable treasures of the created worlds, because it means penetrating one of the infinite secrets of Infinity itself... All the sufferings, all the physical and moral torture that can bear down on a human being, throughout millions of years, could never be worth one single degree of this knowledge. Quite simply, God in his goodness has to bestow this free gift on us. And how can we obtain it? By the least act of submission of our will to the will of our Father in heaven, the smallest act done out of love for him, the least act of obedience, a good desire, an act of self-denial, even a joy accepted in God out of love. The Blessed Trinity is the only Treasure worthy of the name : it offers us incredible riches... Alas! How few accept them by surrendering themselves perfectly to his holy action, by abandoning themselves in faith, trust and love without ever taking anything back! "My God, pour out your love, through Christ, on those souls who are faithful to you ; pour out your love, according to your will, through Jesus and Mary, on my annihilated self."

XXIII
RELIGIOUS LIFE
18 February - 2 May 1925

God contemplated by Jesus in the elect, in the angels, in Mary.
— Participation in the 'mode of eternity'. — God contemplated in
himself. — Formula and content of the vow of total perfection. —
Wiles of the devil. — Action of the Holy Spirit.

18 February. God allowed me to begin to see him through
the eyes of Jesus. I see, but not at all in the way we see with our
bodily eyes. I see, and yet, I repeat, there is nothing perceptible :
no images, but always the inexpressible, the unknown truths that
the human intellect cannot conceive.

The countless multitude of angels and saints is lost in God.
Each of them is absorbed by, permeated by, the infinite Trinity.
The beauty of each of the elect is an emanation of the supreme
Beauty. As I look upon the soul of each of the blessed, it is God
himself that I see ; but I contemplate as many different manifes-
tations of beauty as there are elect : the eternal Master does not
replicate himself in any of his saints. What harmony! In all of
them, there is love, holiness, in the degree that God chooses to
communicate it ; there is perfect happiness. The light that I
admire is soft and pure ; light on earth is mere darkness. What I
see — and it is so beautiful! — is still but a pale glimmer of the
truth. Silence... Silence... Love...

19 February. I see God in his angels, and the angels abiding
in the infinite Trinity. They are unspeakably beautiful...

20 February. I can see the three adorable Persons : Father,
Word and Holy Spirit in the angels ; each of them is permeated

with the Trinity, with the infinite Unity, and radiates through it a rapturous splendour. There are as many varieties of magnificence as there are angels. How beautiful my Guardian Angel is!

It takes an endless eternity, an eternity that lasts for ever, that never comes to an end, to contemplate the perfection of our God, to love him, him alone, in all the masterpieces his love has accomplished. The Trinity is a profusion of wonders... ; it is the Infinite...

Still through the eyes of Jesus, my gaze is fixed on my God. My longing is intense. I feel an irresistible desire to ask Jesus to cut short my exile, to release me from my carnal prison ; but I repress this ardent desire so that my abandonment may be complete. The intensity of my suffering is in proportion to the knowledge I have been given of Goodness itself, that is to say, the more the Trinity reveals to me its attractiveness, the more I love it. I am filled with longing, not because I want to enjoy God, to see him in the fullness of light : if that were the case, it would be self-seeking and my love would be full of self-interest. I am filled with longing, not because I want a life freed from bitterness and suffering : where, then, would be my love for Jesus crucified? I am filled with longing simply for God, for him alone, for his sake alone. It is as if a powerful magnet were drawing me gently towards my unique goal. It is a compelling need to live forever in my eternal home, the Heart of my Creator, of my loving Father, of my beloved Bridegroom. My God loves me, and I love him...!

21 February. I contemplate the Most Blessed Trinity in Mary, in the most fair Virgin, the masterpiece of infinite power and goodness. Purity... Love... Mercy...

At one moment during my meditation this morning, I felt I was so truly immersed in God, that I believed I had been released from the bonds of my mortal body.

22 February. God in Mary... The immaculate Virgin in the Blessed Trinity...

This morning, I received a special grace that I find difficult to describe. I felt taken up into God, as if in the eternal mode, that is in a permanent, unchanging state, contrary to the temporal mode which is a passing state. That does not mean that my soul is no longer free nor capable of self-abandonment. Events take place, succeed one another, around my physical being, but **my soul is no longer involved with them.** Jesus is in control of these events : he sees to everything, he takes care of everything. It is as if my soul no longer had any connection with my body. This grace which the Trinity of my God grants me with so much love is a foretaste of my participation in the divine life ; I say a foretaste, because it is the state of the elect in heaven, yet I, in bodily form, am still on earth. It is a participation in the divine life in the sense that, for the eternal and supreme Being, nothing comes to an end : for him everything is present, since he himself does not come to an end and will never come to an end. "O Jesus, O Mary my Mother, I beg you to give thanks to the Trinity that has shown me such infinite mercy!"

24 February. I contemplate with the eyes of the Heart of Jesus, with the very Heart of my dear Master. Yesterday, by this more intense light, I beheld with wonder the most adorable Trinity in the elect, in the angels and then in Mary, the Virgin of virgins.

Today, it is God himself, God alone that I am gazing upon... Love, mercy, goodness... Through the Heart of Jesus, I gaze upon the sovereign and all-powerful Trinity, fearlessly, since my confidence is that of our Lord himself in his Father. A thick veil still hides the full splendour of its Beauty ; the truth that I can see clearly is but a ray of the infinite Sun. I am in awe of such brilliance, such magnificence!

25 March. For a month, my spiritual state has been unchanged. My soul continues to dwell within the Divinity. Love is more powerfully and sweetly felt.

This morning, I completed the conditions for gaining the precious Jubilee indulgence. I entrusted to Mary, my mother, the task of distributing these treasures as she and Jesus wish.

On this hallowed day, feast of the Annunciation of the Most Blessed Virgin and the Incarnation of the eternal Word, I am inscribing the formula of the Vow of Total Perfection in characters of love in the Heart of Jesus, and as a consequence in the very Heart of the adorable Trinity.

Formula and content of the vow of total perfection

With the grace of God and the help of Mary, my good Mother, I make the vow of total perfection, to the fullest extent possible, in accordance with the light I believe I have received from our Lord.

First of all, obedience is my great rule of total perfection. Accordingly, if there is a choice between sacrificing my own will and enjoying some satisfaction, some natural pleasure, recommended or simply desired by my superiors, I see perfection as residing in the pleasure indulged in under obedience, because the will or desire of my superiors is for me the expression of God's will or good pleasure. When obedience leaves me free to choose, perfection seems to me to lie in self-sacrifice.

I bind myself then to total perfection, under pain of sin, constantly and in everything, that is to say at each moment, in my thoughts, my desires, my words, my actions, my physical movements, whether it be in the most important command or the least intimate and optional detail.

Accordingly, I undertake not to refuse Our Lord anything, not to think of the past or to anticipate the future and, in the present, to concern myself with God alone ; I abandon to Jesus and Mary reparation for the past, preparation for the future and perfection in the present. I undertake not to consent to any useless thought and not to allow myself any voluntary useless movement.

I make the vow of total perfection **freely, with great happiness, out of love**, quite simply to tell God that I love him, that I count on him , that I trust him and that I abandon myself to his action.

My sense of unworthiness is indescribable ; I am keenly aware of my nothingness ; I feel weak, poor, powerless. Because of this, my trust in Jesus is like a boundless ocean, engulfing the abyss of my poverty. With faith and love, I plunge deep into the territory of infinite Mercy. The goodness of God : that is my firm safeguard and my exquisite peace.

I pronounce this vow for the greater glory of the adorable Trinity, for the salvation and sanctification of souls, in a spirit of reparation, of immolation, of thanksgiving and of praise ; in a word, for the intentions of Jesus, abandoning myself totally to infinite Love as a **victim** of love, an **apostle** of love and a **martyr** of love.

I will renew this vow each morning, binding myself until the following morning.

1 April. Painful struggle. Peace in obedience. It was a terrible assault, but divine grace was very powerful, too. But for obedience, I would not have been able to receive holy Communion this morning. Oh! What trickery the devil can deploy! I was not upset. I hid myself in God with greater confidence and love.

While the dragon is prowling round, unable even to brush against me with his infernal wing because I am hidden in God, the Holy Spirit is at work within me. I know nothing of his action ; it is something new, always beyond perception, that I cannot express.

4 April. The demon is, as it were, enraged because Our Lord's action within me is snatching souls away from him and leading them to God. What a great responsibility I have to be faithful to the graces I receive! "O Mary, my Mother, obtain for me constant fidelity according to the desires of Jesus!"

8 April : Aridity, revulsion, darkness. All that fails to drive me out of my divine and heavenly hiding place. Jesus is keeping me there for ever. Today, I feel a great capacity for suffering : I am conscious to some extent of the strength and serenity of my dear Master at the time of his Passion. Souls! Souls! I want them all to belong to God. I do not want a single one to escape the Saviour. I want each one to respond to the Creator's designs for her. I want to plunge impious, blind hatred into pure, atoning love. I want to annihilate evil in the Blood of the infinite Lamb. *My God, may your will be done on earth as it is in heaven!*

10 April. Good Friday evening. Yesterday and today, I was not able even to go to holy Mass. So what have I this evening to offer Our Lord who has suffered so much for me? I feel very poor. The devil, in an effort to disturb me and make me sad, tells me that I am neither generous nor mortified. I will not listen to that wicked angel of darkness. I am nothing, nothing. Oh! What bliss! Nothingness, because it is non-existent, cannot be preoccupied with self. Without looking at myself, I cast all my failings in self-denial into the infinite mercy (of God). I want to occupy myself only with God. I love and I am happy!

13 April. Intense longing. Moreover, an intimate sorrow moves me deeply. "Thank you, Jesus! the more bitter the chalice, the more I believe in your love. Mary, my sweet Mother, I beg you to make reparation for me, to bless me in return..."

20 April. I have a premonition of precious graces, of moments of enlightenment. Recollection, silence... I need to look at God alone. I am as if unconscious, lost in Love.

23 April. Yesterday, still in the Heart of the Most Blessed Trinity, I began a long retreat which will end on 30 April. This retreat consists in keeping my gaze fixed on God as much as possible through the action of Jesus,. Since yesterday, I have been savouring the Infinite. Such sweetness, that human language cannot even begin to suggest! Everything finite is a cup of vine-

gar for me. My immense longing is in proportion to the sweetness of the Good that I am savouring...

28 April. Words convey nothing. What can I write? And yet, I must write out of obedience.

Silence, recollection, love. Today is being spent in preparation for an imminent divine favour, in expectation of a great grace. During my prayer this morning, Jesus allowed me to feel in some way the sweetness and power with which he looks upon me, annihilated in the depths of his Heart. A soul possessed by God is united to him by such strong, tender and intimate bonds that only infinite love can know its capacity.

Our Lord is jealous, in the fullest sense of that word, yes, jealous of my pure and exclusive love. Can he ask anything less of me? If he did not ask so much of me (and, in reality, to please him, the sacrifice of everything is as nothing), he would manifest less tenderness and magnanimity towards me. "My God, you alone! Accomplish in me, through Jesus, your plans and your least desires. Your least wish is like precious spikenard which inebriates me in you."

How can I describe my prayer? — A celebration of love, a glimpse of God, a taste of the Infinite, annihilation in the Heart of the Trinity, an improvisation in harmony with the Spirit of love. No images, no words, no movement. Happiness unknown on earth : Oh! If the world could have any suspicion of the delights of paradise, it would not do violence to itself by vainly seeking consolation anywhere else than in genuine Goodness.

1 May. Monthly retreat in community. First Friday of the month.

2 May. Yesterday, on the day of retreat, I heard the reading of the first meditation in community but Jesus wanted me to be alone with him for the rest of the day, for I was unable to assist at any of the other exercises.

On the first Friday of the month, we draw at random a message from the Guard of Honour of the Sacred Heart of Jesus. I always read this message as if it were a letter from my divine Master. This month, Jesus sent me : **The soul alone with the Sacred Heart**. Each sentence and even each word corresponds so well with the working of the Holy Spirit in my soul that I am copying out this wonderful text :

"Solitude is the homeland of those who are strong! On earth, it is also the paradise of saints! O solitude! O beatitude! cried out St Bernard. Privileged soul, come apart, hide yourself ; with Jesus, escape into the desert! It is there that manna falls from heaven...! Yes, escape...! Escape from futile distractions, anxious cares, useless conversations... **escape from yourself!** And, far removed from this little interior and exterior world which demands all your attention, go into the desert, ascend to the heart of God ; there, hide yourself in the hollow of a rock : the Heart of Jesus! What wonderful works the good Master will accomplish in your dear soul, if he finds it alone with him!

During this month, during your hour of guard especially, your interior task will be to remain so recollected, so alone and silent that, no matter at what moment the Bridegroom comes, he will be able to speak to your heart!"

"Your Heart, O Jesus, will be the sanctuary where I shall live in peace, in love, alone." (25th Office)

My hour of guard is from midday (or midnight) to one o'clock, in union with the Blessed Virgin, for the intentions of the holy Church, of the sovereign Pontiff and of the clergy.

"O solitude! O beatitude!" I repeat with St Bernard. Happy the soul whom God keeps in solitude with him alone!"

XXIV
RELIGIOUS LIFE
2 May - 23 June 1925

Grace of freedom. — Radiating love. — Smiling at Love. — The fullness of love. — On joy. — Demonic attacks. — The price of the cross. — Absorbed into the Infinite. — The Host, a treasure. — This is Jesus!

2 May. The anniversary of my first Communion. My thanksgiving after Communion this morning began in darkness. Suddenly, swift as an arrow, gentle and powerful, I felt my soul was released from every human bond. It was like a grace of freedom. I am free... I cannot explain the true meaning of these words... How admirable God is in the means he uses to achieve his ends! I am free... Jesus does not break the legitimate and sacred bonds that he himself has secured and blessed : on the contrary, he draws them more tightly ; and it is he who keeps them secure in the treasury of his divine Heart. I am free to gaze upon, to savour the blessed Trinity alone.

This seems to me a very great grace, for my life in God is being given a fresh impulse. Oh! If only I could describe the life of my annihilated soul! And, above all, if only I could hymn more worthily the infinite mercy accorded to my nothingness! I note that this favour has been granted to me on the first Saturday of the month, dedicated to the Blessed Virgin. "Mary, my good Mother, thank you, and please thank Jesus for me."

9 May. A week of blinding silence and silent love. Love! Love! Would that I could set the earth alight with pure love, for the greater glory of God. Would that I could convince souls that divine love means happiness, joy, felicity. Love intoxicates me like a heavenly perfume and engulfs me like a turbulent ocean.

17 May. Smilingly radiating Love... Love...! Martyrdom...! Abandonment...! Love...! Happiness...! Peace...! Love...! Infinity...!

27 May. Smiling at Love... Smiling at sacrifice... Radiating joy... Love is cloudless bliss.

5 June. "My God, how I hunger for Love! I am famished not merely for want of love, but for want of the fullness of infinite love. To satisfy my hunger, I must have the fullness of love without measure." Oh! How fervently I pray that God may draw from my being, annihilated in him, the fullest extent of glory! From the feast of the Ascension to Pentecost, my prayers were more ardent than ever. I begged the Spirit of love to fulfil his plans in my soul ; in a spirit of humility, trust and self-abandonment, I begged for love from Our Lady of the Sacred Heart, my dear Mother and trustee of the infinite graces of the Heart of my Jesus and steward of the riches of our Father in heaven. In two days' time, it will be the feast of the Most Blessed Trinity. I am preparing for it by a triduum. Yesterday, the first day, was dedicated to the eternal Father, in union with Our Lord, the Holy Spirit and the Blessed Virgin. Today, the second day, is dedicated to the infinite Word, in union with the divine Father, the Holy Spirit and my immaculate Mother. Tomorrow, the third day, will be dedicated to the Spirit of love, in union with God the Father, Jesus and Mary. And I am united in a special way with the whole heavenly court and the souls in purgatory. Sunday will be dedicated to the most adorable Trinity and to Our Lady of the Sacred Heart whose Solemnity will be celebrated here on that day.

7 June. My ideal continues to be expressed as follows : **The fullness of Love**, that is to say the satisfaction of infinite love, goodness and mercy ; meaning joy, rest in the blessed Trinity, outpouring of the inexhaustible depths of God himself ; the fulfilment of the ideal envisaged by the Eternal to the full extent of his Spirit of love ; in a word, the divine will perfectly accomplished.

I hunger, I thirst for the fullness of love, with unspeakable longing and ardent desire, for the sole purpose of glorifying God. I burn with the desire to receive Love in so far as the Creator desires to grant it to his creature. The substitution of Jesus in my being allows me to put no limit to my ideal, since the Most High can find satisfaction in pouring himself out on his infinite Son. If the inexhaustible love of the sovereign Good could be exhausted, I would venture to desire this for the greater glory of the Divinity and out of pure love for him.

I aspire to the plenitude of Love, for the salvation and sanctification of all souls according to the designs of the supreme Artist for each one of them. My ambition is to achieve the fullness of Love so as to fulfil the words of Our Lord to his apostles : *You must be perfect just as your heavenly Father is perfect.* And relying on that other saying of the Master : *Cut off from me you can do nothing,* I count on Jesus at every moment.

8 June. I am to smile constantly at Love. Especially since yesterday, I feel I am continually in the presence of the adorable Trinity. My soul, annihilated in the Heart of the Indivisible unity, contemplates it with greater suavity, in a purer light, and I am more aware of the power that pervades me. I no longer look directly upon the angels and the blessed, I see them glorified in God ; but it is the supreme Beauty alone which enthrals me. I can understand how the angels and saints can enjoy the beatific vision and yet, at the same time, be concerned about what is happening on earth, without being in any way distracted from the thought of God. I understand how it happens that, beginning with the grace of last 25 January, my soul can dwell in heaven, live there without any backward glance towards the earth, and yet continue to animate my material being. This condition creates no friction in the accomplishment of my daily duties, nor does it inhibit in the least my living out of the common life here on earth,. On the contrary, it is a condition of deep peace, total freedom, complete self-possession. But I cannot explain clearly what, nevertheless, I understand so well : divine grace must enlighten with its luminous rays.

How could I be other than filled with continual joy in the presence of my God? Oh! How good is the Lord! How sweet! What tenderness is his! If only I could convince all timid and fearful souls of his tenderness! If only I could envelop and imbue with boundless confidence the poor souls who do not trust their heavenly Father! The greater our need, the more abundant is his infinite mercy ; and when, through our repentance and trust, we give God the opportunity to exercise his mercy, we give him pleasure. Nothing offends his fatherly Heart more than our lack of trust.

And the Lord is seeking souls who serve him with joy. Darkness and light, desolation and consolation, bitterness and sweetness, all come from his generous hand, or rather, escape from his Heart like a dart aflame with love. Our life should be an unbroken act of thanksgiving, a joyous prelude to the canticle of eternal praise. The divine Master is seeking joyous souls, all across the world ; all the more reason, then, for him to yearn for consecrated souls, those whom he has chosen to console him, to make him known and loved, those whom he calls his privileged Brides. Oh! Jesus speaks to each soul in peace, in silence, in times of recollection. What does he want of us...? Let us listen and be faithful, for he wants us to be happy : whether he offers us a bitter or an inebriating chalice, a crown of thorns or one of roses, a heavy cross or a light one. *Servite Domino in laetitia*, yes, let us serve the Lord in joy and gladness.

15 June. For a week, I have been conscious of being absorbed more and more into the Infinite ; I have a more intense feeling of being in the presence of the divine Trinity and I am learning to smile at Love with more joyful serenity and simple self-abandonment. The word *smile* is but an inadequate expression, a faltering attempt to verbalise a condition which I cannot put into words ; for this smile, like everything relating to my life in God, has nothing material about it.

The devil is not unmindful of me, but Jesus is my unassailable rampart. Not a single morning passes without the wicked angel of darkness setting a snare so as to make me miss my Communion. Each evening, when it comes to the general examen, he returns to the assault. Besides these two regular ambushes, he deploys his craftiness at other times ; he disguises himself the better to deceive me. I do not even bother to show my contempt for him. I remain firmly attached to the will of my divine Master ; I often obey by sacrificing my own judgment, which is in that case an illusion of the enemy, and not only does my peace remain intact but it grows with every fierce assault of Satan. By allowing the evil spirit to tempt me, Our Lord is offering me precious graces of humility ; I am growing continually in awareness of my wretchedness and powerlessness and count only on his infinite Goodness.

16 June. I am still aware of, and even have a clearer understanding of the presence of the adorable Trinity in which I am submerged, and of the same grace concerning the presence of Our Lord in the sacred Host.

18 June. I would like to help all souls, and especially consecrated souls, to understand the **price of the cross**. Moral or physical suffering is an eternal gold-mine ; it is a flaming dart shot by love from the Heart of the Infinite to inflame the human heart and plunge it into the Divinity. The cross! It is the dazzling sceptre of incarnate Wisdom, the co-redeeming jewel of the immaculate Virgin, the radiant palm of the blessed. If only we knew the amount of love contained in each of our crosses, we would hold this infinite treasure in such high esteem that, day and night, without ceasing, we would offer ardent prayers to God to obtain it and rapturous prayers of thanksgiving when it was granted to us. If we understood the value of our crosses, we would be numb with joy and happiness at receiving them ; trials, tribulations, anguish of every kind would call forth songs of gladness and enthusiasm and, spontaneously, we would intone the *Te Deum.*

The Lord is not understood! The loving, kind Heart of the adorable Bridegroom is not understood! Jesus has chosen the cross as a sacred treasure, he embraced it passionately, he loved it to distraction : and all for us. Yet when he offers us a fragment of this mystic treasure, we hesitate to accept, or at least to do so with joy. Alas! Fallen human nature is an abyss of darkness. God knows that, so his mercy always takes pity on our blindness and, in spite of our natural repugnance, offers us, and even compels us to receive, the inestimable favour of the cross. Oh! How happy the divine Master is to hear one single grateful word of appreciation when he offers us a thorn from his crown or a few drops from his bitter chalice! How his sacred Heart rejoices when the wounded and trusting soul kisses lovingly the precious scourge, the lance and nails! Oh! If only the gift of God were understood! Every suffering, every torture, every martyrdom, taken together, would seem sweet to my soul, in thanksgiving to a loving Providence for the least suffering. If only the Heart of the Bridegroom were truly known! "Spirit of truth, I beg you, through the merits of Jesus, to enlighten souls, to teach them to prize genuine good and to recognize infinite Goodness in times of trial and humiliation."

20 June. I feel more and more possessed by Love. A bright light flashes suddenly like lightning and absorbs me totally. My soul is no longer in touch with my material being ; my life on earth is over. What an apparently ridiculous sentence that is, by human standards! But it is the one that perhaps gives some faint idea of my state of life. My body continues to live on this dismal, distant earth, that I no longer inhabit ; it continues to operate through the action and the will of Jesus. My soul, quiescent, consumed, has been absorbed by the Eternal, in heaven. I receive, too, great graces for the glory of God, to pay to the Creator the debt of love that guilty, unfaithful and indifferent creatures refuse to pay him. Through Our Lord, substituted for my being annihilated in him, I have at my disposal the riches of the Infinite. Not only on my own behalf, but in the name of all responsible creatures I must return love for love, and offer up infinite Love in response to the eternal Love of the divine Trinity. How blameworthy I would be if I deliberately failed to follow the inspiration

of the Holy Spirit and, even for a second, escaped from my anni-hilation! My responsibility is immense ; it does not terrify me : I count and rely on Jesus.

I have a far better understanding of the immateriality of the soul and at the same time, a better grasp of the nothingness of my material being. For that reason, I can glimpse something of the unspeakable superiority of the soul over the body. Graces and light in abundance have torn down the veil that separates me from eternity.

This morning, at the moment of Communion, I received a fresh, gentle, clear, unanticipated, powerful illumination. In a soul taken up into Jesus, holy Communion is the outpouring of the Infinite into the Infinite, it is the satisfaction of sovereign Perfection in supreme Beauty, it is the gift of the Eternal to the Uncreated ; it is the embrace of God the Father and his Word, issuing in the Spirit of love, a surge of love passing among the three adorable Persons, an outburst of tenderness from the Heart of indivisible Unity... If only we knew the extent to which under-standing in the light of eternity differs from understanding in temporal obscurity...!

21 June. If only souls realized what Treasure is theirs in the divine Eucharist, tabernacles would have to be protected by unassailable ramparts ; for, under the influence of a holy and all-consuming hunger, they would go by themselves to feed on the Manna of the seraphim ; night and day, churches would be over-flowing with worshippers consumed with love for the august Prisoner.

I have a profound sense of the heavenly atmosphere in which my soul is immersed. The mystery which shrouds the invisible world is melting away. By the light of the All-Powerful, how clear it all is! And my understanding of the unknown is being revealed with such ease and sweetness and truth that I savour it almost without realizing it.

"Yes, my God, I want to make some return for all the

favours you have granted all your creatures, for your unbounded love down the ages, without beginning or end.

Behold Jesus! The Infinite ; I offer him to you through the Heart of the Immaculate Mary, through the flaming breath of your creative Spirit.

Behold Jesus! Into the abyss of his mercy, I plunge the iniquity, the hatred, the impiety of souls.

Behold Jesus! In his redeeming Blood, I bathe the souls of the guilty, the ungrateful and those who do not see.

Behold Jesus! In his sacred wounds, I hide the souls of the fearful, the timorous, the defiant ; in the ocean of his tenderness, I drown the hearts of the cold, the hardened and the rebellious ; and finally, into his burning Heart, I plunge the universal world ; into this purifying and sanctifying brazier, O my heavenly Father, I cast all your creatures who are capable of new birth and per-fection."

22 June. *"Behold Jesus!* O eternal Justice of sovereign Holiness! Be appeased by his superabundant merits ; repay your-self infinitely for what is owing to you ; restore to yourself that glory of which Lucifer and his proud cohorts, as well as guilty and ungrateful souls, have deprived you.

"Behold Jesus! O boundless Love of supreme Charity! May the all-powerful flames of his divine Heart repay you worthily.[1]

O adorable Trinity! For your greater glory, I desire to bring to fruition the riches of the uncreated and incarnate Word. Find your delight in him. Through his atoning, surpassing and inexhaustible treasures, rejoice in the original ideal you had for your creation, delight in the restoration of complete harmony

---

[1] That is : May you be loved fittingly in return.

between every human creature and your holy will, satisfy your insatiable desire to give yourself and, in the name of every creature your love can conceive, receive in return and for ever, without any interruption or diminution, your Christ Jesus, the eternally Infinite!"

23 June. "*Behold Jesus!* My God, nothing I can write or tell you can assuage the vehemence of my aspirations for your great glory. Silence is the best expression of the ardour of my love for you. Take Jesus, and deign to read in his divine Thought, which is your own, the inexpressible characters of fire that your Spirit of love engraves in my soul, annihilated in the Heart of your Unity!"

XXV

RELIGIOUS LIFE
23 June - 20 September 1925

Attacks of the Evil One. — Hunger for the divine Host. — Perfect abandonment. — Satisfaction of infinite Love. — A little beggar for love. — The divine Pearl. — God is Love.

23 June. The enemy's attacks are more aggressive. Last evening, all of a sudden, I felt the presence of the Evil One, to my left, as in real life I would have noticed the presence of a visible person. At the same time, I was aware of his devilish temptations ; he was like a madman multiplying his diabolical inspirations and actions ; he was very close to me, but he could not even brush against me with the tip of his filthy wing. His attacks were as wily as they were vigorous. I was not afraid, for Jesus and Mary were between him, the wretch, and me. I remained annihilated in my heavenly refuge, hiding myself more deeply in the Heart of my God and praying with fervour and confidence. Several times during the night, this angel of darkness tried to make a surprise attack, and I need hardly add that he redoubled his insinuations so as to make me miss my Communion this morning. Our Lord battled with him and protected me : *Deo gratias! Laudate Mariam!*

In the midst of these infernal and humiliating attacks, and my repeated acts of blind obedience, especially during the early hours of the morning, I felt an inexpressible hunger for the sacred Host. At half past four, I would have run to the chapel and stolen a divine Host to sustain myself, had I been allowed. I had to wait two more hours for the Bridegroom to come to me sacramentally. What joy I felt when I received the sacred Bread! My happiness bore no trace of felt joy, but rather of love completely lost in the Beloved.

25 June. (Feast of the Eucharistic Heart of Jesus) A day of intense interior suffering. "Yes, Jesus, I wish to smile joyously always and in every circumstance."

28 June. "My God, fulfil to an infinite degree the perfect ideal you have for all your creatures in time and in eternity!"

I feel a passionate love, still more ardent and yet at the same time, gentle. At times, today, I needed a very powerful grace to enable me to cope with the strength of this inrush.

I have never been so clearly conscious of my poverty, my faults, my imperfections. But that simply increases my confidence in my good Master. Our Lord knows me ; he can be under no illusion in my regard, for he has known from all eternity that I am nothingness and weakness and that, without him, I can do nothing, less than nothing.

The demon is pursuing me like a wild animal. Jesus and my immaculate Mother are thwarting his devilish plans. I remain joyful and at peace within my divine fortress.

1 July. (Feast of the Precious Blood of Our Lord.) The glorious Blood of the divine Bridegroom quenches to some extent my thirst for love. With his purity and his charity, he inebriates me with chaste delights that I never experienced before.

I am also being given fresh light on abandonment. I taste the perfect abandonment of the elect. It is so translucent, so sweet and so divine that it is beyond analysis.

5 July. I am to smile constantly at infinite Love. Oh! How immense is the Lord in his mercy, since he calls me to such a blissful vocation! I need a perpetual and very powerful grace to maintain me in this blessed state : I am enjoying perfect beatitude, and God is granting me simultaneously the inestimable

favour of experiencing all the time intense suffering, grievous temptation and the sharp pain of total renunciation. How happy I am! And how inconceivable is the generosity of God!

6 July. I must not even think of my annihilated self any more. God alone! God alone! It is truly eternity!

19 July. "My God, you alone know how I hunger for love. It is a delectable torment experienced in peace and stillness ; it is an intense and delightful martyrdom."

20 July. **The total gratification of infinite Love!** that is my ideal. *The fullness of love* no longer satisfies me, in that my annihilated being still discovers something of self in this expression. I must no longer think of myself : my ideal, then, must have God alone as its object. Yes, *the total gratification of infinite Love*, and still the same motto : **To love, and let Jesus and Mary have their way!**

28 July. Once again, I have been aware of the felt presence of the Evil One close beside me, on my left. I say *felt* so as to express myself more clearly, for I felt his presence as that of a spirit, owning nothing of the material. It was one night, last week. Sin personified came to me during my sleep. I woke up saying : "Jesus, Jesus, I love you, I love you!", uttered with a feeling of ardent love that I had not known until that moment. At the same time, I felt the infernal angel close beside me. For several seconds, I was numb with emotion, but not with anxiety or fear. I was still in profound peace. The divine assistance, in the form of grace, was very strong. Jesus was fighting for me : I remained hidden in him and protected as always by Mary, my good Mother.

"My God, holy and perfect Trinity, O eternal Charity, satisfy yourself, satisfy yourself! Your glory, your joy, your delight are to my soul like an exquisite manna for which it hungers ever more. Your gratification, O infinite Love, is a heady ambrosia that I continually long for with increasingly pure and insatiable passion. Behold Jesus! O my God, sovereign Good, may you be blessed for ever by him in the name of all your creatures!"

31 July. During the night of the 28th to the 29th, the attacks of the Evil One were as cunning as they were violent. Towards morning, while I was still sleeping, I dreamed about the Blessed Virgin. It was only a dream. "But, O my heavenly Mother, how beautiful you were! No human artist can ever reproduce the delicacy of your features, the goodness and gentleness and tenderness of your expression, the sweetness of your smile. No, the most magnificent work of art that human genius can devise conveys nothing of your beauty nor, above all, of your goodness. O my Mother, how beautiful you were, how beautiful...! And yet it was only a dream ; what, then, must the reality be like...!"

4 August. The annual retreat began yesterday evening. I am not able to join in the community exercises : for that reason, I am making it on my own with my divine Master. The Heart of the adorable Trinity, where I feel ever more submerged in an abyss of silence and loving-kindness, is the meditation book that the Spirit of Jesus presents me.

For several days, a ray of light has begun to reveal my mission to me. While gazing upon God alone, this great word 'mission' has, unprovoked, taken possession of my soul. If God showers so many favours on me, it is so that his power may shine forth in my nothingness, and that he may himself be glorified in souls through Our Lord.

I hunger! How I hunger to give Jesus to souls! I would wish that in each one of them, their supreme Author might recognize the flawless image of his divine Son ; I wish he might behold the eternal Word, risen and glorious, in conformity with the ideal that he had when he created them!

When Jesus leaves lifeless on earth this body of mine that is for him now an *additional humanity*, he will give my soul annihilated in him the true life of eternity. In heaven, I want to satisfy the infinite Love of God. In order to realize my ideal, I must realize the infinite treasures of Our Lord ; this good Master said : *Ask and you will receive*, well, in heaven, **I shall be a**

little beggar for love : that is **my mission!** And I am going to begin it at once. Jesus, in his immense loving-kindness, needs to give himself to souls ; if he could, he would exhaust his treasury of graces for each one of them. **Yes, I want to exhaust the infinite Jesus so as to satisfy infinite Love!**

Exhaust the Infinite, satisfy the Infinite : humanly speaking, those are absurd expressions ; no matter! In heaven, there are no words, love is the sublime language, and whatever I find impossible to put into words, God understands : that is enough for me.

Every heavenly grace comes down to earth through the intermediary of the Blessed Virgin. It is she, our most merciful Mother, who dispenses infinite riches. So I will be a little beggar of love, for the sake of all souls, for the greater glory of our Father in heaven.

6 August. Jesus has said, *Ask and you will receive.* "All-powerful and bounteous Saviour, I am asking for everything, I beg for each soul the abundance of graces that you will to shower on it." Jesus has said, *Ask and you will receive.* "Merciful and kind Saviour, for the souls in purgatory and every guilty soul, I beg the fullest measure of forgiveness that you can grant." Jesus has said, *Ask and you will receive.* "I ask that the inexhaustible merits of the Lamb, atoning for offenses committed against the glory of his divine Father, may be fully realized, and that satanic hatred and the ingratitude and weakness of human nature may be submerged in the abyss of his eternal loving-kindness."

I beg Jesus to grant me the immeasurable and boundless love of his Heart, so as to satisfy his insatiable agonizing desire to give himself to souls. I repeat : Love wants to give itself and, alas! few souls allow themselves to be inundated with its torrents of happiness! Love seeks hearts that are open ; alas! how many rejections it encounters! People do not want to receive it ; they are afraid to abandon themselves to it ; they are afraid of it as soon as there is any mention of renunciation. Self-denial is merely a thin sheath, masking the precious pearl ; if a person is really ready to die to self, the sheath is torn open and the divine Pearl becomes a precious adornment for the soul. A single invocation of Love draws down its favours. So I am going to be a little beggar, pleading for every human heart. It is the Blessed Virgin who will distribute the riches of the Heart of her Jesus ; and, hidden deep in the Heart of Mary, I will ask that they be poured out continually. Yes, in heaven, until the end of the world, I will plead constantly for love.

8 August. When, in God, my soul is recreated for eternity, I will be truly an apostle and a missionary. In the meantime, I remain in annihilation. The action of the divine Spirit within me is more sweet and more powerful all the time. I feel so absorbed in the adorable Trinity and so possessed by it that it is as if I were paralysed.

The evil spirit is hounding me with frenzy. Last night, I again felt his terrifying presence, but neither his impetuosity nor his rage could disturb or frighten me, since he cannot reach me in Jesus and in Mary.

I have begun the second Jubilee of the Holy Year. I will end it next Saturday with holy Communion, on the beautiful feast of Mary's Assumption. I beg from my heavenly Mother the grace to gain the indulgence to the full, and I leave to her its application.

"My God, my good Father, I thank you in union with Jesus and the sweet Virgin for allowing me to be a martyr of love. I want to smile continually at your adorable will, I want to love you and to make you loved with joy, I want to gaze on you alone and, in the name of souls, to beg for all the inexhaustible love of the Heart of your well-beloved Son, so as to satisfy your eternal Loving-kindness!"

6 September. For a month, darkness has alternated with light, struggles with ardent aspirations. The 15 August was marked by an uninterrupted surge of intense love. Then, little

by little, Our Lord let me share in the chalice of his own Passion. I felt an inexpressible hunger for the salvation and sanctification of souls ; at the very heart of my being, I suffered an intense pain. Especially on Friday, 28 August, there was a real agony in every part of my being.

20 September. Am I to speak again of suffering? — No, no, it is over. Still, even if I have no share in it and it is Jesus whom I gaze upon in his suffering, I see in this, alas!, a trace of self!

How good God is! Everything is simple and unambiguous in him. And how delectable is the music of silence in the Heart of the Blessed Trinity! These eternal melodies merge with the harmonies of love. Eternity means stillness ; but, of course, the soul lost in God is for ever enraptured. Eternity means tranquillity : the soul which contemplates sovereign Beauty is speechless with ecstasy. Eternity means harmony : everything is perfect. Eternity means love : God is Love!

XXVI
RELIGIOUS LIFE
20 September - 16 December 1925

Our Lady of the Holy Spirit. — Jesus offers himself to infinite Love. — Total satisfaction of infinite Justice. — Satisfaction of all the infinite attributes. — Renewed offering of Jesus. — Unrestrained love.

2 December. Since 21 September, inaction, physical immobility due to sickness. Intense activity on the part of the divine Spirit. Thanksgiving. Attacks of the demon. Struggles. Graces in abundance. Constant joy. Profound peace. A burning thirst for love, for immolation, for souls, for the satisfaction of the Infinite. Permanent indwelling in the adorable Heart of the Trinity, in heaven. Gaze continually fixed on God alone. Perfect happiness ; such, in brief, has been this blissful period.

On 2 October, the first Friday of the month of the Rosary and the feast of the holy Angels, I felt suddenly inspired to pray to the Most Blessed Virgin under the title of Our Lady of the Holy Spirit. It was a sudden ray of light and a sweet consolation.

The following day, 3 October, the first Saturday of the month and the anniversary of my most personal commitments, Our Lord, in my place, offered himself to his divine Father so as to satisfy to the full his infinite love. Before making this irrevocable offering of himself, Jesus, in his utter kindness, chose yet again to ask for my free consent. At the same time, the evil spirit tried to scare me ; but this assault of the enemy merely increased my confidence and strengthened my will which, after all, is none other than that of my heavenly Master. Without the least hesitation, and with unspeakable fervour and joy, I abandoned myself to the good pleasure of my divine Substitute. He made his offering : Here I am, O my Father, to do your will. *May your infinite Love be fully satisfied in accepting all I have to give.* He offered himself through Mary. The eternal Father accepted his gift, and in my heart I felt certain that my ideal had been fulfilled.

Some days later, the satisfaction of infinite Justice seemed to me to be just as pleasing to God as that of his Love. It was then, in particular, that the evil spirit returned, tempting me in vain to fear and anxiety. I was given the grace not to waver ; and with even greater joy, because I had a premonition of more suffering, I pleaded with the Most Blessed Trinity, if such was its good pleasure, to satisfy its infinite Justice through Jesus, the infinitely Powerful, living in my place.

3 December. On 27 November, the anniversary of the revelation of the miraculous medal of Mary Immaculate, I was praying to my dear heavenly Mother during my meditation ; suddenly, in a flash, I realised that it was possible for me, **through Jesus**, to satisfy not only the Love and Justice of my God, but all his infinite perfections. And since that illuminating grace, my ideal, as measureless as the Infinite itself, has found expression in these halting words :

The satisfaction of all the infinite attributes of the eternal and most adorable Trinity.

The satisfaction of *divine Wisdom* through the passionate love of Jesus for humiliation, suffering, poverty, destitution, and through the sacred folly of his cross and the consuming thirst of his divine soul which knows the true price of the crucifixion and the value of souls.

The satisfaction of the *Almighty Power* of the Creator through the continual substitution of the Uncreated Word for the poor, miserable nonentity that I am ; through the perpetual prayer of Jesus that cannot fail, as he asks and ensures that the whole of creation render to its supreme Author the plenitude of glory ; through the outpouring of the power of Jesus in all its fullness, and its ability to fill to overflowing the fathomless abyss of the divine Trinity and satiate it to the full.[1]

The satisfaction of the *Goodness* of the eternal Father through the substitution of Jesus in souls and the intensity of his life in them, offering to the august Trinity so many sacred fountains of living water[2], from which to satisfy its capacity for giving and pouring itself out ; through the ineffable assimilation of the just into the Divinity in eternal glory.

The satisfaction of inexorable *Justice* through the immolation of Jesus, the infinite Victim, who offers the resolute and sovereign Judge his precious Blood, his healing Wounds, his ravaged and adorable Face, his pierced and ever open Heart ; through the expiation and atonement of this gentle Saviour, making superabundant amendment for the sins, the ingratitude and the weakness of guilty, blind and erring humanity.

The satisfaction of boundless *Mercy* through the exhaustive application, if that were possible, of the inexhaustible merits of Jesus ; through the uninterrupted prayer of the Eucharistic Victim, drawing down on souls graces of repentance and forgiveness in abundance ; by taking advantage of his boundless liberality which delights in raising up prodigies of holiness on the ruins of wretchedness and producing flawless works of art from utter weakness and nothingness.

---

[1] This is what Dina is thinking : God deployed his almighty power in creating the material and spiritual universe. This almighty power has to be "satisfied", that is, it must receive as much as it has given.

[2] Holy souls, on account of Christ's indwelling, are looked upon bt the Trinity as Christ himself, insofar as they are united with him ; consequently they are so many more "fountains" receiving the "water" of God's goodness and, in their turn, making it available to other souls. And the divine goodness communicates itself to them to the extent of deifying them and absorbing them finally into his glory.

The satisfaction of *infinite Love* through the immensity of the Heart of Jesus, capable of containing fathomless depths of eternal loving Kindness and supporting the vehemence of the divine outpourings ; through the burning love of the Sacred Heart ; through the depth of its unceasing sighs offered in the name of all creatures.

The satisfaction of the *Holiness* of the thrice-holy God who sees imperfections in his angels, and in whose presence the pure cherubim hide their face in their wings ; its satisfaction through Jesus, the spotless Lamb, the innocent Christ, the Just One, eternally pure and flawless, offering Holiness itself a worthy tabernacle, a paradise of delight, a sanctuary of rest and contentment.

The satisfaction of the supreme *Good Pleasure* through the fusion of the will of Jesus with that of the heavenly Father ; through his joyous abandonment to the plan of God for souls ; through the fulfilment of the designs of God in all their plenitude, whether actually or by way of atonement.

The satisfaction of the *eternal Trinity*, that is, its delight, its everlasting contentment, for all ages without beginning or end, in itself and through itself ; its superabounding joy, in the whole of creation, through Jesus.

The satisfaction of the *most adorable Trinity*, that is its greater glory through Jesus who alone can render it honour, praise and thanks in keeping with the tribute due to it for its own sake, and merited by it in respect of each one of its creatures and all the beings it could draw out of nothingness by its power, its goodness and all its infinite attributes.

But, alas! How can these inadequate expressions convey my ideal, infinite as my God is infinite! Silence pleases me more and I can sum up everything by begging Jesus and Mary to cry out in my place : *Our Father, who art in heaven, hallowed be thy Name, thy kingdom come, thy will be done on earth as it is in heaven! Amen!*

7 December. "My God, through Jesus and my immaculate Mother, I beg you to take pity on the vastness and ardour of my longing! Take pity! Take pity on the infinity of my desires, on my unspeakable thirst for your joy! O Trinity of love, take pity on Jesus, on yourself, and take your fill."

8 December. (Feast of the Immaculate Conception of the Most Blessed Virgin.) This morning, after Communion, during my thanksgiving, I suddenly felt taken over by a very profound spirit of recollection. Still in the Heart of the adorable Trinity, I sank deep into my nothingness and plunged further into God. There was a moment of heavenly silence and then, through his most pure Mother[3], Jesus offered himself to his Father for the satisfaction of all his infinite attributes : *Father, he said, in the language of heaven, here I am to do your will ; bring to fruition all my infinite merits, and satisfy your divine attributes, for your sake and that of all creatures.* The Most Blessed Virgin recited her Magnificat ; I joined her, but without saying a word ; I could not articulate a single human word. She began the Sanctus which was taken up by all the heavenly choir. She was still holding her Jesus, presenting him to the Blessed Trinity. Then, the eternal Father, looking upon his beloved Christ, said to him : *I will bring you to fulfilment, my Son, and we will be satisfied. (I,* that is the divine Unity ; *we,* the indivisible Trinity.) The whole of heaven sang the Psalm : *Laudate Dominum omnes gentes,* and the *Gloria Patri...*

O the majesty and simplicity of the eternal landscape! But silence...! Silence...! The intimacy of heaven loses its attraction as soon as it is disturbed by an inappropriate earthly utterance.

12 December. Especially in the last few months, I have felt a great desire for the stigmata of the wounds of my divine Bridegroom. Is that not presumptuous? I have asked Our Lord many times to repress this wish unless it comes from him. Far

---

[3] Our Lord offers himself, yet his Mother offers him as well.

from diminishing, my desire is becoming more pronounced and I can no longer resist ; it fills me with peace, serenity and joy, being at the same time humbling and leading me to count on Jesus in boundless trust and total abandonment. I want the stigmata to be invisible to all so that only the adorable Trinity may rejoice in them, I would even want to know nothing about them myself. And besides, if ever my good Master grants me this inestimable favour, it will be he, my divine Substitute, who will receive the imprint of the nails and lance as on the cross on Calvary ; in effect, it will always be he who will suffer in my place. Given this grace, during a prolonged martyrdom, annihilated in him, I will have only to thank him, to smile at him, to love him and to sing Alleluia as it is sung in heaven. I offer this dream of bearing the love wounds of my crucified Jesus in grateful homage to the goodness of God who knows my weakness and nothingness and is aware of my infinite desires.

"Jesus, my dear Jesus, I love you to distraction. Quite often, I speak foolish words of love to you ; I talk nonsense to you. It cannot be otherwise. You are drawing me on and teaching me by your example : It was you who loved me first, and to distraction. You fell in love with my wretchedness, and how could I live absorbed in your love unless in an ecstasy of gratitude and love? It would be absurd."

16 December. "My God, I hardly know how to tell you of my love. Would that I had at my disposal all the symphonies born of silence, all the poetry born of secret suffering so as to sing of my love for you. Would that I had the eloquence of all the martyrs and the simplicity of nothingness so as to set to music my hymn of thanksgiving.

My God, even if you could not possibly know of my love for you, I would love you just the same and thank you just as lovingly : It is for your own sake that I love you, because you are Truth and Beauty.

My God, if after granting me the privilege of suffering every torment you could conceive, every kind of torture combined, whether physical, mental or emotional, from the beginning of the world to the end, even for the duration of myriads of worlds ; if, after that, you were pleased to consign me again to nothingness, I would love you just as much and thank you just as lovingly : it is for your own good pleasure that I love you. And if this absurd supposition were to become a reality and yet added to your good pleasure for only the smallest fraction of a second, I would cast myself into the chaos of non-existence while still loving and thanking you.

My God, if after granting me the immense favour of an eternity devoted to the apostolate, of an eternity filled with every kind of labour and persecution that you can conceive, for the salvation and sanctification of souls ; and if, after that, you could derive greater glory by sending me to suffer in hell for another endless eternity, I would plunge myself into the abyss of the condemned still loving and thanking you.[4]

O my God, so as to prevent the least sin from being committed, so as to eliminate a single imperfection that is a cause of pain to you, so as to ensure you are praised by just one more good desire, however minimal, I am ready for anything : it is for your greater glory that I love you.

O divine Trinity! forgive me these presumptuous outpourings of love, these absurdities and so many more that I would love to see fulfilled if they could contribute to your satisfaction. My God, these extravagances are the expression of a very weak and very cold love compared with the language of your Cross, your Eucharist and your heaven. In my confusion and in my exaltation, my God, listen to your eternal Word, the perfect echo of your song of love, and delight in the flaming breath of your Spirit of love."

---

[4] A hypothesis, a supposition formulated by certain saints, notably St paul, which can not,however, become a reality since love of its nature reaches out to the sovereign Good.

XXVII
RELIGIOUS LIFE
16 December 1925 - 5 March 1926

To suffer and to smile. — Love, suffering, souls!. — The grace of humiliation. — Conversion. — Calvary, my Thabor. — Jesus suffers...— Desire for the cross of Jesus. — Work of the Holy Spirit.

11 January 1926. "Yes, my God, always to suffer more and to smile better! Alleluia in the night! Alleluia in the midst of intimate heartbreak! Alleluia in the satisfaction of your infinite Justice!

Most adorable Trinity, through the Heart of Jesus, I love you with that same love you have for yourself, infinitely, eternally and divinely, for your sake and for you alone, in the name of all living beings and in union with all living beings, in the name of whom and in union with whom you may wish to be loved ; and I pay to you all the homage that can be paid to you according to the immensity of your infinite Spirit."

To live in God alone ; at every moment, to gaze only on God as on a good Father ; to smile at everything, to smile with joy, to smile with gratitude ; to exult with love when the cross enfolds me in its arms : O nameless condescension! O heavenly delights! "My God, my God, still more suffering if it is for your glory! It will always be too little to tell you of my love.

O holy Trinity, may you be for ever glorified for holding me in annihilation, and in the heart of your Heart, continually! It is peace, it is blessedness, it is to be inebriated with eternal love..."

16 January. "Alleluia! Yes, my God, again and always more bitterness in the chalice. I want to savour it as if it were

increasingly delicious honey. O holy humiliation, come, come, I love and embrace you with joy and respect! I thirst. Oh! Never will I be able to explain how much I thirst for **suffering**, for **souls**, for **love**. Suffering, souls, love are three passions whose flame is being fanned at every second, they are my three torments, my triple martyrdom!"

Jesus told me this morning, after my Communion, that *if I knew of all the evil that is committed in the world, I would die of grief.* And yet I cannot die of love in order to console his divine and outraged heart! Death would be too sweet ; life, seasoned with sacred bitterness, is more to his glory.

18 January. Jesus is letting me rest in his Heart. His tenderness is inexpressible. He seems to be moved by my longing. He plunges me into unfamiliar depths of silence and recollection. He reveals new gardens to me, where an abundance of living water makes everything fruitful. We tell one another secrets. Not a single word. There is total silence, and that is why we understand one another so well. My three passions : suffering, souls, love, are growing in intensity. "O my Jesus, take pity on the infinitude of my desires! I want all possible suffering, I want every soul, I want infinite Love in its plenitude for your greater glory. Your own joy, the delight of the Blessed Trinity in you, this is my great happiness. As for the little annihilated nonentity that you allow to rest so tenderly in your Heart, enfold it in humiliation, in hidden suffering, in action or inaction. Give her the grace to smile at everything ; this smile, O my Jesus, is a glimmer of that joy and peace with which you have flooded her." Oh! How happy I am! God alone, God alone is my felicity!

19 January. "My God, how I long for you...! Yet, you are mine, to the extent of my being annihilated in you ; I enjoy your presence continually ; I look upon you without ceasing. You keep me so completely submerged in you that, for a year (all but three days), I have not looked for a single moment on the earth. In your Heart, you make me live the life of heavenly beatitude, and yet I have the temerity to say that I long for you! My God, I give

thanks for the surpassing joy that you grant me in yourself, and also I offer you my hymn of thanksgiving for the interior longing that you yourself cause to increase in my soul. The more you make me long for you, the more I feel that you are plunging me into your adorable Trinity. You are introducing me to new depths of silence and sweetness. There, my three passions can find nourishment as ample as these limitless chasms. Love, suffering, souls! Oh! My God, you who are the magnanimous Author and the supreme Object of my thirst, may you be glorified by the immensity of my desires! This thirst is Jesus' thirst. Listen to the divine voice of your well-beloved Son as he pleads : *Father, I thirst! Sitio! Father, satisfy yourself ! Sitio! Father, quench my thirst with suffering and souls before I cry out : Consummatum est! And then may I be fully sated in your eternal Charity!*"

23 January. "O holy humiliation, in the shadow of your wings which appear to be bristling with thorns, you conceal a wealth of beauty and delights! You offer a cup which appears bitter, but which in reality contains the Bridegroom's choice wine. I love you! Envelop Jesus living in me in the copious folds of your sacred cloak. Penetrate the intimate depths of my soul, shed more light on my nothingness and my poverty. Jesus is using you, O precious humiliation, to give me a further proof of his love. I have a better grasp of the tenderness and wisdom of his Heart. O holy angels in heaven, look with envy on my happiness! You know nothing of the joy of suffering. Mary, my sweet Mother, I beg you to sing your *Magnificat* for me, in thanksgiving. My God, for your sake, I would want every kind of humiliation. I thirst! I have an infinite thirst, in every situation, as at every moment!"

My ideal haunts me continually. All the time, I see only God. My three passions are like three immease fires that the breath of God keeps alight at each second. Words cannot convey what I am going through. Jesus seems to want to smile outwardly. As for his little annihilated nothing, he clasps her more tightly in the depths of his Heart. I am for ever immersed in the Blessed

Trinity. "My God, whatever you wish! Whatever... Whatever... but take all you want!"

25 January. (Conversion of St Paul.) For a year to the day, the adorable Trinity has kept me annihilated in its Heart. "O my Jesus! With your divine voice, sing my canticle of thanksgiving. As for me, silence is a better expression of my gratitude and my happiness."

5 February. The first Friday of the month. The grace of conversion. I lack vitality in the service of God. I should have more spiritual strength. "O my God! My countless failings humble me. Today, I am changing for good. What a long way I am from that moral energy with which the saints serve you! Ineffectiveness is all I am capable of ; poverty is what I possess ; nothingness is what I am. O Jesus, O Mother most pure! Do everything and keep me in a state of conversion.

"I thirst...! O holy Trinity, you alone know how intensely I thirst! My God, I beg you, provided it is for your glory, to give me love, suffering, souls! Always to suffer more and to smile better!"

8 February. "Jesus, I wish I could suffer as much as you yourself suffered! Your sufferings were so vast that no human intellect can understand, let alone measure, them. Nevertheless, oh yes, I wish I could experience the infinite martyrdom of your sacred Humanity, because I love you! In order to satisfy the infinitude of my desire to love, I must suffer infinitely. I wish I could undergo your martyrdom of love so as to save and sanctify all souls, to console you, to bring joy to your Eucharistic Heart, to achieve the perfect fulfilment of your divine will."

The action of the Holy Spirit in my soul is growing sweeter and more powerful ; I cannot define it. The divine work is continuous. No two seconds are entirely similar : The creative Spirit does not repeat himself in any way, his power is infinite. A deep interior recollection plunges me more deeply into God. Jesus as Victim draws me irresistibly ; he enthrals and ravishes me. I pine... I thirst... And I am happy...

11 February. "O immaculate Virgin, my Mother, it is one of your feasts today. Oh! I beg you to give me love, suffering, souls! I wish I could possess the cross of Jesus. The cross! The very word makes me tremble with joy. Oh! If only I could travel the entire universe and gather up all the crosses that God has scattered since the beginning of the world and will scatter between now and the end of time, so as to make them my own, embrace them with gratitude, savour them, present them as an offering of love to the divine Crucified. And yet, not even the multitude of human crosses could satisfy me. To quench my thirst, I would need the divine cross of my Saviour, from the first instant of his Incarnation to the last beat of his sacred Heart on Calvary ; the cross of Jesus suffering in the Host since the institution of the holy Eucharist at the Last Supper ; his mystical and everlasting cross, in the tabernacle, on the altar, in sacrilegious, half-hearted or ill-prepared Communions! My Thabor, Jesus, is your Calvary! It is there, on the blessed hill of your sacrifice, that I am happy to pitch my tent. My gem is your Cross."

20 February. "O my Jesus, I love you! Will you ever make me capable of proving to you all my love? I beg you to take pity on the infinitude of my desires."

21 February. The vow of total perfection is for me not merely the vow of love and abandonment, the vow of immolation and self-offering, the vow of smiling constantly at infinite and merciful Love, but also the vow of **self-forgetfulness**. Hence, I must no longer recall voluntarily my being annihilated in the adorable Trinity. God alone, in everything! God alone, always!

23 February. Jesus is seeking souls to console him. His Eucharistic Heart is suffering.[1] Oh! How it is suffering...! He desires souls that are totally abandoned to his love ; sensitive

---

[1] Since his resurrection, Christ has enjoyed the fullness of beatitude. Yet, when contemplative souls see Our Lord suffering, and even complaining to them about the sins and ingratitude of men, it is no illusion. They *actually* see Jesus, just as he was when suffering his agony, and they are *actually* called to sympathize with him in his sufferings and to share in them. It is thought that the angels who consoled Our Lord in the Garden of Olives did so by showing him the faithful souls who, until the end of the world, would sympathize with him in his sufferings.

souls that not only refuse him nothing, but seize eagerly upon every opportunity to give him pleasure, who anticipate his desires and surround him with attentions, small in themselves yet very great because of the love that prompts them ; souls that offer him all those trifles that his goodness scatters through each moment of an entire day, those thousands of trivia that, fragrant with pure love, are like a brilliant bouquet of a thousand immaculate roses.

Jesus is suffering... How few souls understand the complaint of his Heart in the tabernacle...! Some hear them ; very few, alas, understand them!

27 February. To refuse God nothing : that is certainly not enough for me. I want to give him a surprise. But God knows everything, is it possible to surprise him? I can and I will surprise him with small, spontaneous and kind attentions ; I can and I will give him unexpected joy by these impromptu acts of kindness that love is so clever at inventing.

28 February. "My Jesus, what more do you want from me before giving me more to suffer? I am ready for anything, anything so as to procure a single drop from your chalice, a single splinter from your cross. And yet, as you well know, I wish I could have the whole of your chalice and your cross, without any mitigation. Is it because I am not generous enough that you are not granting me more bitterness and humiliation? Your one desire is to expiate and to give ; expiate my wrongdoings and, in my annihilated being, endure your agony, the scourging, the thorns, the nails, the humiliations, the desertions, every physical and moral agony of your sacred Passion. O Mary, my good Mother, Jesus is saving the thorns for himself and leaving me the roses! The bride has the same rights as the Bridegroom. Tell me, O immaculate Virgin, tell me what surprise I am to give my loving Bridegroom so as to captivate him and obtain from his divine Heart his inestimable gift of suffering."

The Most Blessed Trinity is intensifying the grace by which I am rendered as it were unconscious of everything that is not essentially itself. I repeat, for the glory of my God, that I am not living on earth. How can that be? I am subject to the action of the Holy Spirit. Through the Spirit, my gaze is fixed irrevocably on the adorable Trinity. I cannot explain this state. God works effortlessly in souls just as he pleases. I see nothing, I hear nothing, and, of course, I have no taste for anything on earth. I have no recollection of the past and I do not think at all about the future ; the second that has just elapsed, and the moment to come, have no place in my thoughts. I no longer remember myself ; my being is annihilated in the Infinite. But to all appearances, I am living on earth, yet in reality I am a stranger to it. In all my actions, words, thoughts, desires, I feel I am passive, as if under the influence of the supreme Being, as if urged on, gently yet powerfully, by the Spirit of love. I am entirely free, and there is not the least contention about this state. Simply, grace is so strong that I cannot resist it. Nevertheless, everything evolves on the basis of renunciation. The impulse of grace almost always runs counter to my initial impulse. So, it is time to write ; there are two notebooks before me and the work in both of them is equally urgent ; which am I to take up? — The one that is less attractive to me ; I say less attractive ordinarily speaking, but from the point of view of the supernatural, oh! what delights are in store for me! It is the same with everything, everything. Self-denial in the smallest details is unremitting. Our Lord ensures an unbroken chain of small acts of self-denial and interior mortification in my life. How good it is of him! My privilege is very great. "O Mary, my sweet Mother, sing of my ineffable gratitude and joy!" And in all this, I take pleasure in repeating : Jesus reserves the thorns for himself and leaves me the roses...

5 March. "My God, I want to suffer so much in order to glorify you that only the infinite voice of my Jesus can convey the ardour and immensity of my desire. Eternal Father, through the sacred Heart of Our Lord and the Immaculate Heart of Mary, I thank you for every suffering, tribulation and trial ; in a word, for all the crosses which, in your goodness, you have strewn upon

the earth since the beginning of the world, for those you are multiplying at this present moment and that you will send in the
future, until the end of ages. O what a treasure the cross is! O
what a favour is suffering! How is it that I cannot prevail upon
my divine Bridegroom, in spite of my wretchedness and unworthiness, to suffer in my annihilated being all that he suffered in
his sacred Humanity!"

XXVIII
RELIGIOUS LIFE
5 March - 8 April 1926

Battles. — Infinite reward. — Longing. — Love of obscurity. —
Jesus offered to his divine Father. — Total gift of the Heart of Jesus.
— Increasing thirst for suffering.

7 March. The most humiliating temptations fill my imagination. I remain at peace, solely through obedience ; I believe I am
in the state of grace, through obedience ; I receive communion,
through obedience. Oh! How good it is to suffer! "Thank you,
my God! You know my love, you know it is my will to please you
in everything, to concern myself with you alone. O Jesus, O my
heavenly Mother, I know that it is you who are fighting my battles ; grant me the grace constantly to be faithful in allowing you
freedom of action. How good you are! In spite of all my
wretchedness, you hold me in the Heart of the adorable and
blessed Trinity. O mercy, O infinite tenderness, how inscrutable
you are!"

14 March. The violent storm has subsided. The enemy is
still raging, but I am deaf to his agitation. I quietly contemplate
my Jesus and, through him, the adorable Trinity. No words, no
utterances, just profound silence. In this wordless contemplation, there is gracious love, joy in God alone, while I smile upon
the Infinite, renouncing all that is finite.

24 March. "My God, how I long for you! You keep multiplying the acts of kindness and thoughtfulness shown me by the
charitable souls who surround me. I am very sensitive to all this ;
I even feel confused : I am so undeserving of their thoughtfulness. O my God, may you be glorified and given fitting thanks by

Jesus! Sweet Master, O my divine Substitute, I always rely on your infinite generosity to pay my debts. Not to mention my debts towards God and towards you, I count on your power and your love to repay infinitely my debts towards others. Each word addressed to me, each smile, each delicate attention, each kindness, each service given so unsparingly, every prayer offered for my intentions, every desire to give me pleasure, in a word, every attention of which I am the object, whether I am aware of it or not, this multitude of blessings makes a debtor of me. And you know, O Jesus, that I cannot pay my debts. All these free gifts which I do not deserve at all from creatures, I receive them in your divine Heart.

As for myself, I ask you to grant me the favour of remaining for all eternity under an obligation to each soul who desires to do me good in any way at all or who gives me the least joy, even without my knowledge. But, out of gratitude, I want you not only to settle my debts but to make an infinite return for the smallest attention I receive ; and that, for the past and the future as well as for the present. Besides, your joy and your glory consist in that. I no longer exist ; in truth, it is you who are the object of the loving kindness shown me. Your joy depends on thanking souls and submerging them in your love ; your glory depends on their praising you better. Mary, my good Mother, you are the immortal steward of the graces of my Jesus ; you can see my gratitude ; I cannot put into words the wishes prompted by my gratitude, but you understand my feelings and my desires. For you, I summarize briefly my prayer for all those I love : **Draw on Jesus constantly and to the full for their sake**.

Why then, my God, since everything contributes to my happiness, did I start by saying : How I long for you! It is because every consideration shown me by creatures is more or less brilliant reflection of your sovereign love. The goodness of the human heart emanates from the goodness of your sacred Heart. Since reflections which, in reality, are pale and dim, are so refreshingly sweet, how could the supreme Source fail to draw me? Yes, my God, you draw me more and more. The more you show me your infinite attributes, the more I feel drawn to you, the more I long for you ; but at the same time, I am always happy to do your holy will, and my thirst for love, for suffering and for souls grows in proportion to the knowledge that you give me of yourself.

Silence, darkness, shadow : that is my great privilege. O my Jesus, how mellifluous is your voice when all is completely silent! What a signal favour you grant me when you deign to leave me in the shade! Oh! If only I could be completely forgotten and you alone would deign to think of your little nonentity! This evening is the vigil of one of my favourite great feasts. O gentle incarnate Word, O holy Mother immaculate, I know that you are preparing special graces for me for tomorrow. I abandon myself to your action, I sacrifice every desire, for your joy and your glory.

25 March. "My God, what a great sacrifice it is to refrain from asking you for the grace to behold your heaven soon! You know how much I desire you ; but also, how happy I am to suffer. If only I could endure the immensity of the Passion of my Jesus through all eternity!"

26 March. (Feast of the Seven Sorrows of Our Lady) Oh! How I beg the Blessed Virgin to obtain for me all the suffering that God wishes to send me! Today, I am reciting seven times the Rosary of Mercy to obtain the *satisfaction of the infinite attributes*.

My sweet heavenly Mother is answering my prayer interiorly by inspiring me to offer to the eternal Father, twelve times every hour, through her immaculate Heart and the Spirit of Love, the Eucharistic Heart, the precious Blood and the sacred Wounds of Jesus, to obtain the *satisfaction of the infinite attributes*.

27 March. Last night, I came across a picture of the holy Face in my room. So Jesus wants me to offer his adorable Face to his divine Father.

28 March. (Palm Sunday) This morning, Jesus gave me the infinite riches of his Heart. There is nothing left for him to give me.

29 March. Yesterday, I did not understand the immense favour that Our Lord was bestowing on me. This morning, during my thanksgiving after Communion, my good Master enlightened me. He has given me his Heart! I can do whatever I wish with all his inexhaustible treasures! I am in possession of all his eternal wealth, all his infinite merits! What next! He has given me his Heart and I can dispose of it as I will...! Realising what this ineffable gift meant, I turned quickly to the Blessed Virgin and handed over my divine Treasure to her, saying : "O my Mother, use it to the full, as you think fit, but satisfy the adorable Trinity and satisfy my Jesus!"

I understood, too, that this most generous grace was Our Lord's answer to the offering I was making of him to the eternal Father. It was a Sunday, the day dedicated to the most blessed Trinity.

"O my God, how can I sing my canticle of thanksgiving! Through Mary and your Spirit of Love, I offer you the Heart of my Jesus. Listen to the voice of your beloved Son and read in it my inexpressible gratitude ; at the same time, deign to hear the voice of my wretchedness and my nothingness : I am nothing, Jesus is everything. O holy Trinity, satisfy yourself for ever!"

8 April. How good Jesus is to give me, each morning, his adorable Host! I hunger for his Eucharistic Heart! Oh! How painful it is for me to refrain from asking him to satisfy my hunger soon in eternity! All the better if it costs me so much! I find my joy in sacrificing every desire. That Jesus should rejoice to the full : that is what I want.

Same day. 8 April. "My God, how I hunger for suffering! I sacrifice to you even the least of my desires. Your joy is mine as well."

XXIX
RELIGIOUS LIFE
9 April - 22 May 1926

Active life. — Jesus gives his Heart for souls. — To consume the whole world in love. — Vow of total perfection. — Thirst for the infinite. — Mea culpa.

9 April. This morning, unexpectedly, an opportunity occurred for me to resume teaching. I abandoned myself to the action of Jesus as completely as possible and with great supernatural joy. To return to an active life, however limited, away from the solitude of the infirmary, was an act of absolute renunciation. With a full heart, I accepted this grace, as pleasing as it was crucifying.[1]

12 April. In spite of exterior distractions, Our Lord is plunging me deeper into silence and interior recollection.

14 April. Jesus has given me his divine Heart for souls. He has entrusted his infinite graces to me for souls, not for myself. As for me, I no longer exist, and I have promised to look only upon the adorable Trinity, taking care not to recall my annihilated self. Through the Most Blessed Virgin, I can and I must draw on the Heart of Jesus for the sake of all souls. I feel I have an immense responsibility ; but counting on God and on Mary, my dear Mother, I have no fear ; I love and I am happy.

---

[1] The reader should not be astonished by this expression. For contemplative souls, the transition from the purely contemplative life to the active life causes suffering.

17 April. Jesus is submerging me even more in himself. He is making me savour more sweetly the life of eternity. I am released from everything, everything that is not my God. Indescribable happiness... Unheard of delights....

19 April. I have a clearer understanding of the action of my divine Substitute. In my place, Jesus is living and working on earth. My soul, that he has consumed in his Heart, lives and contemplates in heaven. "O most generous Lord, may you be thanked for all eternity!"

23 April. Through the Blessed Virgin, I am drawing grace and light from the Heart of my Jesus. The Infinite is inexhaustible. Yet, in order to give expression to the ardour of my desires, I can say only this : **I wish I could exhaust the Heart of Jesus the Infinite for each soul!**

30 April. I must give, radiate, inspire love. I must...

1 May. I wish I could consume the entire world in love ; in keeping with the designs of Jesus, I shall consume it.

Today, **I am beginning again to love God.** I am beginning with renewed zest to live life intensely out of pure love. "Mary, my good Mother, I am counting on you."

7 May. The first Friday and monthly day of retreat. "My God, I have an infinite desire to love you infinitely...! Take pity on the boundless immensity of the desires that you yourself inspire. O my Jesus, if the Most Blessed Trinity is not fully satiated through you in my annihilated being, it is not my fault, no, it is not my fault ; I can do nothing, but you can do everything. My infinite desire for love is sincere ; my will to allow you to act freely and to bring you enjoyment is no less so, O my dear Master. But I am unshakeable in my conviction that your power and your goodness are well able to fulfil the multitude of my desires of which you are the sole author and the final goal.

Same day. As certain details of my vow of total perfection have been omitted, I am rewriting it here in its entirety.

Content of the vow of total perfection

With the grace of God and the help of Mary, my sweet Mother, I make the vow of total perfection in all its breadth, according to the light I believe I have received from Our Lord.

First, obedience is my great rule of total perfection. Hence, faced with a choice between an act of self-denial chosen by myself, and some gratification, some natural pleasure recommended or merely desired by my superiors, I see perfection as consisting in the pleasure enjoyed out of obedience, because the will or the desire of my superiors is for me the expression of the will or good pleasure of God. When obedience leaves the choice to me, perfection would seem to lie in self-denial.

I commit myself, then, to total perfection, under pain of sin, constantly and in everything, that is, at each moment, in my thoughts, my desires, my words, my actions, my physical movements, from the most important command to the smallest optional and intimate detail.

Thus, I undertake not to refuse Our Lord anything, not to think of the past, not to anticipate the future and, in the present, to concern myself only with God : I leave it to Jesus and Mary to make reparation for the past, to pave the way for the future and to ensure perfection in the present. I undertake not to entertain any useless thought and not to allow myself any useless physical movement.

I undertake to smile constantly at infinite and merciful Love, to look only on God and not to think voluntarily of myself, annihilated in the Most Blessed Trinity.

I consider the vow of total perfection to be a vow of love and self-abandonment, a vow of self-immolation and self-sacrifice a vow to forget myself and to keep my attention constantly focused on God.

I include in this vow the total gift of myself to the Blessed Virgin in so far as this is in every respect most pleasing to Our Lord.

I make the vow of total perfection **freely, and gladly, out of love**, simply to tell God that I love him, that I count on him alone, that I trust him and that I abandon myself to his action.

I have an indescribable sense of my unworthiness ; I am convinced of my nothingness ; I feel weak, poor, powerless. Because of that, my confidence in Jesus is like a limitless ocean engulfing the torrent of my misery. I cast myself with faith and love into the regions of infinite Mercy. The goodness of God : that is my firm assurance and my sweet peace.

I pronounce this vow for the greater glory of the adorable Trinity, for the salvation and sanctification of souls, in a spirit of reparation, immolation, thanksgiving and praise ; in a word, for the intentions of Jesus, abandoning myself totally to infinite Love as a **victim** of love, an **apostle** of love and a **martyr** of love, for the satisfaction of the infinite attributes of the eternal and most adorable Trinity.

I will renew this vow each morning, binding myself until the following morning.

I do not recite every morning the long formula that I have just written out. This is how I renew my commitment. As soon as I have received Our Lord in the sacred Host, after adoring him for a few seconds, I say to him :

"O my God, with your grace and the help of Mary, my dear Mother, I renew my vows of obedience, poverty and chastity. I make the vow of total perfection. I vow, O adorable Trinity, to refuse you nothing. I vow , O Jesus, to allow you to act as perfectly as you desire to act. I make the vow of love, of abandonment, of self-immolation and self-offering, and the vow to smile constantly, O my God, upon your infinite and merciful Love, the vow to look upon you alone and not to think voluntarily of myself, annihilated in you. O Mary, my dear Mother, I renew the gift of myself to you, included in my vow of total perfection, in so far as this is pleasing to my Jesus."

Then I implore the blessing and the help of Our Lord, of the Blessed Virgin and of all the heavenly court. I ask them to thank God and to obtain for me the grace not to put any obstacle in the way of his designs. Then I recite the *Ave Maria* three times adding each time : "O Mary, my good Mother, deign to preserve me always from the least involuntary imperfection!" And I make the sign of the cross as I receive heaven's blessing.

22 May. More and more, I need everything to an infinite degree. "O my Jesus, my divine Substitute, if the Most Blessed Trinity is not satisfied and if your infinite Heart can not be satisfied, it is not my fault. My sweet Jesus, if such were the case, you would have to say *mea culpa*! I surrender, I abandon myself, I let you, and Mary, my good Mother, have your way ; I am not interfering with anything, for then I would spoil everything ; my only concern is to love you. I am nothing ; and can 'nothing' be responsible? — No, what does not exist can not have any responsibility. You have only one desire, O my divine Master : to give yourself. Give yourself entirely, I beg of you, to souls, for your glory."

Tomorrow is the holy day of Pentecost. I want the fullness of the Spirit of love for souls. Yes, it is for all souls, present and future, for each one of them, that I want the fullness of the Spirit.

Tomorrow morning, with holy Communion, I will end my first Jubilee of this year. "O Mary, my Mother, use it as you see fit for the greater joy of God."

XXX
RELIGIOUS LIFE
22 May - 18 July 1926

Jesus loves me! — The satisfaction of all the attributes of the eternal and most lovable Trinity. — Through the Most Blessed Virgin, to send forth rays from the Heart of Jesus on all souls.

24 May. Jesus loves me! I felt it! It lasted two seconds, perhaps. What a delight! I know the effort his divine Heart must make so as not to let me know how much he loves me. Immediately after this ineffable moment, I felt the burden of darkness and suffering.

25 May. I am suffering greatly, interiorly. "My God, how good it is!"

28 May. My suffering is intense. I cannot express it. How I suffer for want of more suffering!

30 May. (Feast of the Most Blessed Trinity) It is my feast par excellence. This morning, I ended my second Jubilee. I earnestly begged the Blessed Virgin to empty purgatory.

Our Lord is plunging me more deeply into the Heart of the Trinity. Only there am I able to live, in the atmosphere of the divine and the infinite. More and more, I need the air of heaven.

During the prayers in honour of the Most Blessed Trinity, as well as during Benediction of the Blessed Sacrament, I was inspired to change one word in the formulation of my ideal. I need a word that speaks of love. Instead of expressing my ideal in the words : *The satisfaction of all the attributes of the eternal and most adorable Trinity*, I will, from now on, say :

The satisfaction of all the attributes of the eternal and most lovable Trinity.

That changes absolutely nothing as regards my infinite desire to give pleasure to God, but I am replacing the adjective *adorable* by *lovable*, because I need love everywhere and in everything.

4 June. The first Friday of the month. (Monthly retreat) I am making my retreat with the Eucharistic Heart. I am on fire, burning with the desire to love God and to bring others to love him. "Our Lady of the Eucharistic Heart, I beg you to give Jesus to souls!"

11 June. The Eucharistic Heart in the Host draws me more and more. If I merely pass near the chapel, I feel an irresistible force inviting me in. Close to the tabernacle, I experience an indefinable joy. When the Blessed Sacrament is exposed, I feel totally taken over, paralysed, by this gentle Eucharistic Heart. When I leave the chapel, I have to tear myself away from the divine Prisoner. Yet, I never cease to live in him ; all this takes place in the Heart of the Most Blessed Trinity, an immense distance from the earth ; but Jesus wants me to enjoy him in his Eucharist and to grieve when I am far from his consecrated Host.

20 June. Sunday. It was the feast of the Eucharistic Heart last Thursday, the feast of Love par excellence. My joy consisted in loving without any feeling of consolation or interior light. How good that is, for Jesus' sake!

This morning, at the end of my meditation, I was suddenly given to understand clearly that my duty now, and my task in eternity, until the end of the world, is and will be, **through the Most Blessed Virgin, to send forth rays from the Heart of Jesus on all souls**. To do that, I must remain annihilated, love — oh yes! love — and let my divine Substitute and the Virgin of love have their way.

21 June. (Feast of St Louis of Gonzaga) Once again, I told Our Lord during my meditation this morning that he was to

satisfy himself. And, pleading with him, while at the same time casting all my responsibility on him, I said : "Take advantage of my offering, Jesus!" And I added plaintively, "I'm not aware of anything." And with infinite sweetness, he replied :

> Because you are not aware of anything, I am taking all the more advantage of it.

This tender reply consoled me. "Thank you, Jesus! Provided you are content, that is all I desire."

2 July. Immolation, love! These two words recur to me constantly. Love in immolation, immolation in Love! Oh! How good it is to let oneself be immolated by Jesus and for his good pleasure, that is, for the greater glory of his divine Father! How happy I am! My *pure delight* is all the greater in that I am enjoying no sensible consolation. Our Lord is silent. He slumbers, he sleeps and hides himself, it is dark ; he even seems to be deserting me. The more intense the darkness, the more I love him. He and I have the same tastes ; he likes *to play hide and seek*, well, so do I! He enjoys pretending to abandon me, well, I relish this loving desertion on his part because I have more opportunities to shower attentions on him and to give him little surprises. What fun it is to *play with God!*

5 July. When will I finally love God perfectly! More than ever, **I am dying for want of being unable to die!**

18 July. In one instant, Jesus can accomplish an eternal undertaking because his action is infinite. I have just asked him, during my morning meditation, to bring rapidly to completion his work of substitution in my being, if it is to give him more glory ; but that is always the chief and only condition, his great glory, his greater satisfaction. I desire to suffer and labour for all eternity so as to tell God that I love him ; nevertheless, I continue living in a constant death.

Same day. I have just been told that I will be leaving tomorrow for Saint-Michel, for one or two weeks' rest. How much
kindness and consideration is showered on me! How grateful I
am! "My Jesus, as ever, it is for you to pay my debts. Be more
generous than ever today. Let your generosity be in proportion
to my supernatural delight and my natural apprehension about
what is happening. How happy I am! Oh! How good it is to relish an act of self-denial for God's sake! Thank you! Thank you,
Jesus, for allowing me to find so much delight in what human
language terms suffering! In your Heart, my loving Bridegroom,
it is always heaven ; no matter what happens, suffering cannot
gain entrance there... How happy I am! O most lovable Trinity,
I love you because I love you! I love you for yourself. I love you
for yourself alone!"

XXXI
RELIGIOUS LIFE
18 July - 15 August 1926

Private retreat. — Annual retreat. — A new life of love.

20 July. Yesterday, I arrived at Saint-Michel. Our Lord placed me in retreat from this evening until the morning of the 29th. Nothing appears exteriorly, everything takes place in the Heart of the adorable Trinity. My divine Substitute is plunging me into a very deep interior recollection.

25 July. I abandon myself and submit once again to the action of Our Lord, like a mere nothing in the hands of the Infinite.

30 July. Return to Sillery. During my private retreat with Our Lord, at Saint-Michel, his Eucharistic Heart often spoke to me about consecrated souls. He had me pray for them and asked for acts of interior mortification to console him and to obtain for those he has chosen a greater appreciation of the Gift of God. The Gift of God to consecrated souls is the Heart of the Bridegroom! Oh! If only they understood the Gift of God! If only they knew the Heart of the Bridegroom! Not only could they refuse him nothing, but they would contrive to multiply their acts of kindness and thoughtfulness towards him.

4 August. Last night, I began the annual retreat with the community. I began the Spiritual Exercises by abandoning myself anew and totally to God's good pleasure, and by repeating to Our Lord that *my one desire is to give him pleasure.* Besides, what does loving God mean, if not to give him pleasure...

12 August. The Spiritual Exercises came to an end this morning. "My God, thank you for so many graces!" I am not coming out of retreat ; in spite of the seeming exterior distractions, Our Lord wants to keep me interiorly in profound recollection. A continual turning towards God in love : that is my only occupation. What happiness!

13 August. I have never longed so much to be consumed in eternal love. Never has God drawn me into himself so perceptibly. In spite of my indescribable longing to open my eyes at last in his Heart, what I want above all, most of all, is for him to be filled with joy. Every second is like an eternity for me ; in spite of that, I would be prepared to go on pining for the whole of eternity, if that were possible, so as to give him the least pleasure.

15 August. The entire day has been nothing but a longing for eternal union. Another feast of the Assumption of the Blessed Virgin is coming to an end... Jesus has not finished his work : as far as I am concerned, everything is good, so long as he is content. **Nevertheless, I am starting out once more on a completely new life of love**. To die, or to suffer! Since the hour has not come for me to glorify God through an essentially joy-filled love, well, I want to glorify him to the greatest possible extent through a suffering love. "O good pleasure of God, you are heaven itself!"

XXXII
RELIGIOUS LIFE
29 August 1926 - 12 January 1927

The agonizing Heart of Jesus and the chalice of his Passion. —
Intimate union on Thursdays and Fridays.

29 August. During my meditation this morning, Our Lord
plunged me deeper into the Heart of the most lovable Trinity.

There, he said to me, nothing earthly or human can touch you.

Then he prepared me for some great suffering. What is it to
be? I do not know, I can not understand anything...

2 September. Thursday. On Thursday, I pay homage to the
Eucharistic Heart of my Jesus, in particular. At midday, after my
examen, Our Lord spoke to me interiorly, asking :

Do you want to taste the chalice of my Passion?

"O my Jesus", I answered, "oh yes! How kind you are!"
And in an indescribable, gracious tone, he again said :

Do you?

Repeated as it was, this *Do you?* was like an arrow, a shaft of
love. "My Jesus", I replied, "you know well that not only do I
want it, but it is what I am longing for." At that very moment, a
bitter, intimate suffering took possession of my whole being ; it
is a suffering I cannot put into words.[1]

---

[1] The *chalice* which Our Lord gave Dina was a participation in the sufferings of
his agony. This participation was not achieved simply by compassion, but Our Lord
allowed her to experience in reality the sufferings that he himself had endured. Her
mistress of novices said : "At those times, Dina's expression was exceptionnaly sorrowful. She was very pale, and even her lips became white. Now, when I recal the
expression she then bore, I find that she became, as it were, *another Christ.*"

4 September. Until last night, Jesus allowed me to taste the "chalice of his agony". Yesterday was the first Friday of the month. During the night of Thursday to Friday, I was, as it were, penetrated with a deep feeling of compassion for my Saviour. Physical suffering is mild compared with what I felt in my soul ; my suffering was centred in my heart and from there spread through my entire being as if to crush me. I felt an overwhelming sense of weariness and yet, how happy I was! Out of love for my sweet suffering Master, I would willingly drink and have drunk his chalice to the dregs. It takes a great grace to taste even a few drops with joy, so bitter is the potion. But then, as soon as you have tasted it, you feel an insatiable thirst. That is why, although I know I am extremely unworthy of this favour, I thirst, I thirst yet again for this cup of love. "My God, thank you!"

10 September. Friday. Last night, after the examen, Our Lord asked me :

Do you want to drink from my chalice?

"Oh! Yes, my Jesus," I answered with joy.

My intimate suffering is much less severe than last week. I am happy with everything my adorable Master wants.

17 September. Our Lord is acting in the same way this week as last week.

24 September. Like the last two weeks. I want to console my Jesus! Oh! How his Heart suffered in the Garden of Olives!

1 October. First Friday of the month. What mystic delight to be called by him to console him! This compassion for the agonizing Heart of Jesus unites me very intimately with the adorable Trinity.

On the other hand, the devil is redoubling his assaults on Thursdays and Fridays. He is trying as craftily as possible to make me miss my Communions.

7 October. First Friday of the month. Oh, what a surprise! Our Lord handed me his chalice just when I was not in the least expecting it, during my thanksgiving after Communion. Until now, he had not granted me this great grace before midday. He no longer asks me if I want to accept his chalice, so well does he know my answer, but he hands it to me without a word, and with such graciousness.

14 October. Yesterday, I spent the day preparing for the graces of Thursday and Friday, in case Our Lord should again grant me this favour.

This morning, as last week, during my thanksgiving after Communion, the agonizing Heart of Jesus allowed me to sympathize with him in his 'sadness' and gave me this text, spoken by him in Gethsemane, to meditate on : *My soul is sorrowful to the point of death!*

21 October. As last Thursday, during my thanksgiving after communion, Our Lord allowed me to experience something of the "fear that his agonizing Heart deigned to feel". I want to console my dear Master. Oh! How he suffered for souls!

28 October. This morning, my thanksgiving after Communion came to an end without Our Lord's presenting me his blessed chalice. I left the chapel humbling myself, realizing that I am still unworthy of this precious favour, and abandoning myself to the holy will of God. Nothing either, during the recitation of the *Little Office of the Blessed Virgin*. But, O joy! At the elevation of the chalice during Holy Mass, Jesus did the same as before, granting me the same grace as in recent weeks. The text that he is repeating to me and giving me to meditate on is that which he spoke to his Apostles : *Watch and pray.*

4 November. Now I am beginning on Tuesdays to prepare for the intimate union of Thursday and Friday. This morning, Thursday, it was during my thanksgiving after communion. Our Lord allowed me to taste "the weariness that he willed to suffer during his agony."

11 November. What a surprise! Again, just when I was not expecting it at all, as the priest was giving me the sacred Host, at the communion rail, my dear Master gave me his divine chalice. It was at dawn, then, on Thursday, at 6.00 in the morning, because I receive Communion well before the Mass, in the infirmary chapel.

Father, your will be done! That is the text Our Lord has given me to meditate on. But, in addition, my Jesus is complaining! During Holy Mass, distinctly yet intimately, he allowed me to hear two complaints and a promise. The first complaint :

> Very few souls want to sympathize with me in my agony!

Second complaint :

> Very few souls, even consecrated souls, know how to sympathize with the agony of my Heart!

The promise :

> I confide great secrets to those souls who want to console me in my agony.

And these are the insights that my divine Master gave me about these two complaints : Very few souls, that is among all the souls in the world in general, *want* to sympathize with him in his agony ; and, among consecrated souls, very few *know* how to sympathize with the agony endured by his Heart, that is, to console him through the most intimate union. Then, abandoning myself to his good pleasure, I asked Jesus whether he wished to answer my question or not : "Why do so many consecrated souls not know how to sympathize with the agony of your Heart?"

> Because, he said, they do not show me enough consideration, and because they are not sufficiently intent on achieving great per-

fection in all the little things. The agony of my Heart was due to loneliness, neglect and ingratitude!

12 November. Friday. Since yesterday morning, Our Lord's two complaints keep coming back to me constantly. This participation in his chalice keeps me in such close union with him that it is like his real presence in the sacred Host after Communion, and it lasts from Thursday morning until Friday evening. On Saturday, nothing is left of this state, it is over. I am left with an unspeakable love for Jesus, an infinite desire to console his Heart and to satisfy him at the expense of all possible sufferings, but I do not have the same intimate experience as on Thursdays and Fridays.

18 November. My good Master takes pleasure in varying the moment he chooses. This morning, I focused on the moment when the priest gave me the sacred Host, but no. I returned to my place and, as usual, after a very brief act of adoration and love, I renewed my three vows of religion and my vow of total perfection. Just as I said : I renew my vow of total perfection, Our Lord handed me his sacred cup. It was so clear, so distinct that I could not doubt ; in this gesture, there was the peace of heaven, the peace of God!

The same text to meditate on as last week : *My Father, may your will be done!* I can hear, too, the same complaints, and my dear Master has added :

> If religious souls only knew! But alas! They do not know! Some do not know because they are afraid to know! They are afraid of having to give up some of their attachments... I do not call all consecrated souls to enter sensibly and in a special way into my agony ; that is a favour I grant to certain souls that I myself choose. But I call all consecrated souls to console my Heart by obedience, regularity, perfect observance of the Rule, and care to perform every action perfectly out of pure love for me.

25 November. During my thanksgiving after Communion, Our Lord allowed me to share in the "aversion he willingly suffered during his agony."

26 November. Friday. This morning, during Holy Mass, while the community were receiving Communion, Our Lord asked me to make a special Holy Hour each Thursday evening, to console his agonizing Heart and to keep him company. Before Jesus made this request, I felt a deep interior peace take possession of me. Oh! What graciousness and silence there is in divine communications! My good Master wants nothing of this to be seen. It is easy for me to make this Hour in my room without anyone noticing. He also wants me not to stay up beyond the community's bed-time, so (it will be) from eight-fifteen to nine-fifteen. By then, I have completed my prayers of rule because I have no permission to join the community so late.

This request of Our Lord has given me great joy. But I do not want to agree to anything on my own, I want to submit to obedience in everything. Having expressed my gratitude to my Jesus, I told him that I would carry out his wish if he allowed me to be given permission by authority. While waiting, I am praying and I am confident.

27 November. Saturday. (Feast of the revelation of the Miraculous Medal of the Blessed Virgin) I made my request and obtained permission very easily. How easy it is to come to an agreement with God and the Most Blessed Virgin! Or rather, how well Our Lord arranges everything so as to achieve his ends!

2 December. Thursday. Just after renewing my vow of total perfection. For several weeks, on Thursday and Friday, my union with the Heart of Jesus has been like his real presence after holy Communion, while the consecrated Host is still with me. This morning, Our Lord gave me to understand that it is just as easy for him to give himself to me — through his blessed chalice — and to extend his sensible presence over two days — through an interior and invisible act — as it is for a quarter of an hour, more or less, under the appearance of the sacred Host. I am enjoying a deep and unspeakable intimacy with my good Master. Oh! How sweet it is to love an infinitely liberal God and to abandon oneself completely to him!

3 December. Friday. Last night, I kept my hour's watch. An hour of struggle, without any consolation. So much the better, it is I who must console the Heart of my Jesus.

9 December. Thursday. At the very moment of Communion, Our Lord allowed me to share in his "physical exhaustion during his agony." How good everything is when it comes from him!

10 December. My hour of watching, last night, was again an hour of struggle. Oh! How I love to console my Jesus without receiving in return his ineffable consolations! 16 December. This week, I prepared with renewed fervour for the union of Thursday and Friday. This morning, early, Our Lord seemed to take pleasure in hiding from me, so much so that before Communion, I said to him : "My Jesus, it does not seem like Thursday today!" But at the very moment I was receiving Communion, my divine Master made his customary gesture. It was clear, precise, there could be no doubt.

Our Lord asked me, during my meditation, to pay homage during these two days to "the silence of his agonizing Heart." Even if he did utter a few words in Gethsemane, yet how silently he endured everything!

He is leading me into a deeper intimacy with him. It is heaven, it is all the time more like eternity! I feel lost in a limitless ocean where there are no coastlines. This morning, Jesus told me that *a mere nothing can penetrate into the most intimate regions of the infinite.* "Lord, grant that I may become increasingly a mere nothing, and may you be everything in my place!"

23 December. At the moment of Communion, Our Lord spoke to me of "the love of his agonizing Heart." He gave me to understand that, in Gethsemane, in the angel who came to console him, he saw all the souls — especially consecrated souls — who throughout the centuries would want to share in his agony.

26 December. Normally, on Thursday and Friday, my intimate union with Our Lord lasts until I fall asleep on Friday evening. Last Friday was Christmas Eve. Through obedience,

I had to go to rest before Midnight Mass. I dozed. I fell asleep savouring "the sensible presence of my good Master", but, when the rising bell rang at eleven o'clock, there was nothing. It was Friday still but Our Lord had gone into hiding. Then, full of longing, I called to him until my Communion at Midnight Mass.

30 December. Since the beginning of the Christmas holidays, my schedule has changed slightly. I begin my meditation at five minutes to six and receive Communion half an hour later.

This morning, Our Lord did not wait until the moment of Communion ; at the beginning of my meditation in the chapel, he handed me his precious chalice as usual. How kind of him! Today, he made me meditate on the "zeal of his agonizing Heart" for the salvation of souls.

2 January 1927. Last Friday, 31 December, the Blessed Sacrament was exposed in our chapel all day and all night until after morning Mass on the 1 January. As is our custom, the community gathered in the chapel at eleven o'clock at night to spend the last hour of the dying year and to begin the new year at the feet of Jesus-Victim and of his most Blessed Mother. I had permission to make this hour (of prayer). As on Christmas Eve, I had to go to rest after Evening Prayer' but this time, Our Lord allowed me to savour his presence and his chalice until after midnight. Towards the end of the final prayers, he withdrew lovingly, and when I left the chapel, this sweet favour had come to an end. "Thank you, Jesus, for letting it last longer this week!"

6 January. At the beginning of my meditation this morning, shortly after six o'clock. Intimacy with the Heart of Jesus means inexpressible delight! Oh! If souls only knew! "My God, thank you! I want to love you through my divine Saviour and through Mary, my tender Mother, ever more infinitely, and for eternity!"

Our Lord is letting me savour today "the intimate union of his agonizing Heart with his heavenly Father."

XXXIII
RELIGIOUS LIFE
12 January - 12 February 1927

A day without bread. — Feast of the Holy Name of Jesus. — The Forty Hours Devotion. — Offering of Our Lord. — Infinite Justice.

12 January. Wednesday. Since Sunday, Our Lord has kept me in the infirmary. No Communion on Monday morning. It is the most painful fast that anyone can impose on me. I was notified on Sunday evening. My disappointment was very great. I submitted myself to the holy will of my good Master with all the more supernatural joy because I found it painful. A day without Bread! A long succession of hours without Jesus in the Host : Oh! What a trial and what bitter suffering!

On Monday morning, I longed all the more for Jesus. I called to him, I begged him to come to me, with all the vehemence that hunger and the love of God can give. I recommended myself to the Blessed Virgin, saying to her : "O my dear Mother, you are so kind and you want so much to give Jesus, you cannot refuse me, give me my Jesus." When the time came for Communion to be brought to the sick, I felt suddenly imbued with great peace. I realised that Our Lord was approaching and wanted something. O joy! He handed me the chalice of his precious Blood, letting me savour his sensible presence as when I receive Communion sacramentally ; then, he said to me :

> I am going to let you enjoy my presence until your next Communion.

I was filled with consolation. I no longer wanted anything else. And this sense of intimate enjoyment together with Jesus lasted, indeed, until my next actual Communion the following morning, or rather until after my thanksgiving.

This chalice of his precious Blood that Jesus gave me was not that of his agony ; but the grace of his sensible presence was similar to that of Thursday and Friday.

13 January. Thursday. Our Lord presented me with the chalice of his agony at the moment of my Communion, at about six o'clock this morning (the normal schedule for the year having been resumed) ; he has given me for meditation the "devotedness of his agonizing Heart."

16 January. (Feast of the Holy Name of Jesus, in our Congregation.) It is my feast today, since Jesus has taken my place. Since midday yesterday, my sweet Master has been drawing me to himself with unspeakable tenderness. In the main chapel, the Blessed Sacrament is exposed, from morning to evening. Before dinner, I went there to make my examen. Towards the end, I felt that Our Lord wanted something ; at moments like that, the voice of Jesus is preceded by a deep peace, which penetrates my entire being ; and, unless this good Master enlightens me with a very bright light, I understand nothing of his mystical ways.

After my examen, then, I noticed that I was enjoying the sensible presence of my Jesus. And he said to me so graciously :

In honour of my feast!

Oh! How I wish I could put unto words how sweet Jesus is!

17 January. The favour I was granted yesterday at midday lasted until I fell asleep yesterday evening. It is a grace which, increasing as it does my longing for heaven, gives me renewed strength to work and to suffer with joy just for the glory of my sovereign Master.

20 January. The Forty Hours devotion opened this morning in our chapel. At the moment of my Communion, Our Lord let me share in "the intimate union of his Heart with his divine Father."

22 January. Saturday. How can I sing my canticle of thanks-giving! Jesus left with me his sensible presence and the chalice of his agony until ten o'clock this morning, the moment when, beneath the veil of the sacred Host, he returned to the tabernacle at the close of the Forty Hours. What joy was mine, during this last night when, on waking up, I realised that this sweet favour was not yet at an end!

It is for his glory and for souls that Our Lord gives me so many graces. Since last night, I have felt as if I were responsible for the entire world. I have felt this before, but in a less pronounced way. It is as if I had the obligation and the power, through Jesus himself, to console his sacred Heart for all the ingratitude and thoughtless-ness of every single soul. I felt crushed by this responsibility. Then I abandoned myself to my divine Substitute and to the Blessed Virgin, relying on their superabundant merits ; my part is to be nothing and to be constantly faithful to the action of the Holy Spirit.

2 February. For some time, I have been hesitating to reveal all the secrets I share with Our Lord. Is that a snare of the devil? I do not know ; but whatever it is and whatever it costs me, I want to be faithful to my great rule of obedience and self-renunciation, and I am going to tell all.

This last 22 January, was a Saturday, the feast of Our Lady of Fourvière and the conclusion of the Forty Hours. During my me-ditation, before the Blessed Sacrament exposed, I suddenly felt inundated with a great peace. I was already aware of the presence of my divine Master, but there was something more than the usual union, however intimate, of Thursday and Friday. Indeed, Our Lord granted me a signal favour : *the stigmata of love of his sacred wounds.* From his divine Heart, flames radiated on to the feet, hands and heart of my person annihilated in his. The Most Blessed Virgin placed the flames on my hands and feet and Jesus imprinted on them the stigmata of love of his sacred wounds. He granted one of my most ardent desires, but he amazed me by doing so at a moment when I was not expecting it and in a way that I could never have imagined. Since then, my limbs are as if consecrated by a seal of the divine. "Thanks be to you, O my God! O Mary, my good Mother, thank you!"

For several weeks, on Thursday and Friday, Our Lord has taken pleasure in calling me **my little Own Self**. That means that he has taken my place, that he is everything and I am nothing, nothing.

Last Thursday, 27 January, Our Lord did not present me with his blessed chalice at the precise moment of Communion. I returned to my place, submitting humbly and lovingly to his good pleasure. He delayed only a few minutes, giving it to me just as I renewed my vow of total perfection.

That day, and especially the next, were marked by a profound spirit of recollection. On Friday morning, Our Lord asked me to forget myself completely and all that concerned me, enlightening me further regarding my state of annihilation in him. At each fresh ray of light that he gave me, I renewed my vow of total perfection, enumerating in detail my promises concerning forgetfulness of self. I seemed to be submerged in a powerful grace of humility. Then my divine Master spoke to me in words that only obedience can make me write down, for it costs me a great deal to reveal them :

> My Heart is continually thinking of souls, and most of them pay no attention to me! I am seeking a soul to represent the whole of humanity, a soul to whom I can grant the grace of thinking continually of God. I have substituted myself for you ; I choose you, my little Own Self, to be this soul. I want to communicate to your nothingness my eternal thought of God.

At these words, I was speechless with emotion, astonishment and confusion. Jesus asked me to remain interiorly very silent, because he wanted to prepare me for this ineffable grace. For two days, he gave me for meditation "the constant union of his Heart with his divine Father."

The words of Our Lord that I have just quoted often come back to me and each time bring me great peace. They have inspired me to offer to God the Father the eternal Thought of his adorable Word.

Since last September I have, as far as possible, been offering Our Lord to his divine Father three hundred times a day. It is easy to arrive at this number in the course of the comings and goings, the delays here and there or during trivial manual tasks. This does not rule out my daily rosary which is foremost among my devotions not prescribed by the Rule. This is how I make this offering each time :

"Almighty Father, through Mary and your Spirit of love, I offer you the Eucharistic Heart of my Jesus ; or the agonizing Heart of my Jesus ; or the sacred Wounds of my Jesus ; or his precious Blood ; or his adorable Face ; or the eternal thought of your adorable Word." Then I recite the rosary of the five wounds of Our Lord which counts for fifty of my offerings. During the Forty Hours, so as to thank my good Master more than usual, I made my offering five hundred times a day.

That is just one small way of uniting with the Most Blessed Trinity through the Blessed Virgin, and of remaining immersed in the Infinite. I know that Mary, my dear Mother, is constantly offering Jesus in my place, so as to praise and thank God, to satisfy his infinite attributes and to obtain mercy for souls. But I feel, too, that Our Lord is giving me the grace to reiterate this offering which I cannot myself make uninterruptedly, an offering that is pleasing to him and consoles his loving Heart.

5 February. Saturday. I have been preparing, since the beginning of the week, to receive the graces of Thursday and Friday. On Thursday morning, before my Communion, I was thinking of this attentively. A few seconds before I approached the holy table, I stopped thinking about the chalice of my Jesus ; just as the priest gave me the sacred Host, Our Lord gently prompted my wandering mind and presented me with his sacred cup. My distraction caused me to make an act of humility ; and my good Master gave me to understand that he had wanted this to happen so as to give me tangible proof of his action and his presence in spite of my involuntary forgetfulness. What kindness on his part!

The first Thursday and first Friday of the month occurred this week. Our Lord forewarned me of two days of suffering. During my meditation on Thursday morning, he told me that he was going to let me experience something of the justice of his Father, of this "infinite justice which oppressed his agonizing Heart." Though his words were quite clear, yet I did not immediately grasp their true meaning. I endured great interior suffering during these two days. The devil was more aggressive ; this wicked spirit wanted to make me believe that I was not in the state of grace and, by deploying a new ruse, he tried to distance me from the Blessed Virgin, to distract me from the thought of my heavenly Mother and to impair my confidence in her. I hid myself more deeply in Jesus, in spite of feeling unworthy and very wretched. I felt crushed beneath a burden that I could not explain and did not understand. At times, God seemed to reject and abandon me and, in spite of that, Our Lord kept me hidden in his Heart. On Friday evening, at the beginning of the hour of adoration before the Blessed Sacrament, my suffering was unspeakable. Suddenly, shortly before "Benediction", Our Lord, by allowing me to savour his presence, took this immense burden away from me and said graciously :

You have just felt something of my Father's justice.

Then I understood what my good Master had said the previous morning. Oh! How oppressive is divine justice! How terrible it must be for the sinner to appear before the infinitely just God! This grace has increased my desire to obtain mercy for sinful souls. "O infinite justice of my God, take pity, take pity on all your creatures who offend you! Obtain satisfaction through my Jesus! I beg you, by his agonizing Heart, save and deliver from the burden of your eternal justice many poor ungrateful souls! My God, always through Jesus, I am not afraid to submit to your justice, however terrible it may be, I want to satisfy it as I do all your other infinite attributes. To save a single soul and to glorify you, with your grace, I would be happy to suffer, if necessary, all the immense weight of your vengeance instead of that soul. My God, your justice is infinite, but your love is also beyond measure. I trust in you, and I thank you for ever for reminding me, sometimes when I am working, of my blessed title of host and victim".

XXXIV
RELIGIOUS LIFE
12 February - 13 April 1927

Infinite Holiness. — Infinite Power. — Infinite Mercy. — The loving thought of Jesus. — Total gift of self. — Love and sacrifice.

12 February. Saturday. Last Wednesday, just as I was going to leave the chapel after my evening prayer, Our Lord told me with tenderness that he was eagerly awaiting the next day. I need hardly say how these words increased my desire to respond to his divine attentiveness. On Thursday morning, he handed me his chalice just as I renewed my vow of total perfection. He gave me for my consideration "what his agonizing Heart felt in the presence of the infinite holiness of his heavenly Father, when it was burdened and clothed with the sins of humanity".

The love of the Heart of Jesus for souls is for the human intellect a mystery of incomprehensible loving kindness. The Son of God, Holiness itself, loves souls so much that he takes their sins upon himself and, in the sight of his eternal and thrice-holy Father, appears to be not only the most abject and the greatest of sinners, but as guilty[1] as all the sinners of every age! "O love of my Saviour, how little we understand you!"

19 February. Saturday. On Thursday morning, Our Lord appeared at a different moment ; he delayed a few seconds and gave me his blessed chalice when, specifying certain aspects of

---

[1] The expression should not be taken literally. Christ, having never sinned, can in no way be guilty. He took upon himself both suffering and death, punishments which were due to us for our sins.

my vow of total perfection, I said : "My God, I vow to look upon you alone." He then asked me to take all possible care to concern myself only with him. To reflect on during my meditations, he gave me "his Father's power" which, in a single instant, could annihilate all guilty souls or hurl them down to hell for all eternity ; in addition, he proposed "the power of his agonizing Heart" which could disarm his divine Father's just anger and obtain mercy.

The subjects my good Master proposes for my consideration, together with his light and his grace, occupy my mind from one week to the next. How much I need to love my Jesus, in gratitude for so many blessings!

24 February. Monday. As I received Communion, Our Lord gave me for my consideration "the mercy of his Father and the mercy of his agonizing Heart". This does not preclude some consideration of the intimate, perfect and constant union of his Heart with his heavenly Father. This union has been, as it were, the foundation and the focus of all my meditations on Thursday and Friday, for several weeks.

Jesus proposes the **infinite attributes** for my study and contemplation. I realise this now, but I was not aware of it at first. I never understand his divine operations immediately.

3 March. The first Thursday of the month. At the moment of my Communion. As on the first Thursday in February, Our Lord allowed me to feel "something of the justice of his Father". But at the same time, he asked me to reflect on "the loving union of his Heart with his divine Father", which, intermittently, alleviates greatly the severity of his justice.

7 March. Monday. **I am beginning anew a life of infinite love**. Our Lord gave me a better understanding today of the value of each second for his glory and for souls. He is asking me again to pay great attention to him alone. For more than two weeks, I have been offering him to his divine Father five hundred times a day, and I even exceed this number. Oh! How easy

everything becomes with his grace and when, confiding in the Blessed Virgin, we allow him to have his way! But I feel that is very little to console him and give joy to the Heart of the Infinite! Love is torture, infinite as God is infinite. A welcome torture which keeps the soul riveted to sovereign Good!

13 March. Sunday. Last Thursday, the same gesture of Our Lord at the time of my Communion. Since then, I have been tasting "the bitterness of his chalice" : weariness, distaste, everything is painful , humanly speaking, yet everything is a delight for him. I am, as it were, in a state of purification and preparation for some signal grace. All my reflections are concentrated on "the loving union of his Heart with his divine Father".

22 March. Tuesday. Last Thursday, as I received Communion, Our Lord gave me a share in the "loneliness of his agonizing Heart".

25 March. Friday. Since last Sunday evening, illness has kept me once more inactive in the infirmary. Yesterday morning, when he came to give himself to me in the sacred Host, Jesus presented me at the same time with his blessed chalice, giving me again for my consideration "the union of his Heart with his divine Father".

Today, feast of the Annunciation of the Blessed Virgin and of the Incarnation of Our Lord, is the anniversary of the day on which I made the three vows of religion for the first time ; I have had five years of private profession. For a month, Our Lord has been preparing me for this happy anniversary : during the last nine days, at his request I made a novena of love ; from Wednesday evening until this morning, I was in retreat in his Heart, more intimately than usual.

This morning, my thanksgiving after Communion began in aridity. I complained to my good Master, saying that this saddened me, but that nevertheless I was happy with whatever he willed.

Towards the end of my thanksgiving, I was filled with deep peace, a prelude to communications from my Jesus. Indeed, he said to me :

> Through my most holy Mother, I grant you the grace of **thinking constantly of me**, of **thinking continually of God**.

I remained speechless with gratitude, and also with fear : I felt so unworthy of being permeated in this way with the thought of the supreme Being. I made an act of faith in the words of my Jesus, an act of trust in his goodness. And he replied :

> I have communicated to your nothingness my continual thought of God, my loving thought of my eternal Father. My Heart is continually thinking of souls, and most of these, even consecrated souls, forget me so often! I want **you to think of me all the time**, as **I think all the time of you and of souls**.

It is, then, for the joy and consolation of his Heart that Our Lord has granted me this precious grace. He is yearning for love! "My God, thank you! Mary, my good Mother, thank you! Grant me the grace never, never to put even the least obstacle in the way of the action of the Spirit of love."

2 April. Saturday. Last Thursday, it was again as I received Communion that Our Lord allowed me to feel the abandonment that his Heart experienced, the sense of being forsaken by his heavenly Father. All this to console him and to win souls for him. Yesterday in particular, the first Friday of the month, I endured great moral suffering without realizing again that the principal cause of my intimate sorrow was this abandonment that my divine Master made me endure. He made me understand it to some extent yesterday evening, and clearly this morning.

I can no longer put into words my infinite thirst for suffering. Only the multitude and intensity of the sufferings that Jesus endured, from the first moment of his Incarnation until his final moment on Calvary, in his body, mind, soul and Heart, could satisfy me. Love is the sole motive of my desires : I want Jesus crucified to be reproduced in me, so that I may resemble him as perfectly as possible and, through him, apply his inexhaustible merits to souls. Yet, I submit my desires to his good pleasure : just as he wishes, neither more nor less!

7 April. Thursday. I have been confined to bed since 20 March, through illness. This morning, I began my meditation at half past five. Even before Communion, Our Lord gave me the subject of my meditations for these two days, namely, "the suffering caused to his agonizing Heart by the futility of his sufferings" in the case of a great number of souls.

At the time of Communion, he gave me his blessed chalice. During my thanksgiving, he let me see in spirit millions of souls rushing after Satan towards their eternal ruin. And he, the Saviour, was there, surrounded by a small number of faithful souls, suffering for these millions of sinners, but to no purpose. His Heart saw souls falling in countless numbers into hell. Seeing this, I said : "My Jesus, you accomplished the act of redemption to the full ; what is wanting, then, given that so many souls are being lost?" He answered :

It is because devout souls do not unite themselves sufficiently with my sufferings.

I offered myself again to him and through him, to console his Heart, to deliver souls from sin, and, at least by making amends, to satisfy all the infinite attributes. In a most gracious tone, he said :

Will you consent to your whole being, physical and moral, undergoing torture?

I answered : "Counting on you alone, my Jesus, counting on your strength and your goodness, out of love for you, oh yes! I consent." He added :

If only you knew how consoled my Heart is when I find a soul **totally** abandoned to me! I find so few! Even among consecrated souls, there are few that abandon themselves totally to me!

Our Lord then enlightened me regarding this **total gift** of self which, in the case of many souls, is not really total, because it is not in fact unlimited or unconditional. Finally, he said to me :

Remember that, even when I seem to forsake you, to abandon you, to reject you, I will be near you, in you, substituted for your being, to a greater extent, if possible, at those moments than at other times.

8 April. Friday. Our Lord continues to show me in spirit the millions of souls that, during his agony, he saw falling into hell. And he is there, praying and suffering, surrounded by only a small number of souls. What a moving sight!

This morning, during my thanksgiving after communion, he said to me.

My apostles, Peter, James and John, to whom I had just given myself in holy Communion and just ordained priests, were consecrated souls, and they slept during my agony! How many consecrated souls are still sleeping while my Church is persecuted and suffering!

I asked him : "What do you want, Jesus?" He answered :

Love and sacrifice. People say to me, in words : All for you, my God! But, in practice, they very often act : all for self...

Then he repeated his earlier promise :

I entrust great secrets to souls who are willing to sympathize with me in my sufferings and console me in my agony.

XXXV
RELIGIOUS LIFE
13 April - 2 May 1927

Longing. — Tenderness of the Eucharistic Heart. — Holy Week. — Consecrated souls. — Priestly souls. — Saturday offered for priests. — I looked for some to console me and found none. — Thursday offered for consecrated souls.

13 April. Wednesday. Yesterday was a day of struggle. I found everything wearisome. I felt that only God could satisfy me. Everything created left me absolutely empty.

In the afternoon, I felt an intense longing for heaven. And yet, Our Lord keeps me there all the time, in the Heart of the lovable Trinity ; all the same, I was longing for God, so impatient am I to set eyes on my Jesus! I kept saying : "Let me live like this for a hundred years, if that is what you wish ; I want only what gives you most pleasure, but I am ever longing for you..."

Shortly after five o'clock, at the beginning of spiritual reading, a great peace invaded me. I recognised my divine Master. He said to me :

I want you to experience the feelings of my Heart after my triumphal entry into Jerusalem — as today — two days before the institution of my Eucharist and before the sufferings of my Passion. Let me shower you with them. At that time, my Heart was filled with tenderness... It cost my human Heart a great deal to leave my apostles ; the best of fathers, I was about to disappear from the sight of my beloved children. My little Own Self, it costs me a great deal, too, to leave you yearning for me, but you know that I have you in my Heart.

Last night, for this morning's meditation, he gave me the same subject, that is "what his Heart felt before the institution of the holy Eucharist and at the approach of his Passion".

Today, Wednesday, I am filled with his infinite tenderness, with his immense desire to give himself to souls as their food. His Eucharistic Heart communicates to me something of his unimaginable love. All the time, I can hear the divinity saying with a sigh : *I have longed to eat this Passover with you before I suffer!*

He was eager on Holy Thursday, yes, he was eager at the Last Supper to conceal himself whole and entire under the appearance of a fragile piece of bread and to take up his abode in human hearts. Since that moment, to each soul he invites to his table, at each Communion, the Eucharistic Heart says again with the same effusive love he had for his apostles : *I have longed to eat this Passover with you before I suffer!* He is always eager to give himself...

14 April. Holy Thursday. Last night, for this morning's meditation, Our Lord gave me as my subject : "the love and tenderness of his Eucharistic Heart". Shortly afterwards, he said to me :

> My Eucharistic Heart loves to confide in souls, it is like a great need. But I find few pure souls who understand this. To be the confidante of my intimate secrets, a soul must be **very pure**, constantly intent on **thinking of** and **acting for me alone**. I wish I could find many pure souls.

This morning, at the beginning of my meditation, before Communion, I tasted a sweet union with him. At the moment of Communion, nothing more! And his chalice? On Holy Thursday! Nothing. I renewed my vows and, enumerating the details of the vow of total perfection, said, "I vow to sacrifice myself and to be a victim." At these words, the Eucharistic Heart presented me with his sacred cup, reminding me that, especially today and tomorrow, I had to live in union with him, as oblation and sacrifice. In all this, there was an element of unaccustomed tenderness that I did not understand, yet I was filled with divine sweetness. He said to me :

Today, I am giving you, I am communicating to your nothingness, the **thought** of my **Eucharistic Heart**. My Heart is continually thinking of uniting souls to itself through the Eucharist, as it is itself united with my Father through love, in perfect unity and charity.

Father, may they be one in us, as you are in me and I am in you. That, he conti nued, is the prayer which best expresses the thought of my Eucharistic Heart. Keep my thought, then, and, in me and through me, say my prayer.

Then he added :

I am entrusting my secrets to you as I did to John, my beloved, at the Last Supper.

15 April. Good Friday. My good Master is giving me a share in the feelings of "tenderness experienced by his Heart during his Passion and on the cross". The tenderness of the Heart of Jesus! Oh! I never understood it until yesterday and today. Human words can convey nothing of it. The tender feelings of the heart of the best of mothers can in no way be compared with it. The Heart of Jesus is an abyss of tenderness... that is all I can say, because I have no words with which to express what I now understand.

16 April. Holy Saturday. This morning, no Communion for the sick who could not go down to the main chapel. How I hungered for my Jesus. Two days without his Host! But he consoled me. At the time of Communion, he said to me :

Here is my host of love. I am giving it to you. Keep my presence and my thought until you receive my host sacramentally tomorrow.

O bliss! From that moment, I desired nothing more. Jesus is there, I am in possession of him, and I have his thought.

22 April. Friday. Yesterday morning, Our Lord gave me his chalice at the time of Communion. During my thanksgiving, he said to me, or rather his sacred Heart said to me, for when Jesus speaks, it is always the voice of his Heart that I hear :

Let me inundate you once again with my tenderness. Today and tomorrow, I am giving you my thought of God. I want you to console me in particular in the name of consecrated souls. I always want you to console me without ceasing in the name of all humanity ; but, more particularly today, I want you to do so in the name of consecrated souls.

I asked him : "In what way, my Jesus?" He answered :

Always in the same way : **love and sacrifice** ; by constant attention to my good pleasure. I have given you my loving thought of my Father, guard it well. I want you to have some appreciation of the infinite tenderness my Heart feels for consecrated souls.

Then he enlightened me regarding his infinite tenderness... the inexpressible tenderness he feels for the souls he has chosen.

This morning, Friday, he told me about the "sorrow of his agonizing Heart" at the sight of the insensitiveness of consecrated souls, then he added :

My agonizing Heart, suffered much more from the insensitiveness of consecrated souls than from the sins of the worldly, because I enlighten consecrated souls to such an extent and lavish so much love on them!

23 April. Saturday. Last night, the Heart of Jesus opened up its intimate depths to me, like a person who has suffered much and finds comfort in confiding his hidden sorrows to another. He was sad ; it was a sadness that, once again, I do not know how to explain. For half an hour he spoke to me of priestly souls, and of his priests. Among other confidences, he said :

My priests should be replicas of myself. During the agony, my Heart shed tears of blood over a certain number of priests. Several of them are eloquent and learned, humanly speaking, but they lack the most basic knowledge ; that of holiness. They are united to me through sanctifying grace, but they do not live in sufficient intimacy with me through self-denial and unalloyed love.

And in a pleading tone, he added :

O my little Bride, comfort me! I know you love me.

This morning, during my thanksgiving after Communion as well as during my meditation, he continued along the same lines :

My priests, he said, my priests, oh! how I love them! And there are many who love me so little...! If, during the agony, my Heart shed tears of blood for them, it is not simply because they were separated from me through the loss of sanctifying grace, but because they did not live sufficiently in intimate union with me. I call them to be other Christs. **To be replicas of me** : that is their vocation. Many of them are my consolation, my glory, a credit to me. But several, alas! are a cause of sadness... Will you, my little Bride, through my most blessed Mother, offer me this day for priests? Will you in the same way offer me every Saturday? That is to say, through my divine Mother, love me, pray, deny yourself, sacrifice yourself for my priests?

I responded eagerly to the request of my tender Master. I am still profoundly moved by the dependence he chose to convey in the words *Will you?* After all the blessings he has given me, he still respects my freedom! Oh! How infinite is the tenderness of God, shown in his condescension towards poor human nothingness!

The Heart of Jesus continued :

My priests govern the entire religious society. If they were truly holy, the mere sight of them, anywhere at all, in church, in the street or elsewhere, would remind people of me ; they would draw souls to me ; meeting them, people would think : there is another Christ passing by. The Evil One is more afraid of a single soul in whom I can act freely than of a whole army of tepid, indifferent souls in whom my action is paralysed, because in the former I act with power, while I have no choice but to abandon the latter to their weakness.

Finally, he asked me :

Do you want my thought?[1]

"Oh yes, my Jesus", I answered, "you know well that I do."

I will give it to you, he said ; keep it for my priests.

28 April. Thursday. From yesterday morning until this morning, the Heart of Jesus absorbed me, in deep retreat, in preparation for the confidences of today and tomorrow.

This morning, he gave me his precious chalice at the moment of my Communion. After a few moments of darkness and aridity, his Heart communicated to me his "feelings in the garden of the agony, at the sight of consecrated souls".

He showed me thousands of consecrated souls assembled in his presence. Very many of them were heedless of their divine Bridegroom ; a small number, just a few, easy to count, kept their gaze fixed continually on him. He said to me :

> Look at all these souls. You see how very few of them remain totally abandoned to me! On the day of their profession, they give themselves without reserve, but then they take back fragments of themselves. When important things are concerned, in the principal points of the Rule, they do my will, but in little things, they have no concern for my good pleasure.
>
> Do you see these souls (showing me all those who paid no heed to him) : some are looking to the world, to see what is going on there ; others have their ears wide open to hear all kinds of news ; others speak at times of silence so as to make useless remarks or to criticise ; still others occupy their minds with vain thoughts of the

---

[1] The thought Our Lord offered and gave to Dina was not at all the remembrance of his presence. This remembrance, or this awareness of the presence of God, is continual in a fair number of fervent souls. The grace in question here is something quite different ; it was, as it were, the substitution of the faculty of thought belonging to God-made-man for her own. It was, it seems, an inspiration given to Dina so that she would think as he did, as if he were thinking in her, in her place.

past ; in their imagination, others make all sorts of plans for their own personal advantage ; others maintain countless, futile desires or keep a part of their own will for themselves, etc.

And I pass by... My Heart is begging for consolation, and all these souls, taken up with themselves or with the world, do not afford me any consolation. Can you understand now why my Heart uttered, with good reason, this complaint : *I looked for some to comfort me and I found none!* Come, he said, come over with me to this multitude of consecrated souls. (He led me to the left, into the crowd in front of him.) I am going to walk among them asking for consolation... You see, not one of them is thinking of me... I have come back without finding a single one to comfort me.

Certainly, there are some here (pointing to the small number of souls who constantly pay attention to him) who never leave me ; Oh! They are a comfort to me ; but there, on the left, not one...!

I am familiar with human weakness, I always forgive ; when souls turn back to me, I overlook their thoughtlessness, but that does not does not mean that my Heart has not felt wounded. I love consecrated souls so much! As soon as they come back to me, I smile on them because I love them with an infinite love, and my gaze is fixed on them continually.

My wish would be to grant them untold graces ; but lack of self-denial, of perfection, of love in quite small things, in the least significant actions, holds me back. They say to themselves : that is not worth troubling about and all the while they take no account of my good pleasure. Everything that is done for me with great love and attention to my desires, gives joy to my Heart.

Then again, they say : great graces are reserved for a few privileged souls. They are mistaken. All those I have chosen as my Brides, whom I call to consecrate themselves to me, are privileged souls. Their vocation is to be concerned constantly with me. What they call a privilege, or a number of privileges, in certain souls, is simply a reward for their constant attention to my presence and my action in them.

My little Bride, he said, comfort me. Will you, always through my most holy Mother, give me Thursday for consecrated souls?

"Yes, Jesus, as you wish", I answered.

Pray, suffer, love me, he continued, paying attention only to me. Consecrated souls : this includes priestly souls, my priests as well. Saturday will be very specially dedicated to my priests. And I am giving you my thought until Sunday. Soon I will give it to you permanently.

XXXVI
RELIGIOUS LIFE
2 May - 6 May 1927

The devil in action. — The agonizing Heart of Jesus and consecrated souls. — Pray and intercede! — Friday offered for all souls.

2 May. Monday. Last Friday was a day of darkness, except for several moments towards evening, when Our Lord repeated a few words he had said the day before.

The devil is multiplying his wiles. He is determined to try and make me miss my Communions, especially on Thursday and Friday. In an attempt to make me believe that I am not in the state of grace, he acts like someone laying a cloak on another person's shoulders and saying : "You made this cloak", when this is not true. In the same way, the devil tries to attribute mortal sins to my soul, saying : "You committed them." Oh! What trickery there is in his lies! But with the grace of my divine Master, who always sustains me in the battle, I recognize the snares of the enemy.

Last Thursday evening, and especially on Friday, the devil adopted another tactic : he tried to behave in the same way as Our Lord. When Jesus speaks to my soul, his language is divine, devoid of human words ; that means he does not articulate a single word, and I speak to him in the same way, altogether interiorly. Thus the devil does not know what is happening. But when, through obedience, I write my *Canticle of Thanksgiving*, perhaps Satan does not fail to follow my pencil with an attentive and jealous eye.

On Thursday afternoon, I wrote down the morning's divine communications. On Thursday evening, a sudden thought distracted me from thinking of my good Master, advising me with agitation to offer Friday to the Heart of Jesus for souls called to the religious life, that is, for vocations. Not recognising Our Lord's voice, I gave him a gently questioning look and realised that the suggestion did not come from him. The distracting thought vanished. But on Friday morning, during my thanksgiving after Communion, this same thought recurred insistently, accompanied by anxiety and agitation. Jesus was silent, he was leaving me in darkness ; however, I knew he was there, and I was in possession of his divine thought, full of peace, calm and sweetness. I turned to my tender Saviour, begging him to enlighten me. Immediately, a gentle, peaceful, interior light drew my attention to the insistence, the agitation, the abruptness that accompanied the distracting thought and, at this infallible sign, I realised that it was a temptation from the evil spirit.

In reality, what a difference there is between the working of Our Lord and that of the dark angel! Jesus, peace ; the devil, nothing but trouble. Jesus is freedom ; *Will you?* ; the devil, compulsion : *Then, offer yourself!*

"O my divine Master, O Mary, my tender Mother, thank you! Keep me from being caught in the enemy's ambushes. Hide me ever more deeply in yourselves. In everything, I seek only the greater glory of God."

5 May. Thursday. Yesterday evening, Our Lord gave me for the subject of this morning's meditation "the agonizing Heart of Jesus and his vision of consecrated souls". First point : *I looked for someone to comfort me and found no one!* Second point : *In the Garden of Agony, my Heart shed tears of blood over many consecrated souls.*

This morning, he gave me his chalice at the moment of Communion. Then, plunging me into the very depths of his agonizing Heart, he showed me the multitude of consecrated souls, just as he saw it himself in Gethsemane. With his divine eyes, I saw all these chosen souls ; I could see into an limitless, distant future, to the end of time. The Heart of Jesus said to me :

Look closely at all these consecrated souls. Most of them are living in union with me ; the others, alas, are no longer in the state of grace and have wandered away from me. I am going to let you see my life in them, or my separation from them. When I am united with a soul, I more or less reproduce myself in it. Look at this soul.

He pointed to one among them.

You can recognise me there ; but, you see, my hands are tied by threads. This soul loves me, but remains attached to material goods which bind my hands and prevent me from giving great graces.

Look at this other one. Here, I am more luminous and loved more. But, look at my Heart, it is pierced by tiny thorns : these are the small things that it refuses and which prevent me from giving it all the treasures of my Heart.

Consider this one. You can barely see me. My feet and hands are bound with cords ; thorns penetrate my Heart, pressing in upon it and making it bleed. This is a lukewarm soul. Here, my action is paralysed and the soul is very close to leaving me.

And then look here. Do not be afraid, you are with me. This is a soul that has wandered away from me, having lost the state of grace. This is the soul of a priest. I am no longer living there but my image remains imprinted on it ; it is a baptised soul, a consecrated soul. Look at the evil one who is taking possession of my image, encompassing it with iron chains ; he is making a great din, dancing around, sneering ; he is playing with my image and tyrannizing this soul, making it miserable, dragging it right and left ; he is turning it into his prey. You can win it over for me, snatch it from the demon, in union with my most holy Mother, through love and sacrifice. Alas! There are several consecrated souls who fall under the control of the demon! Look there, over there, in the distance... And finally, look at this one.

From the left where he had taken me last of all, he drew me over to the right. Seeing this soul, I said to my divine Master : "O my Jesus, how beautiful you are!" To the extent that I had been terrified by the soul delivered into the hands of the demon, now I was seized with admiration. Jesus was radiant, full of grace and light. After this initial outburst of admiration, I became speechless under the charm of his beauty. He went on :

You see I am totally radiant : this is a soul who refuses me nothing. You can no longer see anything of the soul itself, it is annihilated in me and I have substituted myself for it. I can freely bestow on it all the treasures of my Heart. I make it happy, and it consoles me.

After several moments, he added :

I have let you see five major groups of consecrated souls. This does not prevent each soul from having its own special character, but according to their union with me or their separation from me, they belong to one or other of these major groupings.

Look once more at those in whom my hands are bound. I shine out to some extent around them ; through them, I do a little good to the souls that surround them. Look at those in whom my Heart is pierced with quite tiny thorns. My hands are free ; they love me more, refusing me only quite small things. I shine out more clearly in them, and I do more good, at a greater distance.

Finally, look at the souls that are completely abandoned to me and who refuse me nothing. My rays reach out to all the other souls, far away, very far away ; they reach out even to souls in the grip of the devil. Look, I am going to let my rays fall on the soul of the priest you considered a moment ago. This priest is going to let himself be touched by my grace, he will fall on his knees and I will forgive him.

Our Lord left me with these reflections. The time of my prayer, which had followed my thanksgiving after Communion was over except for the five minutes devoted to an examination of my meditation. I was deeply moved. At every moment of this day, there has recurred to me the appeal of my tender Master : *For consecrated souls!*

This morning, after I had renewed my fourth vow, when I said : "My God, I vow to concentrate on thinking only of you", Our Lord answered gently :

I give you my thought until Sunday.

"O infinite Love, who will ever understand you!"

6 May.   First Friday of the month.   Since yesterday, while thinking over the first category of souls that my divine Master showed me, the souls in whom his hands were tied, I found it strange that he had not spoken of his Heart while, in the second category comprising souls who loved him more, his Heart was wounded by thorns. This morning, I asked him to explain, if he would. He answered :

> When one's hands are bound like those of a prisoner, do you think one's heart can be at ease?

I realised that this was clearly impossible. He added :

> When my hands are bound in a soul because it is attached to something other than me, you can understand that my Heart is wounded.

This morning, he continued to enlighten me about yesterday's subject and said to me :

> I am letting you see the whole multitude of consecrated souls, to the end of time, so that you will understand how even one soul completely given over to me can radiate on all the other souls. You can see that, through it, my rays reach out into the distance, far into the distance, to the furthest end, meaning that I am doing good until the end of time.
>
> I call upon all consecrated souls to abandon themselves totally to me, to let themselves be filled by me, to let me act freely in them and to shine through them as I will. I call upon all of them. And you see how few there are who do not refuse me anything. In all this multitude, in each soul, nothing human should be visible, only me, me alone. When my heavenly Father looks upon consecrated souls, he should recognize and see only me in each one of them. Alas! This is far from being the case!
>
> My little Bride, listen... listen well... **If all consecrated souls refused me nothing**, if they allowed me to act freely in them all the time, **all other souls would be saved**. Yes, all other souls would be

saved. Seeing only me, his well-beloved Son, in consecrated souls, hearing only my divine voice, my heavenly Father could not refuse them anything. Through the voice of consecrated souls, I would pray and implore my heavenly Father to save and sanctify all other souls according to his holy will, and he could not refuse me. If I can refuse nothing in response to my most holy Mother's prayer, with still more reason can my heavenly Father refuse nothing in response to my pleading.

My little Bride, if I see so many souls falling into hell, it is without doubt because they want it, but it is also because conse-crated souls abuse of my graces. Pray and intercede, through my most holy Mother and through my divine Heart, pray and intercede with my heavenly Father to save and sanctify all souls. Pray to him and beg him to sanctify all consecrated souls. My Heart loves each soul infinitely. During my human life on earth, I could do no more for the salvation and sanctification of souls ; and since that time, I have wished to continue the work of redemption through my life in souls. Pray and intercede with my divine Father. Intercede, that means praying earnestly, praying untiringly, praying with the cer-tainty of being given what you are asking. Pray and intercede!

My little Own Self, will you, each Friday, through my most holy Mother and through my divine Heart, pray and intercede with my heavenly Father for the salvation and sanctification of all souls in accordance with his holy will?

"O, yes, my Jesus!" I answered, "just as you wish." He went on :

Make Friday a day of intercession. Pray and intercede!

I can not describe the passion, the astonishment, the suffe-ring that these words produced in me. And since then, every morning, I continually hear my divine Substitute pleading : *Pray and intercede!*

XXXVII
RELIGIOUS LIFE
6 May - 5 August 1927

The influence of consecrated souls. — The state of perpetual immolation. — How to suffer in silence. — The prayer of the Heart of Jesus. — Annual retreat.

12 May. Thursday. Last night, Our Lord again gave me as the subject of this morning's meditation : "his agonizing Heart and consecrated souls", making two main points in particular :

> 1° Do not refuse me anything, my little Bride ; 2° Through my divine Heart, your power is infinite for the salvation and sanctification of souls.

He has made this last consideration the theme of almost all my meditations since the beginning of the week.

This morning, he gave me his sacred chalice immediately after I had received Communion. Without speaking to me, he granted me the grace of seeing once more the tableaux of last Thursday and Friday. At the end of my thanksgiving, he said :

> Do you wish to have my thought?

Full of gratitude, I answered in the affirmative. He continued :

> I am giving you the thought of my Heart, my continual thought of God.

He added :

> Do you want me to give you today a day of suffering for consecrated souls?

I accepted this great favour with joy and love. I had not been well since midnight. Oh! How good it is to be taken up only with the concerns of God!

13 May. Friday. Last night, towards the end of my hour of guard, Our Lord gave me as subject of contemplation "his agonizing Heart and his vision of all souls". He showed me the influence consecrated souls have when he himself radiates through them, and said :

> Through my divine Heart, your power is infinite ; you have a great part to play in the salvation and sanctification of all souls both now and in the future.

This morning, during my thanksgiving after Communion, he pursued the same subject :

> In Gethsemane, he said, my agonizing Heart saw the multitude of other souls, in addition to consecrated souls. Look at them, stretching far out into the distance, to the end of time, look as far as the last soul to be created. Now, consider the influence of consecrated souls through whom I can shine out on all the souls of the world.

> In consecrated souls in whom my hands are bound by threads, in whom consequently my Heart is wounded, my rays reach only some souls living in the world at the same time. In consecrated souls who refuse me only small things, you can see that my rays reach many other souls in the world and extend further. In consecrated souls that have abandoned themselves totally to me, in whom I can act freely, see how my rays reach all souls, even to the end of time.

> Because of the graces and enlightenment that I am giving you, you have a great share in the sanctification of all souls, present and future.

Until this time, I had seen all created souls, without any distinction between the past, the present and the future, just as the Heart of Jesus saw them, since everything is present to him. Now, he made a distinction, giving me a general view of souls who, in relation to me, lived in the past, are now living or will live in the future. Then he went on :

You can see all these souls belonging to the present and the future. They all expect great graces from your faithfulness in letting me act freely in you. You have a great part to play in the salvation and sanctification of each one. I have given you all the treasures of my Heart ; through my most holy Mother, give them to all these souls. Consider how I am treated in them. There are certainly some very devout souls through whom I radiate, but you can see that there are only a few.

Consider the others. You will note that I am bound hand and foot with cords and that my Heart is wounded, or else you can see that the devil has taken my place.

I saw very many souls in whom the demon reigned supreme. and this sight was so repulsive that I scarcely looked.

Do not be afraid, my divine Master said, simply look. Pray and intercede with my heavenly Father. Love me and suffer in silence.

19 May. This morning, Our Lord gave me his chalice at the moment of Communion, and his thought immediately afterwards. He again showed me the earlier tableaux, repeated some of the remarks that I have already written down and added :

I am giving you my uninterrupted thought. I want your life now to be completely otherworldly, as regards your thought and your affections. Let me remain in you, in a state of perpetual oblation and immolation. Let me remain in you, in a state of continual sacrifice. Beg my heavenly Father to let my most holy Mother bestow upon souls the treasures of my Heart. My Heart is so overflowing with love for each one of these souls that it can no longer contain the streams of grace that I would wish to bestow on them ; but the majority of souls will have nothing to do with my love...

After a fervent prayer that I offered just as the Heart of Jesus inspired me, he then said to me :

In you, I want to restrain the avenging arm of my Father's justice and allow my most holy Mother to pour out on souls the treasures of love contained in my Heart. I want to be sure that my mercy triumphs. I want to give to souls graces of repentance, to forgive them and to restore them to friendship with their God.

27 May. Friday. Yesterday morning, the same customary grace from Our Lord, at the moment of Communion. The Heart of Jesus allows me to contemplate the subjects of recent weeks and meditate on what he has been saying. For several days, I have been adding certain words to the offering I make of my divine Master to his heavenly Father ; each time, I say : "Eternal Father, through the Hearts of Jesus and Mary and through your Spirit of love, I offer you the sacred Wounds of my Jesus, or I offer you the Eucharistic Heart of Jesus, etc., etc."

4 June. Saturday. The day before yesterday, Thursday morning, at the moment of Communion, the customary grace of the divine chalice. For the subject of my meditation on both days, Thursday and Friday : "The oblation and immolation of the agonizing Heart of Jesus to satisfy the justice of his Father".

18 June. Saturday. Not a single word from my divine Master on Thursday and Friday of last week and this week, except that, through an intimate light, he gave me again for my meditation "the immolation of the agonizing Heart". He made me spend the first four days of the week, from Sunday on, preparing seriously for the last three days.

The assaults of the devil are violent. This morning, Our Lord consoled me saying that, while he is leaving me in a state of humiliation and struggle, as if abandoned to my own weakness, he is wresting souls from the devil, granting them graces of pardon and purity and saving them.

I am undertaking today a completely new life, a life of consuming love. This is a real conversion that the grace of God is bringing about in me. Less than ever, can I find words in which to express the working of the Most Holy Trinity in my being, annihilated in his infinite Heart.

24 June. Friday. My good Master gave me his chalice on Wednesday evening (the day before yesterday), at six, while I was in the chapel. My joy and gratitude were profound. He gave it to me early because the feast of his Sacred Heart falls this week, and it seemed his love could not wait until tomorrow.

Since last night, and even more today, the Heart of Jesus is allowing me to savour something of "his infinite tenderness" as he did several weeks ago. The feast of the Sacred Heart is not kept until tomorrow, because today is St John the Baptist, our national festival.

26 June. Sunday. Because of the feast of his divine Heart, Our Lord left me with his chalice and his thought until last night. This morning, he withdrew his chalice. Yesterday morning, given this new favour of the Heart of my Jesus in honour of his feast, I did not know how to thank him. I thought of increasing, if possible, the number of times I offered him to his heavenly Father. During the day, I offered him a thousand times, without any strain and without omitting any other prayer or any task. That may seem absurd, but it is the folly of love ; it is nothing compared to the excessive love of the Saviour who went as far as the folly of the cross and the folly of the host.

1 July. Friday. Yesterday morning, Our Lord gave me his chalice but he remained profoundly silent.

2 July. Saturday. Through his very silence, Jesus is teaching me to suffer in silence, to accept everything, to bear everything with the meekness of his Heart. Oh! What beautiful wisdom that is! "Thank you, my God."

10 July. Sunday. The grace of the chalice of the Heart of Jesus in agony and that of his thought are now two such regular graces on Thursdays and Fridays that I will not refer to them any more. But if it should please my good Master to take them from me I will mention it.

The thirst to be immolated and the desire to console the Heart of Jesus still haunt me with increasing intensity. On Thursday morning, more lovingly than ever it seemed, I offered myself once more to the eternal Father, through Our Lord and in him, as a victim, in reparation for all the sins of souls throughout the centuries, from the beginning of the world to its end, as if I were the only soul capable of loving God.

On Friday morning, I felt so united with the agonizing Heart of Jesus that not only was I associated with his immolation but, like him and to the same extent, I was commissioned to make reparation for all the crimes, all the sins, all the voluntary abuses of grace. With him, I felt I was laden and covered with all sins, past, present and future. At the same time, he communicated to me his infinite power of expiation with regard to his Father.

While I was being taken over by the action of my sovereign Master, he himself interceded with his divine Father :

> Father, he said, take pity on the many souls who offend you, *forgive them, for they do not know what they are doing.* Satisfy your justice in me. Strike me, but spare these guilty souls. Let my Heart pour out on them my graces of repentance and conversion. O Father, save them.

Jesus also prayed for his Church and for his priests. I find it impossible to convey, even very imperfectly, the graciousness and ardour of the prayer of Jesus. In these words alone : O Father, there was an unutterable tone of infinite confidence, power and love!

5 August. Friday. Yesterday morning, Our Lord allowed me to explore new depths in the Heart of the Most Blessed Trinity. For several days, The working of Jesus in my soul has been so heavenly that it is totally beyond my poor means of expression. Yesterday evening, I began to follow the exercises of the annual retreat. I feel so taken over by God that it is as if I were living in him the life of eternal bliss enjoyed by the angels and the blessed. This morning, Our Lord said to me :

> I want your retreat to be devoted to the great concerns of my glory. As you know, I have given you my Heart, do with it whatever you will ; do whatever you will with all my treasures for the sake of souls. During this retreat, continued my good Master, look and see : the arm of justice of my Father is upheld, it has been checked and my mercy is going to pour out on souls the graces of my Heart.

At these words, I seemed to see rivers of grace flowing from the Heart of Jesus.

XXXVIII
RELIGIOUS LIFE
5 August - 15 August 1927

In the infinite confines of the Most Blessed Trinity. — Struggles. — A vision of my actions. — Absorption into the divine. — Confirmation in the permanent state of humiliation and suffering.

5 August. Friday evening. Once again this morning, Our Lord said to me :

> Come into **the infinite gardens of the Most Blessed Trinity** where only a few privileged souls can enter.

Then, my good Master took me into an infinite expanse where the light is so brilliant that I have been dazzled ever since that moment. Since then, too, I have been united with the Most Blessed Trinity in a new and far more intimate way. I am united with each one of the divine Persons individually, with the Father, the Son and the Spirit, and at the same time immersed and annihilated in the unity of God. And, turning towards me, Jesus added :

> Silence and renunciation, my little Own Self, refuse me absolutely nothing...

6 August. Saturday evening. Today has been a day of humiliating temptations and very painful struggles. Our Lord, in his goodness, is keeping me *in the infinite gardens of the Most Blessed Trinity*, but he is making me go through a period of purification before opening my eyes to this light which dazzles me. Today, my good Master has asked me for several acts of

humility and several exterior humiliations, apart from the interior humiliations to which I am subjected. How I thank him! Everything good comes from him and belongs to him, and I am nothing but weakness and sin.

7 August. Sunday. Yesterday's storm lasted until this morning. At the moment I received Communion this morning, Our Lord restored calm to my soul, and with what authority! "Silence!" Jesus said, and at once the evil spirit's suggestions ceased. A little later, during the morning, the battle began again. The devil tried to make me lose confidence in the mercy of God. But at midday, after I had once more suffered a humiliation, Our Lord restored me to calm, in the goodness and tenderness of his Heart.

The sense of my weakness and of my poverty arouses my love. I have never loved God as much as I do today. I can understand how expiatory love in the hearts of those who undergo a conversion can exceed in intensity the innocent love of pure souls. I can understand how a repentant Mary Magdalene could, through the ardour of her love, reach such heights of sanctity. I can understand, too, that it is sometimes salutary to commit certain faults — impulsive rather than deliberate, it is true, but still humiliating to the will — because then our poor nature, deploring its weakness, leans more lovingly and trustfully on God, its only strength. I love my God infinitely, through the Heart of Jesus, and I desire to love him infinitely more. The infinitude of my desires is increasing infinitely.

8 August. Monday. Since last night, I am no longer at peace, except in my will. So that means more struggle.

Our Lord continues to keep me *in the infinite regions* of the Most Blessed Trinity. This morning, he said to me :

> Here, everything is total self-denial, and everything is absolute joy in God alone.

At the same time, he gave me to understand that this meant complete self-forgetfulness and a constant, wholehearted seeking after God alone, in everything ; in other words, perfect purity of intention. Then, in the presence of the infinite holiness of the adorable Trinity and in the divine light of eternity, I saw my actions...! Oh! My poor actions were tainted with self-love, vanity, hidden self-seeking! Seeing the holiness of my God, I would have hurled myself into the flames of purgatory, so as to purify my numerous imperfections. I realised how this infinite Holiness could easily discern blemishes in his angels. And I saw my poor actions... and Our Lord kept me there...

In spite of my confusion and shame, I needed to acknowledge my misery ; I said to my good Master : "My Jesus, I am very guilty!" He answered :

> Do not look at yourself. Trust in my mercy. It is precisely because you are weak and helpless that I have chosen you.

I turned my eyes to Jesus, my divine Saviour, and kept them fixed on him, resolved — needless to say — to act for God alone.

10 August. Wednesday. Last night, I sensed the maternal protection of the Blessed Virgin in quite a special way. My heavenly Mother seemed to be preparing me for some divine favour, and I was, as it were, enfolded in her immaculate cloak. My guardian angel also seemed to be covering me with his most pure wing.

This morning, from the beginning of my prayers, Our Lord has been asking me for the most complete silence. Absolute interior silence, the silencing of all my faculties, of my imagination and every desire. Whenever the slightest disturbing thought threatened to distract me, my divine Master would repeat tenderly :

Silence!

Since yesterday, I have also felt that Our Lord was drawing me closer to the Most Blessed Trinity. Yet, I was still in his adorable Heart but, at this very centre, there exists an expanse, infinite as the infinite Being himself. This morning, at the beginning of my first meditation, still in the presence of the Most Blessed Trinity, of the three distinct Persons of the Unity, near to it and *in its infinite regions*, I was like a canvas, absolutely still, waiting for Our Lord to act ; Jesus repeated :

Silence...! Silence...!

and with his sacred hand, with a fine paintbrush, he worked at reproducing his divine traits in me. At one moment, the Most Blessed Trinity drew me gently towards it then, with unspeakable graciousness, it absorbed me entirely, or rather, it absorbed Jesus in me. I was absorbed by my God into an indescribable union and intimacy with each of the three divine Persons.

Submerged in the most profound gratitude and in the consciousness of my unworthiness, together with the Blessed Virgin, for this good Mother never leaves me, I recited the *Magnificat* slowly, not articulating the words but in a silence significant of eternity. At the end of my meditation, Jesus said :

Silence, in gratitude and humility!

Since this favour, the Most Blessed Trinity has kept me absorbed in its divinity, at depths which are new to me.

11 August. Thursday. This morning, during holy Mass, in my abode of absorption in the divinity, Our Lord, having taken my place, offered himself and consequently offered me to the Most Blessed Trinity as a host and chalice, immolated. During my meditation, my good Master said to me :

Here is the centre of Life. Everything contributes to the glory of God. Your mission as victim is becoming more and more urgent. I have brought you into this divine Abode, my little Own Self, for the greater glory of my Father and the benefit of souls.

The state in which I find myself is a state of continual self-denial, uninterrupted self-forgetfulness. This is nothing new, but

Our Lord is, I would say, intensifying this state in me. Oh! How good he is! Apart from the self-abnegation that is characteristic of religious life, my divine Master is inspiring me to make all kinds of little sacrifices. He is asking me these continually and, the more he asks, the more I desire to give him. Certainly, he is giving me countless sweet delights, yes, but in some way he allows me to savour them while combining them with mortification. My happiness is in him, in God alone. And how indescribable this happiness is!

12 August. Friday. This morning, at the beginning of my meditation, Our Lord asked me again for the most complete silence : silencing of the least desire, silencing of every thought other than unique attention to his action, an attention devoid, as far as I am concerned, of any knowledge of the immediate future. A feeling of fear possessed me but, in confidence, I counted on my divine Master and on the most Blessed Virgin. Our Lord said to me :

> My little Bride, the offering of myself in you is pleasing to my Father. Because of that, for his greater glory, for the glory of my divine Heart and for the salvation and sanctification of souls, I am confirming you in a permanent state of humiliation and suffering until the moment I open the eyes of your soul in a glorious eternity.

After the grace of perfect and constant union of my will with that of God, no personal, divine favour could cause me greater joy than this confirmation of the state of humiliation and suffering. I was unspeakably grateful. Through the most Blessed Virgin and the Spirit of love, that is, the Holy Spirit, I offered my divine Master ; I offered the Heart of my Jesus to the eternal Father in thanksgiving. And Our Lord said to me :

> My little Own Self, all for God alone!

At the same time, I was enlightened anew concerning the manner of acting in everything for God, solely for his joy alone.

XXXIX
RELIGIOUS LIFE
15 August 1927 - 2 January 1928

Wednesday for vocations to the religious life. — Tuesday for my Congregation. — In the enclosed garden of the Most Blessed Trinity.

29 August. My longing for God is becoming more intense. The torment of the Infinite overwhelms and strengthens me : it overwhelms me through the burning desire for perfect union with my God ; it strengthens me by the ever more determined will to please my sovereign Master in everything.

Our Lord said to me this morning during my meditation :

My little Bride, if only you knew how few consecrated souls take time to think of me! They are taken up with their own interests, with all kinds of trivialities, but they do not bother thinking of me. Each time that you concentrate your thoughts on me, I allow you to penetrate further into the Heart of the Most Blessed Trinity. At the same time, I give you the grace of my thought, I grant you, in return for your faithful correspondence with grace, the favour of entering more deeply into my Heart.

I answered Our Lord : "My dear Jesus, you do everything and yet you reward me!" And he added :

That is the generosity of God!

23 September. Friday. Since yesterday morning, the Heart of Jesus has been taking me with him on his campaign for souls. It is he who is doing all the work, and I offer him my longing, my small sufferings, I have only to let him have his way and to refuse him nothing. Certainly, he warned me yesterday morning that one cannot set out to conquer souls without experiencing great fatigue and difficulties, but with him and for him everything is so good!

4 October. Tuesday. Monthly retreat. At the end of my meditation this morning, Our Lord said to me :

> There are very few souls, even religious, who are willing to subsist on infinity during their earthly pilgrimage! Yet, only infinity can satisfy their heart!

8 November. Tuesday. For the last month, longing all the time, a longing for the eternal! This morning, Jesus said to me :

> Let me immerse you in humiliation while you concern yourself only with me. If you only knew how many consecrated souls refuse to submit to authority, because of their pride! Let me immerse you in humiliation and, during this time, I will give many consecrated souls the grace to leave their pride behind.

Oh! How these words of my good Master, while hurting me because they expressed a grievance, comforted me because for several weeks Our Lord's silence had overwhelmed me. So this morning, I took the opportunity to say to him : "My Jesus, when you speak to me, everything is sweetness and light ; but when you keep silence, everything is burdensome, and then I am always afraid I have caused you pain." Jesus answered :

> No, do not be afraid. I know your great weakness, and I take account only of your intention. I know very well that you love me.

12 November. Saturday. For several weeks, the Heart of Jesus has been offering me his sacred chalice on Wednesday evening, as and when he pleases, most often during Benediction of the Most Blessed Sacrament. This week, he gave it to me on Tuesday evening, saying :

> Console my agonizing Heart... for I am sad.

24 November. Thursday. This week, Our Lord offered me his chalice on Tuesday afternoon. This morning, through a deep feeling of peace, he forewarned me of his divine confidences. The devil tried to disturb me, making me fearful, apprehensive. But Jesus said to me :

> Do not worry, this fear is from the devil.

And there was perfect peace. Then, my divine Master made a request :

> Will you give me Wednesday for vocations to the priestly and religious life? Many vocations are being lost in the world : people are afraid of renunciation and sacrifice, they want to be free to enjoy (life) and are afraid of abandoning themselves to my love.

"Yes, my Jesus", I answered, "I want to do that. I want everything that you want."

> That is not all, Our Lord went on. Will you give me Tuesday for your Congregation?

"Oh, yes, my Jesus," I answered again. "I love my dear 'Jesus and Mary' so much!"

> And it is so dear to my Heart! replied my good Master in his turn. Pray much for your Congregation ; for you, this is a duty, and for me, it is a pleasure to pour out upon it my abundant graces.

I then asked Our Lord to explain about Wednesday. "My Jesus", I said, "do you want Wednesday to be only for the souls you call to the religious life and who are still in the world, or is it also for the souls who are already in novitiates?" He answered :

> I want your Wednesday to be for all who are called to the religious life, those still in the world and those already in novitiates, those called both now and in the future.

29 November. Tuesday. Last week, Our Lord left me the great grace of his chalice until Saturday evening. At about six o'clock, he gently took it from me. I would have liked to keep it... This morning, he gave me the same favour at the moment of my Communion. During my meditation, I asked my good Master : "My Jesus, you told me last week that it was a pleasure for you to pour out on my Congregation your abundant graces. If it should be your will, I would wish not only an abundance but the plenitude of your graces." Our Lord answered :

> If only one religious in a Congregation refuses me some small thing, that prevents me from pouring out on the entire Congregation the plenitude of my graces.

I went on : "My Jesus, please, do whatever you will in me and with me so as to make reparation, if need be, for what is wanting in my Congregation, so that you can pour out on 'Jesus and Mary' the plenitude of your graces." And he then said :

> That is my great desire... but pray and let me have my way.

19 December. Monday. Last week, two great and extremely tragic fires, which broke out within forty-eight hours of each other during the night, afflicted the Good Shepherd Sisters ; two of their houses were burnt down in Quebec, and the first fire resulted in numerous deaths. On Saturday evening, I was terrified by what had been said about them. On my last visit to the chapel, I told Our Lord that I was afraid. He kindly replied :

> Do not be afraid, remain secure in my Heart. I am going to protect you (referring to our convent in Sillery) from this scourge of fire.

I answered my good Master, saying that I wanted to believe what he said but, as I am always frightened of being under an illusion, asking for the grace of faith if this answer was really from him as I believed it to be. At that moment, I was still in possession of the grace of his divine chalice. Our Lord replied :

> As a guarantee of my word, I am going to leave you my chalice until tomorrow morning. Do not be afraid, I am going to send you other trials, but I will spare you that of fire. I need reparation to be made, and I choose religious souls. Offer me reparation.

In fact, my Jesus left me the favour of his chalice until the following morning, that is, until yesterday morning. At the moment of Communion, he took it from me. During my thanksgiving after Communion, he said :

> I need reparation. My Father's justice is enkindled. Offer me, offer my Father my merits and my Blood to appease his justice. How many Catholics make no attempt to do penance during this holy season of Advent! How many Catholics do not think of preparing for my coming at Christmas! Give me this day in a spirit of reparation. Offer it, too, in a spirit of thanksgiving, to thank my Father for all the gifts that he pours out on souls : for there are so many souls who do not even think of thanking him!

21 December. Wednesday. This morning, my Jesus pleaded with me :

Give me love!

A little later, he went on :

My Father's justice is being appeased. Give me love so that I can offer it to him.

"My Jesus", I answered, "through Mary, I am giving you all the infinite love of your Heart."

25 December. Christmas. Sunday. In preparation for the beautiful feast of Christmas, I had to offer Our Lord struggles and aridity. It was the same when I received Communion at Midnight Mass. Towards the end of the last Mass, my good Master broke his silence, telling me that he wanted to take me into **the enclosed garden of the Heart of the Most Blessed Trinity**. A great fear took possession of me. My wretchedness terrified me. It could be said that everything in me dreaded this grace. By an act of trust in the infinite mercy, I abandoned myself completely, with my worthlessness and my fears, to the will of God. The Most Blessed Virgin was there, for this power-ful Mother does not leave me. Our Lord then said to me :

Come into the enclosed garden of the Heart of the Most Blessed Trinity.

And he led me into these new and infinite depths. In this place of abode, my union with the adorable Trinity is even more intimate than *in its infinite gardens.* The atmosphere, too, seems to induce more silence and love. But, truly, I do not know how to express these divine phenomena or describe the nature of these heavenly dwelling places.

XL
RELIGIOUS LIFE
2 January - 7 March 1928

Sunday in a spirit of reparation. — Monday in thanksgiving. — Uninterrupted grace of the divine chalice. — In the sanctuary of the Most Blessed Trinity. — In the tabernacle of the Most Blessed Trinity.

2 January 1928. Monday. On Saturday, the day before yesterday, the last day of the year, during my adoration of the Blessed Sacrament at night, Our Lord said to me :

Will you give me Sunday in a spirit of reparation for all the sins of the world and for all the graces that are scorned and refused?

I promptly agreed to my good Master's request. Last night, Sunday, he said to me :

Will you give me Monday in thanksgiving for all the favours that my Father bestows on souls, both spiritual and temporal?

I gratefully answered that I would. To the Heart of Jesus, everything is present. His intentions embrace at one and the same time all that is spoken of in human terms as past, present and future.

Thus, my divine Master assigned a special intention to each day of the week. I will list his requests :

Sunday :	A day of reparation.
Monday :	A day of thanksgiving.
Tuesday :	For my Congregation.
Wednesday :	For vocations to religious life.
Thursday :	For consecrated souls.
Friday :	For all souls.
Saturday :	For priests.

To my great surprise, Jesus gave me the chalice of his agonizing Heart this morning, Monday, during Holy Mass.

3 January. Tuesday. This morning, Our Lord said to me :

Let me have my way in the *enclosed garden of the Infinite* ; there, I am going to prepare your entry *into the sanctuary of the adorable Trinity.*

4 January. Wednesday. I found it strange that, in the intentions for the week, Our Lord did not mention the souls in purgatory. This morning, I asked him : "My Jesus, in your intentions for each day of the week, you make no mention of the souls in purgatory?" My good Master answered :

The souls in purgatory have a share in each day of your week. Through the offering of indulgences that you make each morning, my divine Mother, according to her wise choice, applies the merits of your prayers and actions. You have no merits apart from my merits, and my merits are infinite, inexhaustible. The intentions for each day of the week do not deprive the souls in purgatory who are dear to me of anything. My merits can be applied to them as well as to the special intentions of each of your days.

18 January. Wednesday. Last week was one of violent struggle. The devil seemed to be intent on the same aim all the time, that of making me miss my Communions. At one of these moments of profound desolation, when I could find peace only in blind obedience, Our Lord consoled me, saying that this state, through which he was allowing me to pass, was a state of purification.

Last Saturday evening, my good Master allowed me to keep the precious grace of his chalice ; on Sunday, the feast of the Holy Name of Jesus in our Congregation, he left it with me for the entire day. Towards the end of the afternoon, during my private adoration before the Blessed Sacrament, he asked me :

Do you want to keep the grace of my chalice?

"My Jesus", I answered, "you know how much I desire it provided it is your will."

Love me, my little Bride, and keep it for ever, he said.

Indeed, all week this grace has been uninterrupted. On Monday morning, Jesus said to me :

You are letting me have my way in you. Well then, I am going to let you have your way in my Heart. All my infinite treasures are yours. Through my most holy Mother, give them to souls.

Offering Jesus to his divine Father has become a compelling duty for me. Through this offering, I feel I am all-powerful as regards the eternal Father, meaning that this power is that of Our Lord to whom his divine Father can not refuse anything. I always make this offering through the Hearts of Jesus and Mary and the Spirit of love. Then I understand that the Most Blessed Virgin is offering Our Lord to his eternal Father with one hand, and with the other hand is pouring out on souls the treasures of the Heart of Jesus. I ask the Blessed Virgin to make this offering for me unceasingly. As a result, when I look at this good Mother, I now see her — in keeping with the image I have just described, that is to say, in my place — offering her divine Son continually to the eternal Father and, as a result of this infinite offering, drawing from the Heart of Jesus with the other hand and pouring out on souls its inexhaustible treasures, in conformity with the intentions and desires of the sacred Heart. As for me, I no longer feel inspired to keep count of my daily offerings. Now that I have made it a habit, keeping count seems to me superfluous.

Our Lord has also given me to understand that just because, through this offering, fitting reparation, thanksgiving and intercession are given to his Father, it is a consolation for his Heart. His Heart ardently desires to distribute its treasures and to apply its infinite merits to souls. When a soul in whom he is living freely and divinely, offers him to his Father for his glory, the eternal Father, on the one hand, can refuse his well-beloved Son nothing and, on the other, is satisfied with this infinite offering.[1] So the Heart of Jesus, to whom his Father can refuse nothing, is able to pour out his riches on souls as he wills, with all his immense love, and that is his consolation.

---

[1] An infinite offering in the sense that it is the Infinite that is offered.

20 January. Friday. The Forty Hours devotion has been taking place in our chapel since yesterday morning. This morning, Our Lord asked me to strive after the most perfect exterior and interior recollection today. Then he said to me :

> The enclosed garden of the Most Adorable Trinity is vast, but my love can lead you through it quickly.

21 January. Saturday. (Final day of the Forty Hours.) Yesterday and early this morning, battles and aridity. At the same time, I knew that Jesus was preparing me to receive some new grace. During my meditation before the Blessed Sacrament, I told him again quite simply of my love then, after I said *I love you, my Jesus,* he replied :

> And I love you, too, my little Bride, my little Own Self.

One word from Jesus is light and joy!

My good Master again made me cast all my miseries, which I find ever greater, into his divine Heart, so that they are abandoned to his mercy and consumed in his love. The Most Blessed Virgin clothed me in her purity, my Guardian Angel covered me with his wing and, above all, the Holy Spirit hid me in its shadow. Jesus said to me :

> Come, my little Own Self. **Let me take you into the sanctuary of the Most Blessed Trinity.**

My canticle of thanksgiving consisted first of all in silence..., then in offering Our Lord. In this new divine dwelling, what strikes me, because I have a better grasp of them, is the power, the greatness, the immensity of God's attributes. The Infinite seems to me to be more and more infinite...

9 February. Thursday. From the time I entered the sanctuary of the Most Blessed Trinity until this morning, Our Lord has remained silent, and the assaults of the devil have been more and more aggressive and artful. Last night, towards six o'clock, a powerful grace of love invaded me. I realised that my divine Master was preparing me for one of his intimate communica-

tions. This grace persisted this morning, increasing in particular during Holy Mass. The devil was still trying, in vain, to disturb me. When the community were receiving Communion, I was completely taken over by the action of Our Lord. But in this kind of invasion by the divine, even though I have no doubt that the action comes from God, I totally distrust myself. So, this morning, I said to Our Lord : "No illusions! You know that I want none of them, my sweet Jesus." And breaking a silence that had lasted for almost three weeks, he answered :

> Do not be afraid, it is I. **My love desires to lead you into the tabernacle of our Most Blessed Trinity.** Come, it is I, do not be afraid.

Abandoning myself to my divine Master, and in the company of the Most Blessed Virgin and of my dear Guardian Angel, through a gentle and powerful grace, I found myself, as it were, in an immense furnace of delights. This latter expression, *an immense furnace of delights*, is very inadequate, but, I am growing more and more incapable of expressing in human words what I discover in the depths of the Infinite. My Jesus said to me :

> This is the heart of the divine fire, it is the centre of infinite Love. My little Own Self, consumed in me you must live only on pure love and immolation. And I have brought you here for the glory of my Father, for the consolation of my Heart and for the good of souls.

21 February. Tuesday (Shrove Tuesday). In the tabernacle of the Most Blessed Trinity, not only does the Blessed Virgin offer Our Lord unceasingly to the eternal Father in my name, but I offer my divine Master continually with her and through her. My offering is far more active than in the preceding dwellings where the love of my sovereign Substitute led me.

This morning, I could not reflect on the Heart of my Jesus without feeling sad, and I said to him : "My good Jesus, you are making me suffer!" (in the sense that I grieve when I look at you, because you seem to me to be suffering.) He answered :

I am forgotten! I am forgotten! It is not only people in the world who offend me, it is religious souls who forget me. They pray, they act with a kind of superficial devotion ; in their prayer and work, their love is lacking in depth. My Heart is so sensitive to the genuine love of souls who are consecrated to me! I am sensitive to their selfless love, to their love which in all things seeks only my interests!

I said, "My Jesus, today is Tuesday, it is the day dedicated to my Congregation. Will you grant me the grace that in my Congregation not a single religious soul, professed, novice or aspirant, will forget you? That each one will correspond perfectly to all your desires for her?"

In response to my request, Our Lord seemed like the most tender of fathers, like the infinitely kind Bridegroom who would have preferred not to answer rather than share a secret that gave him sorrow. At first, he kept silence. And his silence distressed me... Yet, I had a dread that in his confidence there would be a complaint... Eventually, he said :

In your Congregation, as in other religious Communities, there are souls who forget me ; but you have in my Heart everything you need to make up for their neglect.

24 February. Friday. This morning, I felt the same sadness as during the preceding days when I thought of Our Lord. I said to him : "Are you still suffering greatly, Jesus?" He answered :

I want love, I am seeking for it and I find so little! I am treated like Someone who is absent, when I am really present with and in souls!

Then, in a tone of infinite tenderness and supplication, he said to me :

Oh! My little Bride, let me give you all my love! I love and I need to give myself completely!

Then I felt crushed by an immense weight, the weight of this divine Love, and I found myself in a state of deep intimacy with my good Master, greater than I ever imagined. I thanked him, using one of those extravagant expressions of love that I often use with him and adding : "What I am saying to you, dear Jesus, makes no sense, but I know you understand me."

Then addressing the eternal Father, always through the Blessed Virgin and the Spirit of love, I said : "My God, it is Friday, the day dedicated to all souls. I beg you to let Mary, my good Mother, give all the treasures of the Heart of your divine Son to souls. I would so love **to exhaust my Jesus** for every soul, if this were possible!" Then, Our Lord said to me with indescribable tenderness :

> This prayer is so pleasing to me, my little Bride, that if possible I would exhaust myself completely for you.

XLI
RELIGIOUS LIFE
7 March - 3 April 1928

Jesus kept bound in many consecrated souls. — Perfect renunciation. — Felt presence of the evil spirit. — Thirsting to be immolated in the same way as Our Lord. — Martyrdom of the Heart of Jesus.

7 March. Wednesday. Again this morning, I could not think of Jesus without feeling sad. I said to him : "My Jesus, you are sad! Your Heart in particular seems to me to be sad!" He answered :

I am kept imprisoned in many consecrated souls. Sever my bonds.

"How?" I asked him.

With love and by offering my Heart, he said. In these consecrated souls, who are too attached to their own will, my divine will is bound, and so I can not act freely. Love me on their behalf ; and, by offering to my Father the infinite love of my Heart, you can obtain for many of these consecrated souls the grace to be detached from themselves and allow me to act freely in them.

8 March. Thursday. Jesus said only one thing this morning, but in these few words, his divine Heart traced out for me the whole programme for today :

Come with me, he said, to win for me perfect freedom in consecrated souls.

Yesterday, his divine complaint and his request : *Sever my bonds*, were for me a powerful grace of compassionate love. My duty, as well as my sole ambition, was to respond to his desire and console him, at the cost of every form of self-renunciation.

So yesterday, at the midday examen, I felt physically crushed by fatigue and sickness. And, as a result, my eyes quickly filled with tears. But were I to hold them back, would this not be one way of freeing my divine Master in some souls? I took on the challenge. It was very painful for me. I asked Our Lord for the grace to sever his bonds in as many souls as the number of tears I held back. Although that meant a great number, it was still too few to satisfy my love. Thinking only of the infinite mercy of God and the need to console the Heart of Jesus, and with that boldness inspired by boundless trust, I asked this good Master for the grace to set him free in the same number of consecrated souls as each of the tears that I was holding back could be divided into for his sake. It was a fierce struggle, but Our Lord granted me the grace to conquer my weakness. And, O joy! what is more, he let me know of the efficacy of my prayer (an efficacy due to his merits because of my union with him) and of the joy it gave him. His bonds had been severed in many consecrated souls, now he was free in them, and his Heart was consoled on that account.

I did not rest content with the joy of this consideration. I received this grace from Jesus with deep gratitude, but I was so haunted by the desire for him to be freed in the greatest possible number of souls that it scarcely eased the grief caused by his complaint in the morning.

16 March. Friday. Yesterday morning, Thursday, intimately united with the Heart of Jesus, I could not help being sad. I said to him : "My Jesus, I do not know why but I feel sad when I think of our Community." He answered :

> In all religious Communities, there are many consecrated souls who do not understand what perfect renunciation means.

I asked him : "My Jesus, will you grant me the grace to understand perfect renunciation, and help me to practise it, for the sake of all consecrated souls, especially those who do not understand it?"

> Offer to my Father, he said, the perfect renunciation of my Heart. There in my Heart, you have always all you need to make abundant amends for every failing and every negligence.

Then with unspeakable tenderness and profound sorrow, he added :

> Oh! My little Bride, even among consecrated souls, there are very few who understand the love of my Heart. I cannot give them the grace to understand it because they are not sufficiently detached from themselves. There are very few consecrated souls to whom my Heart can communicate itself as it desires!

At the end of my meditation, when it came to making a resolution for the day, I asked my good Master : "What do you want, Jesus?"

> Perfect renunciation, he answered.

I find this perfect renunciation in him ; only the renunciation of his Heart is divinely perfect. While giving him, then, my poor efforts, united to his love and his merits I should, in response to his request, offer the perfect renunciation of his Heart.

18 March. Sunday. During the week that has just come to an end, the attacks of the Evil One have been very aggressive. On Friday evening, before falling asleep, I could feel the presence of the evil spirit. He was on my left, tormenting me like someone actually present. At the names of Jesus and Mary, he fled, but immediately tried to return. I begged Our Lord to keep me well hidden in his Heart. Sustained by divine grace, I defended myself with the sign of the cross, and the demon ceased to make his contemptible presence felt.

21 March. Wednesday. Yesterday morning, **Our Lord made me penetrate to new depths in the tabernacle of the Most Blessed Trinity**. He had granted me a similar favour ten days ago. I am overwhelmed with Love, totally submerged in the Infinite...

I have a consuming thirst for immolation. I rely on Jesus alone in my unspeakable and burning desire for suffering, for I know nothing about suffering. More and more, to satisfy me, it would take all the sufferings, the humiliations and the anguish that my Jesus endured throughout the whole of his life on earth, from the Incarnation to Calvary ; and throughout his eucharistic life, from the institution of the adorable Sacrament at the Last Supper until the end of time. It is true that, since his Resurrection, Our Lord, in the Host, is no longer able to suffer ; but the insults, the contempt, the hatred, the neglect, the indifference and ingratitude affect him all the same and wound his Eucharistic Heart. Oh! Why can I not suffer all the torments inflicted on his sacred body, all the afflictions of his holy soul, even the martyrdom of fathomless love endured by his Heart! I love Jesus, and because I love him, I wish I could suffer for him, in union with him, as much as he willed to suffer for me. He loved me and still loves me to folly ; to respond to this excessive love, I want to love him infinitely, and if it pleases him to give me the grace, I will love him with his own Heart to an infinitely infinite degree.

Jesus loves souls so much that he would be ready to endure again and suffer all the humiliations and pain that he has already endured, as many times as there are and will be created souls. Like him, with the help of his divine strength, I would be ready to live his crucifying life and to undergo his cruel Passion as many times as there are and will be souls to save and sanctify. But, I repeat, all my desires to be immolated are dependent on his divine strength alone, on the infinite strength of Jesus. The more this divine Master consumes me in himself, the more I understand my absolute powerlessness and my constant frailty.

23 March. Friday. During the first few days of this week, I experienced at times something of the suffering love of the Heart of Jesus. Yesterday morning, Our Lord seemed to be weighed down by his love for souls. He remained silent, and his silence was a heavy burden for me. Towards the end of Mass he said :

Love me!

I replied "My Jesus, you are suffering yet you do not wish to complain." After a few minutes of silence, he repeated :

Love me!

His despondency overflowed onto me. A little later, during the last part of my meditation, I said to him : "My good Jesus, I am undergoing the suffering of your Heart." My sweet Master answered :

> Do you want to retain this intimate suffering of my Heart that I have been giving you at different times for several days?

I replied, "My Jesus, I would desire to retain it always if you wish to grant me this grace."

> Keep this suffering of my heart constantly, he continued. Use it to console me. I will increase it in proportion to the strength that, by my grace, I give you to bear it.

"O my Jesus", I said, "if it is your will, increase it until it makes me die of love!"

24 March. Saturday. Our Lord told me this morning.

> Offer to my Father, for my priests, the spirit of prayer of my Heart, my spirit of prayer, the perfect union of my Heart with him. This is what most of my priests lack, the spirit of prayer of intense interior life.

26 March. Monday. My divine Master kindly said to me this morning :

> The suffering of my Heart is the martyrdom of love ; and that, my little Bride, is what I am giving you.

"O my Jesus, how good you are," I answered : "I have been wanting the martyrdom of love for so long!"

XLII
RELIGIOUS LIFE
3 April - 31 May 1928

Fear of illusion. — The divine chalice and the real presence of Our Lord. — In the essence of the heart of the Divinity. — The reproduction of Jesus in souls. — Smiling interiorly and exteriorly.

3 April. Tuesday. For eight days, the devil has been trying desperately to torment me. Apart from his ordinary temptations and his subtle ruses to make me miss my Communions, he has been trying to make me believe that I have been under an illusion and thus to destroy my faith in Our Lord's action.

During this time, Jesus, my divine Master, has remained silent, causing me to experience something of the rigorous justice of his Father. On Thursday last, from the first moment of the day, when the devil was lying in wait for me with one of the most cunning of infernal snares, Our Lord took more complete possession of me through the suffering of his Heart, making me feel it more deeply. To give some idea of my state, I could think only of this expression : **my sorrow is like a flood of bitterness**. It lasted all day.

Yesterday afternoon, Monday, Jesus as Victim gave me a sign of his tenderness through a dart of light. This grace helped me to bear the burden of divine rigour and the struggle against the evil spirit. But this morning, Jesus spoke to me just when I was least expecting it, for my good Master had been so silent.

Remain united to my agonizing Heart, he said.

Oh! How gentle and powerful was this word! It consoled and strengthened me and has remained with me as renewed confirmation of my intimate union with the Heart of my Jesus.

5 April. Holy Thursday. The day began in dryness. But Our Lord deigned to break his silence at the end of my thanksgiving after Communion. He said :

> The grace of my chalice is my real presence which I am giving you, as in the sacred Host. I have already told you this, but I did not let you understand it fully : you are constantly and really in possession of me as during those few minutes following sacramental communion. My power and my goodness are infinite. It is as easy for me to give myself to you through an interior, intimate grace that is apparent to no one, as it is to conceal myself in the consecrated Host, or in the chalice on the altar under the appearance of wine. My little Bride, I love you. Because I love you, I want to shower graces on you. And always with the same purpose : the glory of my Father, the consolation of my Heart and the salvation and sanctification of souls.

After these words of my sovereign Master, spoken by him with an effusion of divine tenderness, silence is a better expression of my emotion and gratitude than faltering words.

6 April. Good Friday. This afternoon, Our Lord said to me :

> The grace of my chalice is a perpetual communion with my divine Person, but it is also a perpetual communion with the agony and the sufferings of my Heart. My little Bride, I am giving you the continual grace of my real presence, so as to associate you more intimately with my Passion and the redemption of souls.

22 April. Sunday. Struggles and longing for more than two weeks : what precious sustenance for love! Our Lord grants me uninterruptedly his great graces, meaning his life in the Most Blessed Trinity, his thought, his chalice and real presence and the suffering love of his Heart. Those are certainly ineffable consolations ; yes, far beyond any human description, but also quite independent of what are ordinarily termed felt consolations. So, in spite of the continuity of these divine favours, I can still experience, and I very often do experience, violent attacks of the devil, dryness, desolation and great moral anguish.

This morning, during High Mass, I was totally absorbed by one of those divine invasions that always precede Our Lord's communications. Immediately after Mass, I made the second part of my meditation. A feeling of peace and love continued to penetrate me at depth, with unspeakable sweetness and power.

All this came from my Jesus, of this I could have no doubt, yet I was fearful. I said to my good Master who was forewarning me of some great new favour : "My Jesus, how fearful I am of illusions! You know that I seek you alone, purely and honestly. I do not seek you for my own sake, I am seeking you for your sake alone. I do not seek you because of your consolations, no ; you know well that my prayers and my desires are that you should reproduce yourself in me, O my crucified Jesus, with all your sufferings and your sacred wounds. I believe and trust in you ; I want what you want, keep me in close union with you."

Hearing me express fear, Jesus answered me with infinite tenderness :

> Fear not, it is I. In vain is the devil raging against my power and my goodness. He cannot touch you in me ; he cannot achieve anything.

Then my fears faded away and I said to my Jesus : "I abandon myself to you." Our Saviour continued :

> My little Bride, I want to lead you further into the depths of the Most Blessed Trinity. **Come into the essence of the Heart of God, into the very essence of the Divinity**. God is indivisible ; he is completely himself, everywhere. But I use expressions like these to help you to understand the intimacy into which my Father wishes to admit you. For this, my Father needs to see me unceasingly, me alone, in your place.

I was quite overcome with gratitude and with the assurance that this new dwelling place afforded me when Jesus said :

> It is time now.

This remark astonished me. Was it already time to end my meditation? I thought instead that I was just beginning it. I looked at the clock. Yes indeed, the time prescribed had already slipped by ; just five minutes remained for the examen after the meditation, as our Holy Rules require. This remark of Our Lord, offering me the opportunity to sacrifice the ecstasy of an indescribable joy in obedience to the Rule, gave me great joy. If my divine Master had delayed by even half a second to make me obey the Rule, I have no hesitation in saying that I would have been very anxious, wondering if the favour I had just received and which I believed to be from him, came in reality from his action. But, by this act of perfect obedience to the Rule, Our Lord put the seal of the divine, as it were, on his work and confirmed my faith in him.

30 April. Monday. I am very tired physically. How good everything is when it is for Jesus! This morning, I again asked my good Master, with all the joy that love gives, for the grace to be consumed and entirely spent by him and for him, according to his holy will. In spite of my genuine interior joy and the joy of my will, my eyes filled with tears. And I am very much afraid of tears, they are a weakness that I find very humiliating ; and I am afraid of them in particular because I am always afraid of lacking in generosity and causing my Jesus sorrow.

So this morning, I begged Our Lord, if such was his will, to wipe away my tears. If such was his will... for if he prefers this humiliation, then I prefer it for his sake. If such was his will... for at times like this, I take pleasure in smiling at God and asking him : "My God, again and always more suffering, if such is your will, with your grace and your love."

In the end, this morning, I said to Our Lady : "My good Mother, do not let me cause Jesus any pain." Our Lord deigned to answer :

> If only you knew how much pleasure you give me by accepting joyously the humiliating condition to which I have reduced you!

2 May. Wednesday. Our Lord spoke to me this morning about the happiness he finds in reproducing himself in souls.

> Apart from the eternal and perfect happiness that I enjoy in my Father and in myself, my happiness is to reproduce myself in the souls that I have created out of love. The more a soul allows me to reproduce myself faithfully in her, the more joy and contentment I find. The greatest joy a soul can give me is to allow me to raise her up to my Divinity. Yes, my little Bride, I take immense pleasure in transforming a soul into myself, in deifying it, in absorbing it wholly into the Divinity.

16 May. Wednesday. For the last two weeks, temptations to discouragement, moral anguish, physical exhaustion, everything has been bothersome and trying, everything has been burdensome and painful. While blessing the divine good pleasure, my constant refrain has been not merely an act of submission, but an insistent supplication : "Yet again and always, O my Jesus, more suffering!"

Yet, it was a hard struggle. My will rejoiced in desolation ; interiorly, I was happy, with the true happiness that pure love gives. But alas! Exteriorly, how many involuntary failings I committed! I was unable to hide my troubles beneath a pleasant smile. Several times, I found myself sighing, as if overcome by a burden that was repugnant to me ; I made reparation for this natural reaction by kissing the ground and humiliating myself. How these weaknesses make me more convinced of my powerlessness and my poverty!

One afternoon last week, wearied and in desolation, I went to the chapel to tell Our Lord again that in spite of exterior failings, I did not want to cause him the least pain. I asked him what he wanted from me in these circumstances in which everything was proving difficult. He deigned to reply :

Smile... Smile whatever happens, even when I am wearing you down...

At another time, he asked me :

Do you want to suffer all the time?

At the time, I was feeling crushed. With his grace, I answered eagerly : "Yes, my Jesus, I want to suffer as you did right to the end. Grant me this grace, I beg of you."

Yes, right to the end, just as my divine Master did, right to the very limit according to his holy will, and to an infinite degree by his sovereign power, for his glory and for souls.

This morning, as I was forming a resolution, during my meditation, he said to me :

My little Bride, will you let me spread abroad exteriorly the joy that I am giving you interiorly?

By the tone of his *Will you?* he was asking for my consent. What mysterious goodness on the part of God! "Yes, my Jesus", I answered.

Endeavour, he continued, to smile at everything. In silence, repress your anxieties, your weariness, your moral and physical suffering, and concern yourself only with pleasing me by smiling.

At midday, after the examen, he returned to the same subject :

My little Bride, forget your suffering while you are enduring it. That means : do not let suffering prevent you from smiling exteriorly just as you are smiling at me interiorly ; do not let suffering distract you from thinking of me. Bear it without the least self-pity, and with great joy and gratitude to my Heart which is giving it to you. You no longer exist, my little Bride : hence, you no longer have any right to think of your suffering, since in reality it is I who am suffering in your place.

O admirable tenderness of my divine Substitute! With what loving kindness he teaches me how to let him live in me! With what delicacy he reprimands me for my failings! Though his sacred words have enlightened me, they have not resolved my problems, and how happy I am about that! This morning, at the end of my meditation, after I had said to Our Lord : "I love you and I want what you desire", I immediately added by way of responding to his request and still engaged in a struggle : "My Jesus, do everything, because you know how difficult it is."

But his words have left me in great peace, and he alone is the object of my thoughts.

XLIII
RELIGIOUS LIFE
31 May - 14 June 1928

The satisfaction of the infinite attributes and the reproduction of Our Lord. — I am not sufficiently loved for my own sake. — The reign of the divine at 'Jesus and Mary'. — The Eucharistic Heart of Jesus and the Congregation of Jesus and Mary.

31 May. Thursday. **Silence and smiles** : these are the two words, I think, that best sum up my efforts during the last two weeks in particular. Yes, I want God and the Most Blessed Virgin to be the sole witnesses of everything... I do not want any creature to rob them of the least fraction, however minute, of my life of love.

Yesterday morning, Our Lord said to me

The satisfaction of my infinite attributes in a soul involves my being perfectly reproduced in that soul. Only I can accomplish this perfect reproduction ; in order to accomplish it, souls must let me have my way in everything. Since you want to satisfy me to the full, my little Bride, let me have my way constantly and perfectly.

Having reflected on these words of my good Master, I said to him : "Yes, my Jesus, I want you to be fully satisfied in me, but I want you as well to be fully satisfied in every soul. I want you to be fully satisfied for your own sake and that of the adorable Trinity, and for the sake of each one of your creatures, and I want this *infinitely*, *eternally* and *divinely*." I will explain briefly what I mean by these last three words :

"O Jesus! I want you to be fully satisfied, and I want it *infinitely*, that is, multiplied to an infinitely infinite degree, to the full capacity of the desires of your power, of the desires of your heart, even of the passing fancies of your tender love, in a word, in the measure of the fathomless immensity of your boundless comprehension.

I want it *eternally*, that is, for all ages without beginning or end, throughout your divine uncreated existence, for ever and uninterruptedly, at every moment of this eternity which will know no ending.

I want it *divinely*, that is, through you alone. Only a God can satisfy the Infinite. Yes, Jesus, through you I want to satisfy the eternal and sovereign Trinity : the most holy Father, your adorable Word and the Spirit of love.

O my God, through Jesus, I want to satisfy you fully, for your own sake, because you are my God, because you are the Infinite, because of each one of your attributes and perfections."

When I tell God of my desire to love him, I need to add these three adverbs. In that way, Our Lord understands that, for the glory of his Father and the adorable Trinity, I desire everything that a human creature can ever desire through the Spirit and the Heart of a God ; that, for the consolation of his Heart, I desire the salvation and sanctification of all souls just as he himself desires it.

1 June. Friday. This morning, Our Lord was sad, very sad. After I had said to him with compassion : "O my Jesus, how sad you are!", I addressed myself to the Blessed Virgin : "O my good Mother, how sad the Heart of Jesus is!" My divine Master answered :

> I am not loved sufficiently for my own sake. Too often, people love me for their sake. There are so few souls who, while giving me love, love me for my own sake.

I replied : "O my Jesus, forgive these poor souls who love themselves too much, forgive them, it is because they do not know you ; if they knew you, they would love you for yourself."

> The Heart of Jesus continued : If I am so sad, it is because there are so many consecrated souls who love me just for their own sake ; it is because there are so many priests who put their own personal interests before mine.

Then I said to the Blessed Virgin : "My good Mother, console Jesus! He must be consoled!"

Turning to Our Lord, I interceded in these words : "My Jesus, let my Mother, the Most Blessed Virgin, draw from your Heart and shed on souls, especially consecrated souls and those of priests, graces of enlightenment and pure love, graces so powerful that no one will be able to resist them."

A little later, Our Lord pursued his complaints, saying again with still more ineffable tenderness :

> Ah, my little Own Self! Most souls are fearful of loving me for my own sake. Even a great number of consecrated souls, a great number of priests, dread my divine overtures. Too many religious and priestly souls fail to understand that the sacrifices I ask of them are flames of love, escaping from my divine Heart so as to draw and sanctify their human heart.

4 June. Monday. The day before yesterday, Saturday afternoon, I asked Our Lord to kindly tell me what is lacking in our religious family of Jesus and Mary, if he is to hold complete dominion over each of us as he desires. Yesterday morning, the feast of the Most Blessed Trinity, my good Master replied as follows :

> Lack of union with me. A great number of my Spouses too often act independently, forgetting to take care to be united with me. I can not bless their prayers or their work as I wish, because their attachment to their human desires places an obstacle in the way of the plenitude of my graces.

Following this reply, I put another question to him in the afternoon : "My Jesus, what does one need in order to obtain the grace of close union with you, the grace of complete detachment from self, in a word, the grace of your perfect dominion over her?" Our Lord said to me :

> You must ask for it. I give my grace to every soul who asks me for it, and above all to every religious soul who is or wants to be my Spouse.

"How are we to ask you for it?", I added.

Let each soul simply ask that I may reign in her as I wish.

"Then, Jesus, when you have given your grace, what are we to do?"

Correspond with it very lovingly.

"Yes, my good Jesus, but you know how great our human weakness is, we often fall, we fail many times to correspond with your grace. What then?"

> Rise up again with much love, always come back to me, count on me. A great number of religious do not count on me enough : that is what is lacking in you. You must count on me in everything : in your difficulties, in your troubles, in your struggles, even when you fall and fail. Count on me and never be afraid of counting on me too much.

This morning, when I reached the chapel shortly before six o'clock, I found Our Lord content. He seemed to be comforted. His joy consoled me greatly. A little later, through an interior light, he wished to show me his divine Heart in the sacred Host, and our Congregation of Jesus and Mary in relationship to him. But I put up some resistance to this light for fear of being deluded. I tried to drive this image away, saying : "My God, no illusions, no imagination, I want none." The image haunted me. Finally, while the community received Communion, during Mass, I found it impossible to resist the power of this light any longer, and I abandoned myself to Our Lord recognising his divine action.

Our Lord, God made man, showed me his adorable Heart in the sacred Host. I did not look upon his sacred Face, but I was captivated by his Heart and the Host. Both his Heart and the Host were perfectly united, so united with one another that I could not explain how I could distinguish between the two. From the Host, there emanated an immense number of rays of light. From his Heart there came forth a tremendous number of flames, issuing as if in dense floods.

The Most Blessed Virgin was there, so close to Our Lord that she seemed to be absorbed by him, and yet I saw her as distinct from him. Oh! How pure she was! How pure she was...! I could do nothing but repeat these words : *How pure she was!*

All the light from the Host and the flames from the Heart of Jesus passed through the immaculate Heart of the Most Blessed Virgin. Our Lord said to me :

Yes, make me reign at 'Jesus and Mary'.

At these words, still interiorly, I fell prostrate, as if annihilated in love in the presence of my God, and in a tone of supplication that was new to me, I said : "O Eucharistic Heart of Jesus, through Our Lady of the Eucharistic Heart, I beg you to reign in all souls as you desire."

Then Our Lord showed me, a little below him and his most pure Mother, all the religious of Jesus and Mary, gathered together as if on a plain. The light from the Host and the flames from his Sacred Heart, passing through the Heart of the Blessed Virgin, flowed down onto the religious of our Congregation ; and, from the religious, they radiated out to a countless multitude of souls, who surrounded them on all sides, as far as eye could see and they were turned towards them. Our Lord said to me :

My Heart is overflowing with graces intended for souls. Bring them to my Eucharistic Heart.

In addition, the Most Holy Virgin was drawing souls towards her so as to lead them to the Eucharistic Heart. Finally, I saw a countless multitude of angels around the Eucharistic Heart, a multitude also reaching as far as the eye could see. In their heavenly language, they repeated : **Glory to the immortal King of ages!**

XLIV
RELIGIOUS LIFE
14 June - 16 August 1928

Benefits of the Redemption. — Invasion of the divine. — Annual retreat. — Temptations. — Vainglory. — Darkness. — The life of eternity. — The share allotted to nothingness. — The desire to reproduce Jesus crucified.

14 June. Thursday. For several days, I have been feeling genuine regret at the thought that, throughout eternity, God will be hated and blasphemed by the wicked angels and the dammed. I wish there were not a single spirit, not a single soul who did not love God. I say, and I keep on saying to Our Lord, that if it were possible without offending the most sacred justice of his Father and if the demons and the dammed could be redeemed, I would want to save them all through him, my Jesus. I would be ready to endure anything, as many times as there are and will be souls in hell, if I could bring all rational creatures, without exception, to love and glorify the adorable Trinity.

When I told Our Lord again this morning how desirous I was of his infinite and eternal glory, to the highest degree, my good Master answered :

> The glory that my Father has received since the Redemption is, in spite of human sinfulness, far greater than if humans had never sinned, because the reparation that I offer my Father is infinite, and it makes up infinitely for all the sins of the human race. Each time a soul unites itself to me to glorify my Father, it gives him infinite glory through me.

2 July. Monday. My period of probation began yesterday. I am completing my fifth year of religious profession ; my first vows of religion expire this year. I shall have the happiness of renewing them on 15 August, and this time for ever.

I want **my period of probation to be marked by consuming love**. In my annihilation, I abandon myself anew to all the desires of infinite Love. I abandon myself to the infinite satisfaction of all the divine attributes. I am pining... How I pine! Yet, I am already living in heaven. Oh! If only Jesus and the Blessed Virgin would open my eyes soon to eternity... soon! But, I desire nothing... No, nothing... Neither death nor life. I want to sacrifice everything, even my consuming desire to see God, so that my love for him may be more perfect and my apostolate more efficacious for his glory.

7 July. Saturday. A week of struggles. Temptation to discouragement. Am I really a good nun? I see my defects, my failings, and the devil would like me to lose confidence in the mercy of God. But, in keeping with the desire of Our Lord, I am not stopping short at my imperfections ; while humbly regretting them, I abandon them all to him, I cast them into the furnace of his love, and I concentrate on looking at him, at his divine Heart alone.

My good Master remains silent ; still, he is active. Last evening, I experienced one of those mystic invasions, the sources of which come from the bliss of heaven. Speaking in human terms, I was overwhelmed with love. God alone! All for God alone! Everything purely for him! Jesus alone, infinitely and divinely taking my place for the joy and glory of his Father : such are the consuming desires that this ineffable grace has again increased and multiplied.

23 July. Monday. On Thursday morning, from the first moments of the day, I felt crushed by an interior suffering that at first I could not understand. I was concentrating on remaining closely united to Our Lord when, thanks to a divine light, I realised that it was quite simply the suffering of his Heart that he was graciously increasing. How tedious were those hours! My longing was like a crushing weight. That day was a holiday for us 'probationists'. The recreations in which I took part did not distract me in any way from the action of my divine Master.

Exteriorly, I appeared relaxed and lively ; interiorly, I was sharing in the sufferings of my Jesus. In the evening, while exteriorly I was engrossed, chatting and laughing, I was closely united with the agonizing Heart of my God, keeping him company, trying to console him ; neither of these simultaneous thoughts was difficult. No. I had only to follow the divine impulse. On the one hand, I was at recreation through obedience : Jesus wanted me to be cheerful and full of joy. On the other hand, his Heart wanted me to taste the bitterness of his agony : he himself gave me the grace and kept me mindful of his intimate action.

I find nothing new in this synchronization of very different thoughts, but if I mention this, it is out of obedience and for the glory of my good Master, because the suffering of his Heart so preoccupied me on Thursday last that he had to give me at the same time a very powerful grace to cope with my exterior actions. The following day, Friday, was painful and oppressive, too. On Saturday, the immense burden was lightened ; the pain of love that Jesus has left with me is almost normal.

26 July. Thursday. For several days, Our Lord has been teaching me, through his salutary action, to accept everything, especially interiorly, in a spirit of sweetness and gentleness. It is like a light from the Holy Spirit, a very sweet and powerful illumination, enlightening me in my actions and especially in what vexes me, and filling me with the gentleness of the Heart of Jesus. This grace seems very precious to me.

Yesterday, Wednesday, at midday, Our Lord took possession of me with great power, increasing the suffering love of his Heart. As last week, an immense weight bore down on me. Last vening, deigning to break his silence which had seemed to me to be very prolonged, he said sadly :

Console me... Remain closely united to my agonizing Heart.

This morning, Thursday, he told me why he was sad :

My Heart has so many graces to bestow and the majority of souls do not even think of accepting them.

7 August. The long annual retreat which, for me this year, is the retreat in preparation for my perpetual vows, began on Sunday evening. I am still abandoned to the good pleasure of my divine Master. I asked him earnestly, if such was his good pleasure, to grant me a retreat marked by suffering.

Yesterday was a painful day. In addition to physical weariness, there was the temptation to discouragement. The demon made an aggressive, frontal attack on me, suggesting that I leave religious life when my temporary vows expire. Oh! The wretch! I had the grace not even to dwell on this infernal thought. With firm trust, I had recourse to Our Lord and the Most Blessed Virgin ; in them, I am at peace. As for the demon, he made a great din and disturbance. I was very much ashamed of this temptation, and I took advantage of it to humble myself profoundly before God, to acknowledge with greater clarity that it is he who has chosen me and to thank him ardently.

This morning, Our Lord wanted to give me joy through his divine words. During my thanksgiving after Communion, I was concentrating on remaining closely united with him but I was not at all expecting his intimate communications. I was taken by surprise when he first spoke to me, and was all the more pleased! He said :

> I want to absorb you, my little Spouse, to the extent of taking your place, with all the attributes and all the perfections of my Divinity.

Later, he added :

> I want to deify you in the same way as I united my humanity with my divinity in the Incarnation.

He just said to me at midday :

> The degree of holiness that I want for you, is the infinite plenitude of my own holiness, it is the holiness of my Father brought about in you through me.

After his first words to me this morning, my divine Substitute repeated the reason for the favours he is granting me :

It is, he said, for the greater glory of my Father, to give joy to my Heart and for the salvation and sanctification of souls.

14 August. Tuesday. By the light of the retreat, I realised that a certain vainglory is creeping into some of my actions ; it consists in small instances of self-seeking, hidden, intimate, not intentional but very real. With God's grace, and in so far as it depends on my will, I will put an end from now on to these despicable acts of vainglory. Nevertheless, if it should happen that I have again to regret these weaknesses, because such fruits are all I am capable of producing, given my human imperfections, I will use them to humble myself and profit from them for the glory of God through greater confidence and love.

For some days, the devil has been redoubling the intensity and craftiness of his attacks. What a day of struggle yesterday was! I received Communion purely out of obedience. At the general examen of the day, last evening, I could see nothing, understand nothing, because the evil spirit was so anxious to make me believe that I was not in the state of grace. Obedience soothed my anguish and enabled me to remain at peace. How good Jesus is to have given me, in authority, this great rule of obedience, granting me, when necessary, the grace to practise it! At times of real interior turmoil which happen so frequently, I submit blindly, and go forward trampling my fears underfoot, since they are always, as in this case, groundless fears that the demon invents and multiplies, and I sacrifice my own judgment, telling God again and again that I love him.

I need a great grace to obey at these times when the infernal enemy goes out of his way to lay snares for me. But even if Jesus seems to be sleeping, I have faith in this divine Master, and the assurance that in him and through him, I can not perish.

While the devil is causing a disturbance externally, Our Lord is continuing with his life-giving action. He has plunged me still deeper into the intimate depths of the Essence of the Most Blessed Trinity. I have a better understanding of my state of life in God and how Our Lord is living in my place. I find it impossible to describe this state of life accurately, just as it is ; here are a few words which give some idea of it : God has absorbed my entire being ; annihilated in Christ Jesus and through him, I am living the life of eternity in the adorable Trinity ; **he, Christ Jesus, is living on earth in my place**.

Yes, that is exactly the case : Jesus is living on earth in my place. He has substituted himself for me, and I no longer exist. Hence, complete oblivion of my being in all that concerns me ; besides, in reality, nothingness can not be concerned about anything at all. As a result, I have no anxieties, it is the concern of Jesus.

If a stone is struck, the effect of the knock or the impact it has received can be seen and observed. This is not the case with nothingness. What is non-existent can not betray any evidence of damage. I am this nothing. In suffering, weariness, illness, opposition, labour, loneliness, in a word, in my entire life, I have to disregard myself as nothingness is disregarded ; in everything, I must look upon Jesus, God alone must occupy my thoughts, it is on him alone that my attention must be focused.

Tomorrow morning, I will pronounce my perpetual vows of religion. I tell God continually that I am abandoning myself entirely to him, to his holy will, to his joy, to his good pleasure. Tomorrow, too, is the feast of the Assumption of the Blessed Virgin. To die or to suffer! I want only what God wants. But, while waiting until he is pleased to open my eyes in his eternal light, I am lonely, and my desires for suffering are growing beyond measure. The more I ask Our Lord to take away these desires if they are not from him, the more they increase and intensify.

My thirst for sufferings is as infinite as the sufferings of Jesus ; as far as I am concerned, it is like madness, but I keep telling my good Master that it is he who has set the example of this madness. I am the spouse of a crucified God, so I can desire nothing but to be crucified and crowned with thorns, while my whole being is subjected to martyrdom like himself!

XLV
RELIGIOUS LIFE
16 August - 14 September 1928

Perpetual vows. — Sadness of the Heart of Jesus. — Joy of the Heart of Jesus. — A blossoming of divine life. — Participation in the eternal canticle of the glorious Heart of Jesus. — The joy of eternity.

16 August. Thursday. By making my perpetual vows yesterday, I have become the spouse of Christ for ever, I belong for ever to my dear Institute of Jesus and Mary! *Magnificat!* How can I render thanks to the Most High! Only through the most pure voice of the Immaculate Heart of Mary and the infinite accents of the Heart of Jesus can I worthily intone my gratitude to God. May I now become a holy religious for the glory of the Lord and the honour of my Congregation!

Another Assumption has passed... *Fiat!* The first grace that I asked of God yesterday was the same as always : **that of the perfect satisfaction of his infinite attributes**. But then I begged Our Lord to reproduce himself in me together with his sufferings, as far as he willed, of course, and to be within my being the Jesus of the agony, of the passion and of Calvary, to live in my place as the crucified and redeeming God. This morning, he graciously deigned to answer me :

> Yes, I have chosen you so as to reproduce myself in you and to satisfy my love. No one will wrest you from my Heart.

23 August. Thursday. Last Sunday, the Heart of Jesus was sad. I was trying to console him for the offenses committed against him in the Holy Eucharist when he said to me :

> I am far more sensitive to the lukewarm love of souls consecrated to me than I am to the sinful sacrileges and desecrations committed against me by my enemies. I give so many graces and lights to the souls consecrated to me!

I asked him, "What do you want, Jesus, by way of consolation?"

Offer me to my Father, he answered. Offer the love and patience of my Eucharistic Heart. Through the offering of my Heart, you atone infinitely for every outrage committed against my Father and me ; you atone for the lack of love in consecrated souls.

24 August. Friday. Last evening, Thursday, at the end of my hour of vigil, the Heart of Jesus seemed to be experiencing joy. In the last few moments, he said to me :

If only you knew how pleasing you are to me when you desire to console me!

I answered, "My Jesus, you know very well that it is my constant desire."

Offer me to my Father, he continued. While you are offering me, I am pouring the graces of my Heart upon souls, through my most holy Mother.

This morning, from the earliest hours, Our Lord was pleased. His Heart seemed at peace and full of joy. He communicated his joy to me by such an outpouring of indescribable tenderness and love, that I asked him : "Why are you allowing me to enjoy your love in this way?"

Because I am pleased, he said. I am pleased with my 'Jesus and Mary'. Beautiful sacrifices are being made in your Congregation, sacrifices that are purely for my sake, consoling me and making up for the neglect of so many souls. Offer me to my Father in thanksgiving.

Just as he asked me to do, I offered him to the eternal Father, in thanksgiving for all the divine blessings he has bestowed on our Congregation. When I had offered him three times, my good Master continued :

Offer me to my Father, too, to atone for the lack of thoughtfulness shown me by certain souls in your Congregation. If I am pleased, that does not mean that all my spouses of 'Jesus and Mary' refuse me nothing. Offer me on behalf of those who are still too attached to themselves, and in whom I desire to act freely.

I corresponded at once his desire. Then, he added :

> Continue to make me known and to establish my reign. I am so pleased that at this moment I am showering down on you a superabundance of my graces.

26 August. Sunday. The action of Jesus within me is taking on a new character ; nothing has changed regarding what I have written up to now, but it is becoming more intense.

It is very difficult, not to say impossible, for me to express in human words the divine life of Jesus, substituted in my being, annihilated as it is in his infinite Being. The new character is this : it is like **a blossoming of the life of Our Lord** in place of my poor life which has totally disappeared. My divine Substitute seems to have removed from my being even the least obstacle which could slow down his work of deification, however slightly. I am indifferent to everything. I am content with everything. Or rather, I am in every circumstance content with God. My eyes are fixed on Our Lord ; everything that, to all appearances, is intended for me is not, as I see it, really intended for me but for him. Oh! What a blissful life! What unspeakable ecstasy to be living in heaven while Jesus is living on earth in one's place!

5 September. Wednesday. How good Jesus is to me! Yesterday morning, while pondering his great blessings, I said to him in an effusion of gratitude, and deeply aware of my poverty : "O my Jesus, how good you are, and how wicked I am!" At once, he deigned to answer me :

> Do not look at yourself. Look at me.

O infinite tenderness...! My good Master accompanied this remark with a grace of very lively trust in him, and of humble, simple abandonment to his divine action.

6 September. Thursday. Since yesterday afternoon, moral and physical exhaustion which increased yesterday evening and has persisted today. I observed that this state of anguish coincided with Thursday but, as I am always extremely wary of being deluded, I did not want to pay too much attention to this

thought. But this evening, Our Lord gave me to understand clearly that this coincidence was indeed intended by him, that today is the first Thursday of the month, and tomorrow the first Friday, and his Heart desires to be consoled.

My intense longing for Jesus crucified to be reproduced in my entire being is increasing. I can no longer tell my divine Substitute that I love him without telling him at the same time that if it is pleasing to him and for his glory, I desire the plenitude of his sufferings : his crown of thorns, all the wounds of his scourging and crucifixion, all the indignities he suffered in his Passion, the anguish of his Heart, in a word, all his sufferings from the cradle to Calvary. Extravagant love on my part! Yes, an irrational desire, I admit and understand. But when one loves, one wants to be like the person loved ; I love my Jesus, and I want to be like him so that he and he alone may truly take my place. When one loves, one seeks the glory and joy of the person loved ; I love my Jesus for his glory, his enjoyment and that of his Father. Like him, I am ready for anything, in order to draw souls to him, to save and sanctify them through him.

8 September. Saturday. (Feast of the Nativity of the Most Blessed Virgin.) The day began in aridity. Towards the end of the 15-minute particular examen, before midday, and following an invasion of the divine accompanied by a very sweet joy, Our Lord said to me :

> I want my life in you to be a canticle of praise for the glory of my Father. From now on, I want you to sing with me the eternal canticle of my sacred and glorious Heart. Let me radiate through you the love and joy of eternity.

12 September. Wednesday. Jesus is allowing me to participate in "the joy of his Heart in heaven, the joy that he derives from perfect divine union with his Father". Oh! How sweet and gentle is this joy! Yet, it does not rule out my free cooperation and renunciation, far from it. Our Lord is generously offering me this unspeakable grace of sharing in the joy of eternity ; I accept it with gratitude and I delight in it, while abandoning myself

utterly to his divine action. When events prove painful, this grace does not lessen the struggle ; sometimes it even increases it, because it presupposes very pure love, joy in God alone, the sincere seeking after his infinite glory and consequently complete self-forgetfulness. Oh! If we only knew the sacred bliss the elect find in God, we would stop at nothing to obtain even the smallest degree!

This morning, I was closely united with Our Lord but, nevertheless, how fearful I was of being deluded! I was so afraid of mistaking the voice of my divine Master that I felt fearful of hearing it. The fact is that I was hearing a voice which was attempting to imitate his but, as it was frenzied, I did not recognize the voice of Jesus and thought with conviction : *it is not he.* I can see now that it was a clever snare of the devil.

Battling and in fear, I turned to the Blessed Virgin, saying to her : "My good Mother, I beg you to preserve me from delusion and not let me put the least obstacle in the way of my Jesus's action." O joy! Jesus willed that his most blessed Mother should herself answer me :

> My daughter, said the Blessed Virgin, as long as you remain closely united to me, have no fear of being deluded ; I will always preserve you from that. As long as you strive to seek God alone with great uprightness and great purity of intention, have no fear of contradictions ; my divine Son will know how to make them contribute to the glory of his Father and the reign of his love.

I can not express the sweetness of my heavenly Mother's words. Silence is always the most faithful echo of these heavenly confidences.

13 September. Thursday. This morning, Our Lord spoke to me about joy :

> A soul, he said, cannot approach my Heart without being happy, because I am the Furnace of joy and happiness. Even at those times when I associate a soul most intimately with my Passion and my sufferings, I can change all its bitterness into sweetness. My little Own Self, I am holding you in my Heart and *in the depths of the Essence of the Most Blessed Trinity* ; so from now on,

I want you to be filled with joy as I am, in so far as you suffer with me, love me and console me. Perfect and constant joy in me is the greatest proof of perfect and constant union with me. You sincerely love me, it is I who am acting in you and for you, so I want to prove this by radiating my divine joy.

When Our Lord speaks to me intimately and at some length, and because in obedience I have to write down every word, I sometimes say to him : "My Jesus, help me to remember all that", or else : "My Jesus, will you write that down yourself because I will not remember everything."

This morning, I did not forget to repeat this request. I felt so powerless to retain faithfully the words he had used that my good Master let me note them down immediately after his last sentence.

The same day. Thursday evening. Our Lord has just added the following to his communication of this morning :

My joy, in which I am allowing you a share, can be found in aridity, in anguish, and in darkness, because it is the joy of perfect union with my divine will, it is the joy of my love, the joy of my Heart.

XLVI
RELIGIOUS LIFE
14 September 1928 - July 1929

14 September. Friday. How God would love to see all souls happy! Here is what Our Lord said on that subject, this morning

> Suffering is the indispensable ransom for sin. But God's love for souls is so great that his happiness consists in changing all their sufferings into joys. He wants souls to be happy while still on earth, through divine love, even when they are suffering. That is why souls that really love God find so much happiness in the cross, in spite of their natural repugnance. It is because they find and love God in everything that goes against their nature.

15 September. Saturday. Our Lord continued this morning :

> Souls are only unhappy in so far as they distance themselves from God. My Father's great desire, and mine, would be to see all souls happy, even on earth. When our divine Justice inflicts distress or punishment, it is always out of love, and always to bring souls nearer to God, to their sovereign happiness. Oh! My little Spouse, work with me to make souls happy!

This last sentence was spoken in a tone of grievance as well as entreaty.

20 September. Thursday. When Our Lord speaks of divine glory, he speaks of the glory of his Father rather than of his own glory or that of the Holy Spirit. Now, as the three divine Persons are equal and equally entitled to the same homage, I asked my good Master, last Monday, in obedience, if he would kindly give me an explanation. The following morning, he replied :

> The glory of my Father is the glory of God. My Father and I, and our Spirit of Love are One. To glorify my Father is at the same time to glorify me and to glorify the Holy Spirit, because our Unity in the Trinity is indivisible.

11 October. Thursday. This morning, the Heart of Jesus seemed weary and tired. He wanted to rest. Then, he grew sad, very sad...! I tried to console him with and through the Most Blessed Virgin. In a tone of profound sorrow, he said to me :

My priests! My priests...! Offer me to my Father for my priests.

I offered him and I offered the perfect union of his Heart with his Father. When I had made this dual offering three times, he continued :

My priests! I love them so much and, in return, there are so many who seek their enjoyment apart from me! There are so many who do not know how to love me!

A little later, he said :

The wickedness of the world incites my divine Justice less than the sins and deliberate failings of consecrated souls. Oh! My little Spouse, I have given you all the love of my Heart. Offer my infinite love to my Father to mitigate his wrath and restrain the arm of his anger.

Since hearing these words, I feel that the arm of divine Justice is raised, and to prevent it from striking, Jesus is urging me to offer him, to beg for grace and mercy.

The same day. Thursday midday.

My priests...!

This grievance of Our Lord's haunts me. I have just asked him : "My Jesus, what do you want for your priests?" He has replied :

Love! Love! I am thirsting for souls! A great number of souls are lost because my priests do not love me enough. They do not touch hearts because they are not sufficiently united with me. They rely too much on human means and on their own activity, and not enough on my divine action.

12 October. Friday. Since yesterday, the Most Blessed Virgin has been sad, too. Our Lord is still sad today but a little less so than yesterday because of certain consolations he receives, but his Heart is still wounded by the lack of love in his priests and consecrated souls.

The arm of divine Justice, though still raised, is less heavy ; the uninterrupted offering of Jesus by the Most Blessed Virgin and the Spirit of Love is restraining it and making it lighter. How I wish I could convey the loving sadness of the Heart of Jesus! And the sadness of the Most Blessed Virgin, too! This morning, I wanted to try and offer my heavenly Mother some consolation ; but immediately, with gracious tenderness, she made me understand that her desire was that I should offer every consolation I could to Jesus himself, through her certainly, but not to her, and that to console Jesus is to console her too.

13 October. Saturday. The sadness and the words of the Heart of Jesus during the last two days have given me an inexpressible thirst to win him love. I would travel all over the world crying out to everyone : Give me love, all the love you can, for God.

27 October. Saturday. Our Lord's silence has lasted for almost two weeks...! How heavily this silence has weighed upon me! One day, however, the Heart of Jesus gave me to understand that he was finding some relief. But on Thursday especially, the day before yesterday, the weight of his silence increased.

That day, Thursday, was painful. Time passed without my wanting to waste a second, but I was a long way from using it all as I had expected. In the evening, one thought gave me cause for anxiety : Was Our Lord content? I was in agony. Suddenly, his divine voice said to me :

> You have not done what you would have liked to do, but you have done what I wanted. Be content. I am content. While you were allowing me to have my way, I saved some souls and purified others according to my desires.

Oh, joy! How good Jesus is! Yet the devil is continually on the offensive ; and the following day, yesterday, Friday, he tried to disturb me, wanting me to believe that the words spoken the previous evening were not Our Lord's and that I had been wasting time. In this insinuation, I recognised a snare and the restless action of the evil spirit, and I paid no attention to it. Shortly afterwards, Jesus said to me in a tone of sweet peace :

> You have not been wasting your time, because you have not ceased to love me and remain united to me. It is not the visible result that counts in my eyes, it is the interior action, total submission to my will.

On hearing these words, I was so absorbed in divine peace that I exclaimed, in an outburst of intense faith : "Jesus, it really is you!"

This morning, Saturday, Our Lord was full of joy. He told me why :

> I receive love, he said, true love, pure love. It is consecrated souls, souls that are very dear to me, who are consoling me. It is also the tiny souls of children that are still spotless and love me for myself. My heart loves souls so much that, in order to secure the love of a single soul, even the most wretched and the most unworthy, I would have suffered infinitely more than I suffered throughout the whole of my human life, if that had been possible. I want you to love souls with the same love that I have for them and, consequently, to let me suffer in your place so as to save and sanctify them.

30 October. Tuesday. Last Sunday, the day before yesterday, we were to have exposition of the Most Blessed Sacrament all day in our chapel. Then we were informed that this privilege, on the feast of Christ the King, was limited to parish churches. We were extremely sorry, and prayed earnestly to Jesus in the Host. Finally, we were given permission. That was Saturday.

On Sunday morning, not knowing about the final decision, I hastened to the chapel. What joy! The altar was prepared for the exposition of the Most Blessed Sacrament. I thanked Our Lord fervently and he replied :

If just one of my spouses in your community had asked for this favour with faith and love, my Heart would not have refused, so great is my desire to shower you with graces.

21 November. Wednesday. Our Lord had remained silent for three days. Last evening, I asked him the reason for his silence.

I just wanted to prove to you that it is indeed I who am speaking to you ; you cannot hear me whenever you please.

22 November. Thursday. I had just told Jesus how good he is when he replied :

Remain faithful to me and you will see more and more how good I am.

24 November. Saturday. Since Last evening, profound desolation.

25 December. Christmas. What happiness! Our Lord has fulfilled one of my great desires, after having asked me to sacrifice it. At Midnight Mass, after I had received Jesus in the Host, I finally made the vow of total perfection for ever. My Communion was preceded by a great struggle, no doubt initiated by the devil, and so intense that my Communion was an act of pure obedience. My supreme offering was an act of love, made in aridity, and to which Our Lord made no response either by word or consolation. Yet, I experienced a joy totally rooted in the will : the joy of abandoning myself to God as completely as possible, through his grace and for ever. In addition, even the silence of Jesus afforded me a supernatural joy, since it offered me some delicious drops of bitterness to savour for his sake.

"Lord, to fulfil my commitments, I count entirely on you and on the help of Mary, my good Mother. O Jesus, be my life, my divine Substitute, always! Keep my whole being, with its powerlessness and weakness, annihilated in you, in your love and in your mercy!"

3 January 1929. Thursday. Great sadness on the part of Our Lord.

> My priests...! My priests...!

4 January 1929. First Friday. Exposition of the Blessed Sacrament in the novitiate. With joy :

> I am pleased with the novitiate. I am happy here. I reign, and I find souls that give me joy.

22 April. Monday. Jesus, come quickly and give me courage.

> I am here, take it... Let me have my way. The suffering that I am giving you is of infinite value for souls. Pray that my grace keeps you perfectly faithful to your mission until the end.

23 April. Tuesday (evening). With joy :

> If you only knew the joy you give me when you let me have my way! There are very few souls who allow me to have my way in everything as I wish at times of great sacrifice.

24 April. Wednesday (morning). While suffering : "How good it is to love you, Jesus!"

> If only you knew how good it is for my Heart to be loved!

30 April. Tuesday. Perceptible presence. **"I love you !"**

5 May. Sunday. No words, but I understood that Our Lord wants to take me **into the essence of the Essence of the Most Blessed Trinity**. He is keeping me *in the essence of the Heart of the Most Blessed Trinity*, but he wants to take me, as it were, into the very heart of the infinite Essence. I can find no words in which to describe these divine phenomena.

Our Lord is showing me the depths into which he has allowed me to penetrate, in the Essence of the Most Blessed Trinity, since last Tuesday when it pleased him to put me into exterior isolation because of illness. How good he is! And how happy I am!

14 May. Tuesday (evening) My extreme weakness made me fear the night, as I could not call anyone to help me. I abandoned myself to my Jesus, and I felt his presence, to the right of my bed, as he said :

I am coming to spend the night with you ; I am going to take care of you.

20 May. Monday. A breath or a grace of the Holy Spirit in a soul is an abyss of love that only a God can measure.

27 May. Monday. The divine Trinity constitutes the glory and felicity of the elect in heaven to an infinite extent, in so far as the soul has been the temple of the Trinity on earth.

30 May. Thursday. The holy Eucharist brings heaven to earth, and very few souls offer the Sacrificial Eucharistic Heart a heaven of joy and consolation.

11 June. Tuesday.

My Eucharistic Heart has two great desires whose ardour would cause it sudden death if it could still die : the desire to reign in souls through love, and the desire to communicate to souls the immensity of its graces. Spouse of my Heart, alleviating one or other of these desires means renewing each time the joy that my Eucharistic Heart experienced when instituting the adorable Sacrament.

July 1929

No invocation responds better to the immense desire of my Eucharistic Heart to reign in souls than : *Eucharistic Heart of Jesus, may your kingdom come through the immaculate Heart of Mary* ; and to my no less infinite desire to communicate my graces to souls than : *Eucharistic Heart of Jesus, burning with love for us, inflame our hearts with love for you.* When you say *our hearts,* have in mind all souls, of the present and of the future.

July 1929. "What is the secret of touching the heart of Our Lord through prayer?"

Love. The more sincerely a soul loves me during lifetime, the deeper the love in prayer, the greater the influence exerted over my Heart. When a soul loves me to folly, I can refuse it scarcely anything. Yet I have wishes that must of necessity be carried out ; in this case, the soul that loves me always receives, for itself and other souls, in response to its prayer, an immense amount of grace for its own sanctification and for the good of souls.

I was reflecting on the great kindness shown to me by my superiors and on the charity of my "sisters". I felt the most profound gratitude, and I told Our Lord of my distress at being unable to thank them. He answered :

I will repay your debts.

"You will repay them as God?"

Of course, I will repay them as God, I will repay them with my Heart. To each person who has rendered you the least service or given you the slightest pleasure, I will give graces in return. But, in heaven, you will also pay your debts yourself. I will give you my Heart for ever. Thus you will distribute my riches through my most holy Mother.

XLVII
EPILOGUE

From July on, our dear Mother Ste-Cécile de Rome (Dina Bélanger) no longer had the strength to hold a pencil and describe what was taking place in her soul.

We believe we should now complete her *Canticle of Thanksgiving* by giving an account of the final weeks of her life.

When we went to her room in the infirmary, we felt we were entering a sanctuary : everything in it radiated a spirit of recollection and sacrifice. We found her engrossed in thought, gracious, smiling. Our Lord had asked her to "suffer with joy and gratitude...", "to smile at him in the midst of suffering..."

When she suffered a particularly severe attack, or after a sleepless night, she would say : "How good it is!" Her love of suffering took delight in every crucifying eventuality ; she found there genuine, supernatural joy.

She would often say to her superiors : "How good it is to abandon oneself to Jesus! How faithful he is! How generous! How thoughtful in the slightest details! How touched I am by his goodness...! How good it is to be consumed for him...! My task is to suffer... How happy I am! Oh! What happiness it is to be a religious...! I am going home to God to work for my 'Jesus and Mary' until the end of the world... for other souls, too... I will give joy... This general weakness, this sense of oppression, these violent spasms of pain... they are all a consummation of every moment (of my life)... I feel I am being torn to pieces and destroyed for him... How good it is...!"

When she was in pain, she kept saying : "As long as he is pleased!" She often repeated this request : "Pray that I be faithful to the end."

On one of the visits her parents (Mr and Mrs Bélanger) paid her, her father said : "We have had many Masses offered for your recovery, we have prayed a great deal... but it seems you are not helping us much." "Papa", replied the dear patient, "I want only God's will."

In a "Preparation for Death", this sentence made a deep impression on her : **the last graces are the best** ; she often referred to it and experienced the truth of this reflection particularly on the two occasions that she received the sacrament of the sick.

"It seems to me that the Blessed Virgin is going to come for me", she said to one of her superiors. On the feast of the Assumption, in the evening, Our Lord asked her if she wanted to suffer still more or else go to heaven. She agreed to suffer so as to ransom souls and obtain graces for 'Jesus and Mary'.

On 4 September, Wednesday morning, she was extremely weak throughout the recitation of the Litanies, the Rosary etc. Her gaze remained fixed on the picture of the Eucharistic Heart which hung opposite her bed.

A few hours before she died, when urged to have courage, she answered in a tone of deep conviction : **Jesus is praying**.

She was fully conscious to the end, joining in the prayers, smiling at her Sisters and tenderly kissing the crucifix that was placed on her lips. At about three o'clock in the afternoon, there were signs that the end was near. "I am suffocating", she said. The 'Mothers' arrived just in time to receive her last breath. She died in the same posture as St Thérèse of Lisieux : almost sitting up in her bed, with her head thrown back and her eyes fixed on heaven. It was one last point of resemblance with the little Flower of Lisieux whom she had imitated so perfectly.

Her funeral took place on Saturday, 7 September, in the presence of a great number of her relatives and friends from Quebec, her home town. Mother Ste-Cécile de Rome left us in the thirty-third year of her earthly life and the ninth of her religious life.

Expressions of admiration and veneration came from every direction ; they came from priests who had known and directed her, teachers and fellow-students she had edified and parents and friends who appreciated her greatly.

APPENDIX

GENEALOGY OF DINA BELANGER

The Bélanger Family

The Bélanger (Bellanger) families, in Canada, have two distinct lines of descent, that of François and that of Nicolas. Up to the present time, no relationship has been found to exist between these two forbearers. Dina's ancestor, Nicolas Bélanger, came from Saint-Thomas de Touques in Normandy. In the census of 1655, he is listed as a voter in the domain of Robert Giffard, in Beauport.

Nicolas Bélanger, *whose parents are unknown, married Marie de Rainville, daughter of Paul and of Rolline Poëte, 11 January 1660, in Notre-Dame de Québec.*

Nicolas Bélanger, *son of Nicolas and of Marie de Rainville, married Marie Magnan, daughter of Jacques and of Ambroise Doigt, 2 November 1699, in Charlesbourg.*

Jacques Bélanger, *son of Nicolas and of Marie Magnan, married Marie-Jeanne Proteau, daughter of Michel and of Suzanne Bédard, 1 September 1749, in Charlesbourg.*

Jean-Baptiste Bélanger, *son of Jacques and of M.-Jeanne Proteau, married Françoise Garnier, daughter of Michel-A. and of Marie-A. Bruneau, 3 February 1795, in Beauport.*

Jacques Bélanger, *son of Jean-Baptiste and of Françoise Garnier, married Marguerite Chartré, daughter of Pierre and of Marie Laflamme, 9 August 1842, in L'Ancienne-Lorette.*

Olivier Bélanger, son of Jacques and of Marguerite Chartré, married Dina Belleau, daughter of Honoré and of Madeleine Matte, 26 July 1869, in Neuville.

Octave Bélanger, son of Olivier and of Dina Belleau, married Séraphia Matte, daughter of Joseph Matte and of Virginie Delisle, 22 June 1896, in Neuville.

Dina Bélanger, daughter of Octave and of Séraphia Matte, born 30 April 1897, deceased 4 September 1929.

The Matte Family

On the side of her mother, Séraphia Matte, Dina Bélanger is descended from Nicolas Matte, son of Charles and Barbe Harache. Her ancestor, Nicolas, from St-Saire (near Neuville-Ferrières) in Normandy, was baptised at Ste-Geneviève-en-Bray, 8 December 1636. At the time of the 1666 census, he was living at la Pointe-aux-Trembles (today Neuville, in the Province of Quebec, Canada), where he was granted land in 1702 by Jean Bourdon, Lord of Dombourg.

Nicolas Matte is one of the founders of Neuville.

Nicolas Matte, son of Charles and of Barbe Harache, married Madeleine Ouvray, daughter of Antoine and of Marie Le Normand, October 1671, in Notre-Dame de Quebec.

Nicolas Matte, son of Nicolas and of Madeleine Ouvray, married Angélique Coquin, daughter of Pierre and of Catherine Baudin, 24 April 1705, in Neuville.

Nicolas Matte, son of Nicolas and of Angélique Coquin, married Marie Godin, daughter of Jean-François and of Genevieve Lefrançois, 19 January 1739, in Neuville.

Jean-Baptiste Matte, son of Nicolas and of Marie Godin, married Josette Grenon, daughter of Joseph and of M.-Madeleine Hébert, 28 July 1766, in Neuville.

Nicolas Matte, son of Jean-Baptiste and of Josette Grenon, married Angélique Mercure, daughter of Thierry and of Françoise Trépanier, 22 January 1798, in Neuville.

Nicolas Matte, son of Nicolas and of Angélique Mercure, married Anastasia Létourneau, daughter of Jean-Thomas and of Marie-Barbe Pagé, 15 January 1833, in Les Ecureuils.

Joseph Matte, son of Nicolas and of Anastasia Létourneau, married Virginie Delisle, daughter of Nazaire and of Flore Gingras, 17 January 1860, in Neuville.

Séraphia Matte, daughter of Joseph and Virginie Delisle, married Octave Bélanger, son of Olivier and of Dina Belleau, 22 June 1896, in Neuville.

Dina Bélanger, daughter of Octave and of Séraphia Matte, born 30 April 1897, deceased 4 September 1929

APPROBATION OF THE 1934 EDITION

Reverend Mother St Peter Claver
Provincial of the Religious of Jesus and Mary, Sillery

Reverend Mother,

It is with the most lively interest and the greatest edification that I have perused the notes on the interior life of one of your young religious, called home by God about a year and a half ago.

These pages, radiant with faith and divine love, reveal to us the increasingly profound working of Our Lord in the soul of his "little Bride". To read and meditate on these writings can bring only profit, especially to souls consecrated to the Lord.

May God increase the number of these generous, immolated souls in your beautiful Congregation and in the heart of his Church!

I bless you, Reverend Mother, as well as all your Sisters, and I earnestly recommend myself to the prayers of your fervent community.

Fr. R.-M. Card. Rouleau, O.P.
Archbishop of Quebec

Quebec, 21 February 1931

PREFACES
TO EARLIER EDITIONS

Canadian edition 1934

A soul consumed by suffering and by love of Our Lord : That is the story related in the work you are about to read.

This soul is that of a Canadian religious. She lived quite near us, among us, in our city of Quebec, and then in the Convent of Jesus and Mary, Sillery, where she offered herself as a holocaust, where she continually grew in holiness through intimate communion with God, and where, amidst the darkness and light of our earth, she penetrated the ecstasy of the Most Blessed Trinity.

We must be grateful to the Religious of Jesus and Mary for having been willing to make this Sister better known ; she lived with them and edified them by her heroic virtues. Now that, through death, the door of her cloister has been thrown open, she can and must travel across the world, spreading the blessing of her example and her very precious spiritual teaching.

Our society has a real need to know souls that will remind them of the meaning of life, souls who are close to them and can exemplify, as alive and necessary, virtues that they believe to be superfluous or impossible to practise.

It might also be said that, when God seems to be more abandoned by a world seeking happiness independently of him, he is pleased to increase the number of men and women saints who seek their greatest joy in him and who seem and are truly completely happy. Our Province of Quebec, and Canada itself are rich in these noble souls, insufficiently known by the generality of people ; by their premature virtue they edify those who witness their daily life. In recent times, we have seen the wonder of

young saints all around us : young men and women, young religious, both men and women, even children who have lived only
to love and serve God. It is the marvel of lilies! The marvel of
virgin souls who have offered themselves as scented flowers on
the altar of their youthful sacrifice, and whose holiness, like a
perfume, is already purifying the atmosphere of contemporary
life.

Marie Ste-Cécile de Rome was one of these privileged souls.
Born to live the religious life, to offer herself unreservedly to the
mystical Bridegroom of virgins, she was born, too, to be an
example, to those in religion first of all, then to the world, and,
through the fame of her virtue, to radiate that supernatural ideal
of which the world stands in such great need. Having been nurtured in the heart of one of our deeply Christian families in
Quebec, and transplanted at the age of twenty-four to the spiritual garden that was the convent at Sillery, she was truly the
mystic flower fit to adorn the altars of Jesus and Mary ; above all,
she was a soul recollected, immolated, sacrificed, a soul such as
we need today to counter, by a display of virtue, dissipation,
egoism and sensuality.

This display might well have been presented only to God and
the angels, had Marie Ste-Cécile de Rome not received one day
from her superior the command to write about her spiritual life.
She submitted, in spite of the deep repugnance that stemmed
from her humility ; and this act of obedience has provided us
with an autobiography, of which many extracts can be read in
this book. Our Lord himself told her one day that, through her
writings, she would do much good in the world. Indeed, it is
these writings which have revealed to the world the secret of her
life and the lessons she has taught.

Among all the teachings contained in the notebooks left by
Marie Ste-Cécile de Rome, there is this, above all : the overri-
ding appreciation we should have of spiritual values. If we draw
attention to this before all else, it is because it is the most rele-
vant of all the lessons that our frivolous, materialistic society

could be reminded of, heedless as it is of true riches and eternal values.

Marie Ste-Cécile de Rome wanted above all to possess God. This was the immense treasure that she never ceased to augment, seeking through meditation and contemplation to add to this gift of God. "Through Our Lord substituted for my own being, I am in possession of the riches of the Infinite," she wrote one day. Indeed, she reached this point, through her union with God and God's gift to her ; she even experienced and verified the gentle substitution of Christ in her. Thus she joins St Paul who experienced, as we know, the phenomenon of his mystical incorporation into Christ : "It is no longer I who live, but Jesus who lives in me." And Our Lord would say one day to Marie Ste-Cécile de Rome : "You will not be in any greater possession of me in heaven, because I have absorbed you entirely."

To possess God, to be annihilated in him, to allow him to take full possession of our souls, that is the highest degree of christian perfection ; it is also the most precious treasure we can covet. Moreover it is something the world scarcely understands, busy as it is with seeking material, ephemeral possessions, which leave such deep traces of disappointment in souls.

Marie Ste-Cécile de Rome did not want to enjoy this supernatural treasure selfishly. And we find in her notebooks the very interesting doctrine of using God.

First, she makes use of her union with Our Lord to give glory to the Blessed Trinity, and to respond, through this offering of the love of Jesus burning in her heart, to the eternal loving kindness of the three divine Persons. She makes use of God, too, to obtain from him her own perfection, and the salvation and sanctification of other souls. Like Mary of the Incarnation, she takes delight, too, in contemplating the Blessed Trinity ; but like her, too, she immediately transforms these movements of her soul towards the august Divinity into a supernatural apostolate.

And if this example and these lessons are not generally accessible to the laity, they should be accessible to those who are consecrated to God, those who will want to read and reread the autobiography of Mary St Cecilia of Rome.

This young religious teaches those consecrated to God, as well as lay persons, how to carry out a mission of suffering. She herself was a victim who paid for the natural satisfaction which the world so awdly ressues with her desire for suffering and the joyful acceptance of afflictions that crucify the flesh.

On the day of her clothing, Marie Ste-Cécile de Rome had asked Jesus for the gift of a spiritual chalice containing the instruments of his Passion. On the day of her religious profession, Our Lord gave her this magnificent chalice, overflowing with treasures, with the merits of his Passion, and into which she was to pour her own suffering. From that moment, she shared in the sufferings of the agonizing Heart of Jesus and accepted, with the smile characteristic of the victims of divine love, all the sorrows that her short, pain-filled life was to bring her.

How profitable it is, in our age of sensuality, of pagan naturalism, this example of a soul which offers atonement and finds, in making reparation and accepting suffering, the joy that others seek in the deceptive excesses of self-indulgence!

In this, as well as in all the other aspects of her religious life, Marie Ste-Cécile de Rome is a model that can be presented to people of all ages.

This devout child from the parish of Jacques-Cartier in Quebec City, who was the precious adornment of the family home ; this student at the convent of Bellevue who asked God, as she was entering the school, the supreme grace of never committing the least deliberate venial sin ; this young artist who, in New York, knew how to combine the demands of musical studies with a deep spiritual life ; this religious of Jesus and Mary who became such a great mystic, one of those virgins of the cloister who have penetrated deeply into the heart of the Bridegroom : all these persons who successively take shape in the life of Dina Bélanger are surely models that we do well to offer children, young women, all young Christians, every person in the world and, above all, souls consecrated to God.

Besides, it was for these souls that Marie Ste-Cécile de Rome prayed especially. It was to make up for their inadequacy that she sacrificed herself so generously. She learnt from Our Lord himself the extent to which his Heart suffers from the luke-warmness, neglect, dissipation, and lack of recollection and prayer in those whom Jesus has chosen to be his ministers and his spouses. May priestly and religious souls learn from reading this book to serve more generously a Master to whom they have given themselves! May they remember, on seeing the particu-larly profound joys of this chosen soul, that it is in God that they should seek both the fruitfulness of their apostolate and the hap-piness of their lives.

May Marie Ste-Cécile de Rome, who lives again in the pages of the book you are about to read, be among us, as a virginal lily spreading her fragrance through the cloisters of the world, an example reminding us always of the supernatural meaning of life, and glorifying that infinite Beauty towards which every soul seeking happiness must ascend.

Camille Roy, priest.

Canadian Edition 1983

The vocation to sanctity is not reserved to a few privileged souls : it is the concern of each and every Christian : "Be perfect, as your heavenly Father is perfect" (Mt. 5,48). The Lord has made it a precept for us, not a counsel.

Vatican II reminded us of this most important truth, in "Lumen Gentium" (Ch. 5).

The life of Dina Bélanger, a young girl from our own country, allows us to gain a better grasp of what this universal call means and of the response which we should bring to it.

Such a life does not set before our eyes some abstract definition of the state of grace, but it makes us rrealize the wonder it really is : deep, personal intimacy with Christ and, through him and in him, with the Father and the Holy Spirit.

In truth, it is the beginning, here on earth, of the happiness of heaven towards which we must strive if we are to possess it for all eternity. That is the only real way of succeeding in life : "What will a man gain, if he wins the whole world and suffers the loss of his soul?" (Mt. 16,26)

This question is valid for everyone in every age, but even more, one might say, in our age when, as a result of the attraction exercised by material goods and creature comforts, there are so few who are as concerned as they should be with the real meaning of life, in the light of eternity.

Dina Bélanger is for us all a lamp that "shines for everyone in the house" (Mt. 5,15). Her radiance will help us to live, with her, as sons and daughters of light.

+... Albert Vachon
Archbishop of Quebec

12 December 1983

CONTENTS

Continuationy studies.— Desire for failure. — Purpose of studies. — Darkness. — Decision to enter the Congregation of Jesus and Mary. — Submission to her parents. — Departure.

Entry to the Convent. — First impressions. — Snares of the Devil. — The power of grace. — A visit to the novitiate. — The retreat. — Two graces received during the retreat.

Life in community. — Love of the Rule. — Teaching. — God's work. — The Game of Love and the Game of the Cross. — The daily cross. — The retreat prior to clothing. — Betrothal. — A 'new name'.

A portrait. — Private profession. — Motive for devotedness to the pupils. — Literary endeavours. — Abandonment. — Friendships. — Divine love. — Annual retreat.

A sacrifice. — Fresh graces. — Writings. — Dina's ideal. — A promise at Christmas. — Intimacy with the Master. — Zeal for souls. — Complaints of the Heart of Jesus.

Communion. — Retreat. — Different kinds of thanksgiving. — Martyr, victim, apostle. — A maxim. — Life in community. — Preparation for profession and death. — My bridal bouquet.

The value of each moment. — Annihilation and life in the most adorable Trinity. — Fresh knowledge of God, of heaven. — Jesus in the Host. — God alone! — Longing. — The only Treasure.

God contemplated by Jesus in the elect, in the angels, in Mary. — Participation in the 'mode of eternity'. — God contemplated in himself. — Formula and content of the vow of total perfection. — Wiles of the devil. — Action of the Holy Spirit.

Grace of freedom. — Radiating love. — Smiling at Love. — The fullness of love. — On joy. — Demonic attacks. — The price of the cross. — Absorbed into the Infinite. — The Host, a treasure. — This is Jesus!

Attacks of the Evil One. — Hunger for the divine Host. — Perfect abandonment. — Satisfaction of infinite Love. — A little beggar for love. — The divine Pearl. — God is Love.

Our Lady of the Holy Spirit. — Jesus offers himself to infinite Love. — Total satisfaction of infinite Justice. — Satisfaction of all the infinite attributes. — Renewed offering of Jesus. — Unrestrained love.

A day without bread. — Feast of the Holy Name of Jesus. — The Forty Hours Devotion. — Offering of Our Lord. — Infinite Justice.

Infinite Holiness. — Infinite Power. — Infinite Mercy. — The loving thought of Jesus. — Total gift of self. — Love and sacrifice.

Longing. — Tenderness of the Eucharistic Heart. — Holy week. — Consecrated souls. — Priestly souls. — Saturday offered for priests. — 'I looked for some to console me and I found none. — Thursday offered for consecrated souls.

The devil in action. — The agonizing Heart of Jesus and consecrated souls. — Pray and intercede! — Friday offered for all souls.

The influence of consecrated souls. — The state of perpetual immolation. — How to suffer in silence. — The prayer of the Heart of Jesus. — Annual retreat.

In the infinite confines of the Most Blessed Trinity. — Struggles. — A vision of my actions. — Absorption into the divine. — Confirmation in the permenent state of humiliation and suffering.

Wednesday for vocations to the religious life. — Tuesday for my Congregation. — In the enclosed garden of the Most Blessed Trinity.

Sunday in a spirit of reparation. — Monday in thanksgiving. — Uninterrupted grace of the divine chalice. — In the sanctuary of the Most Blessed Trinity. — In the tabernacle of the Most Blessed Trinity.

Jesus kept bound in many consecrated souls. — Perfect renunciation. — Felt presence of the evil spirit. — Thirsting to be immolated in the same way as Our Lord. — Martyrdom of the Heart of Jesus.

Fear of illusion. — The divine chalice and the real presence of Our Lord. — In the essence of the heart of the Divinity. — The reproduction of Jesus in souls. — Smiling interiorly and exteriorly.

The satisfaction of the infinite attributes and the reproduction of Our Lord. — I am not sufficiently loved for my own sake. — The reign of the divine at Jesus and Mary. — The Eucharistic Heart of Jesus and the Congregation of Jesus and Mary.

IMRIMÉ AU CANADA